The Struggle for Auto Safety

The Struggle for Auto Safety

Jerry L. Mashaw
David L. Harfst

Harvard University Press
Cambridge, Massachusetts
London, England
1990

Library of Congress Cataloging-in-Publication Data

Mashaw, Jerry L.
    The struggle for auto safety / Jerry L. Mashaw, David L. Harfst.
        p.   cm.
    Includes bibliographical references.
    ISBN 0-674-84530-7 (alk. paper)
        1. Automobiles—Safety regulations—United States.
    2. Product recall—Law and legislation—United States.
    3. Automobiles—United States—Safety measures.
    I. Harfst, David L.   II. Title.
    KF2212.M37   1990
    343.7309′44—dc20
    [347.303944]   89-78109
                                                        CIP

For Alice and Richard Harfst and Samantha Herron Mashaw

Contents

Preface

Is the private automobile (a) a public health menace, or (b) a technological embodiment of America's political freedom? This was the question that safety activists and vehicle manufacturers put to Congress in 1966 as they struggled over passage of the proposed National Motor Vehicle Safety Act. Without a single dissenting vote in either house, Congress chose answer (a). Henceforth automakers would build and market their automobiles under the watchful eye of scientifically sophisticated federal regulators. The job of these public health guardians was to "socialize" the output of an almost completely nonregulated industry—an industry whose "irresponsible" products were implicated in the deaths of fifty thousand Americans every year.

But as is often the case, the legislative process leading to the 1966 Motor Vehicle Safety Act had framed a defective question. The correct answer—"(c) both of the above"—was missing from the choices available. In the rush to ratify a vision of automobile safety that combined science with law to remake the world, answer (b)'s emphasis on freedom was rejected, suppressed, almost forgotten. But worlds are not so easily remade. The private motor car is more than just another "consumer durable." It has permitted an impatient people to conquer space and time and to display individual taste and social status while maintaining maximum personal privacy. That the automobile was, and should be, preeminently a "freedom machine" was not a notion easily tossed aside. Legislation can emphasize, even exalt, new ideas. But it cannot repeal history; nor can it long suppress deeply held social values. The 1966 act thus was not to be the culmination, and indeed was just the beginning, of the struggle for motor vehicle safety.

This book is a chronicle and an analysis of that struggle. Its special focus is on the legal and institutional armaments with which America's domestic policy battles are waged. It emphasizes, in particular, those structural elements of the American legal system, the separation and division of powers and judicial review, that empower resistance to political change. *The Struggle for Auto Safety* is thus a story of the reemergence of suppressed political values through the medium of legal and institutional inertia. It is a tale of government checks and balances that work with a vengeance and of America's constitutionally enshrined ambivalence about whether government is the source of or the solution to social ills. In such a polity even minor shifts in the existing freedom-security equilibrium can provide adversaries an occasion for prolonged contest. And as a result of such struggles, the regulatory scheme for automobile safety that survived to begin the 1990s is not the one envisaged in 1966. It is instead a quite different enterprise, shaped by the environmental constraints of the American legal culture.

Because regulating risk while preserving freedom is in some sense the generic problem of American governance, to examine two decades of experience with auto safety regulation is to examine America's experience with other regulatory regimes as well. If our analysis of the history of auto safety regulation is correct, then the same analytic framework should be applicable to environmental regulation, workplace health and safety regulation, general product-safety regulation, and a host of similar regulatory regimes. Indeed, we believe this to be the case. We believe, further, that what we here call the "legal culture hypothesis" is superior to its analytic competitors as a means for understanding why regulatory regimes in the United States tend to take the forms that they do.

But analytic frameworks are not complete histories. The legal culture referees the regulatory struggle and shapes its rules, but law itself is not a participant in the regulatory contest. The legal culture does not succeed or fail; it does not innovate, manage, or compete. Innovating, managing, and competing are the actions of particular people in particular legal institutions, having particular sets of legal powers, social relations, and economic and human resources. Every regulatory struggle is thus a struggle that defines a unique regulatory regime as well as a struggle mediated by the broader currents of the American legal culture.

The story of the National Highway Traffic Safety Administration (NHTSA) and its administrators, supporters, and antagonists, like most political histories, contains accounts of political idealism and personal ambition, of scientific commitment and professional competition, of long-range vision and political opportunism. By turns both tragic and comic, NHTSA's tale is also richly ironic. Exercising a legal mandate designed to produce a dramatic break both with prior conceptions of auto safety and with prior modes of regulatory action, the agency has achieved its modest legal and political successes largely by returning to the ideas and the regulatory modes of the past. To understand why is, we hope, to begin to understand how to arrange a more successful regulatory future.

In providing this account we have been assisted by many individuals and institutions. We cannot acknowledge them all here, but to some we are particularly indebted. The National Science Foundation (through its Program in Social Science and Law) and the Yale Law School (through its Center for Law, Economics and Public Policy) supplied essential research support. Covington & Burling provided David Harfst with a year's leave of absence from the firm in order to complete work on the manuscript. Our students in several auto safety seminars, and our student assistants over a number of years, have contributed materially to our understanding of auto safety regulation. We are particularly grateful to Daniel Esty and Albert Wells for their work respectively on the legislative history of auto safety regulation and on the effects of products liability on manufacturers' design decisions, to Mark Barnes and Peter Benda for their tireless investigation of NHTSA's Federal Register notices, and to Amy Russell and Janine Crawley for systematic pursuit of both errant syntax and fugitive references. Theresa Cerillo and Patricia Page expertly and cheerfully typed and retyped a flood of manuscript pages without consigning any of them to that dread word-processing purgatory of unretrievable electronic images. Participants in the legislative, administrative, and judicial battles over auto safety policy patiently responded to hundreds of our (sometimes impertinent) questions.

Through it all our families and friends applauded our progress and suffered with us through our setbacks. They seldom had the bad grace to ask when we would be finished, or to remind us how long this project was taking. For these indulgences no author can ever be sufficiently appreciative.

The Struggle for Auto Safety

ONE

Regulation and Legal Culture

The National Traffic and Motor Vehicle Safety Act of 1966 was a dramatic attempt at legal transformation. Indeed, it represented the convergence of two revolutionary movements. The first was a decisive shift in the intellectual conception of motor vehicle safety; the second was a broad-based campaign for reform of federal administrative regulation. To understand the ups and downs of motor vehicle safety regulation since then, and the dynamics of many similar regulatory systems, we must first examine the ambitions that these new ideas represented.

The Revolution of 1966

The New Science of Accidents. In 1966 the use of law to regulate automobile safety was hardly novel. Traffic rules backed by legal sanctions were not only traditional; they were, and are, probably the most often encountered and most often violated legal norms ever enacted. Our streets and highways are alive with legal communication. Stripes and arrows, broken and solid lines adorn the pavements. Signs and flashing lights provide constant reminders of required speeds, stopping places, areas of caution, required and prohibited turns, and so on.

The law encourages good driving behavior in other ways as well. All states license drivers; many either require or strongly encourage driver education courses. These routine forms of vehicle safety regulation are punctuated by episodic, high-visibility enforcement campaigns, during which the police crack down on speeders, drunk drivers, and other vehicular malefactors. Much of this activity is given heavy play in the press.

Yet virtually no driver would claim to follow all of the rules all of the time. And despite gargantuan efforts at legal control, most of it directed at preventing accidents by modifying driving practices, the number of automobile accidents and the resulting death and injury toll have mounted unceasingly. By 1965 the number of vehicular deaths per year had topped fifty thousand. That awesome figure was expected to double within the next decade. Limiting motor vehicle injury and death by regulating driver behavior simply seemed inadequate to the task.

In 1966 Daniel Patrick Moynihan, then assistant secretary of labor, described the traditional law enforcement approach and its increasingly problematic efficacy:

> The entire pattern of State Police management of the automobile complex is derived directly from the model of the prevention, detection, and punishment of—crime. From the cowboy hats, to the six gun, to the chase scene, the entire phenomenon is a paradigm of the imposition of law on an unruly and rebellious population. This involves intense concentration on the guilt of individuals, as measured by conformance to statutes, and of the efficacy of punishment, either threatened or carried out, as a means of social regulation. There is not much evidence that this works. More to the point, the police have almost no tradition of controlled inquiry that would find out. Thus, in 1955 the Connecticut State Police began a crackdown on speeders that soon brought nationwide attention. In a curious way the efficacy of such an effort is somehow presumed. Yet by any measurable standard the Connecticut program has been [a] distinct failure. [Moreover] it is clear that the Connecticut State Police do not, in any meaningful sense know this, and do not intend to find it out. Their response to the gentlest criticism is simply wholesome Hibernian apoplexy.[1]

As Moynihan (but few other public officials) understood, two distinct sets of professionals had begun to take a radically different approach to automobile safety—an approach that sought to ignore driver behavior. One group was composed of highway engineers. Although design safety standards had in some sense always been a part of highway engineering, the significant increase in money and attention devoted to interstate highways in the 1950s and 1960s provided an opportunity for substantial upgrading of highway safety design. And it was clear by the early 1960s that conscious efforts to design highways for safety had produced results. The interstate highways were, in general, three times as safe as other highways.

For our purposes the second group was more important. It comprised the medical profession,[2] especially the members of the profession concerned with epidemiology and public health.[3] From a medical standpoint the mayhem on the highways looked statistically like an epidemic. Automobiles not only were the leading cause of accidental death but were, for the population below age forty-four, the leading cause of death. The efforts of these professionals to understand and control this epidemic of accidents produced an entirely new way of thinking about automobile safety.

Epidemiologists analyze problems of injury or illness in terms of a conceptual triad that includes the *host* (the person who becomes injured or ill), the *agent* (the cause of the injury or illness), and the *environment* (the setting within which the host and the agent interact). In an automobile accident the epidemiologist sees a host coming into contact with an agent, that is, an occupant being subjected to rapid energy transference. Notice that this is an interaction that occurs *after* the moment of what is conventionally called the "accident." The epidemiologist thus is led almost inexorably, when asked to describe the cause of injury to an automobile occupant, to concentrate on the cause of the injury, not the cause of the accident. From this perspective preventing the accident is only one of many strategies for preventing or ameliorating the injury. A small point, perhaps, but one with enormous significance for public policy. It suggests that legal regulation might focus on the car rather than on the driver.

William Haddon, the man who became the Motor Vehicle Safety Act's first administrator, wrote extensively on the etiology of accidental injury.[4] Although much of his work related to the epidemiology of accidents generally, Haddon became increasingly active in the field of automobile accidents. It was clear that he believed he was on to something more than just another strategy for legal control of vehicular injury and death. Like other epidemiologists, he already had a professional bias in favor of interventions that did not rely on changing human behavior. In a 1962 paper, for example, he wrote, "it has been the consistent experience of public health agencies concerned with the reduction of other causes of morbidity and mortality that measures which did not require the continued, active cooperation of the public are much more efficacious than those which do. Consequently, a much higher value and, hence, priority should be placed on proven measures in the 'passive' than in the 'active' area."[5]

By "proven measures" Haddon was referring to more than the increasing evidence of the efficacy of highway safety design. Building on Hugh De Haven's pioneering research at the Cornell Medical School,[6] and borrowing engineering technique from aeronautical engineers, teams of doctors and safety engineers had by 1962 designed or redesigned the interior of the automobile to make it much more forgiving of its human occupants in the event of a crash. Considerable work had also been done on determining the structural characteristics of automobiles that would make them more "crashworthy." This research was widely known within the automotive engineering fraternity and by state and federal officials who were particularly interested in automobile safety. Popularly described as the "second collision" approach (referring to the energy transfer after the "first" collision, the accident itself) to automobile safety, these ideas were also coming to be understood by the insurance industry, by medical professionals who dealt with automobile trauma, and by the American Trial Lawyers Association.

Yet nothing much seemed to be changing in the design of the automobiles that were being produced—at least not in their *safety* design. In the 1950s and early 1960s, automobile "design" meant automobile "styling." The urgent design questions seemed to concern tail-fin height and the shape of the grill. For the reform-minded, the epidemiological approach therefore suggested a radically new role for automobile safety law. Rather than attempting to modify driver behavior, the law should attempt to modify the motor vehicle.

Regulatory Reform. When the revolution in the substantive conceptualization of motor vehicle safety came to be translated into law, it converged with a concurrent revolution in the form of legal regulation.[7] The regulation of vehicle design thus was expressed in the language of a new approach to the design of legal institutions. From the perspective of regulatory reform, the 1966 act should be seen as creating the first of a new breed of federal regulatory agencies (NHTSA, the National Highway Traffic Safety Administration) concerned with health and safety, a breed that now also includes such familiar regulatory actors as the Occupational Safety and Health Administration (OSHA), the Environmental Protection Agency (EPA), and the Consumer Product Safety Commission (CPSC).

These agencies, and the multiple statutes that they administer, have much in common; they are the institutional offspring of a distinctive political-intellectual union. The first parent of regulatory reform was the "liberal" political activism of the 1960s and early 1970s that viewed most social issues, whether civil rights, poverty, pollution, or product safety, as problems to be solved by the application of federal governmental power. The second parent of reform was an intellectual climate created by governmental critics of both the Left and the Right. These, mostly academic, analysts described venerable federal agencies such as the Interstate Commerce Commission (ICC), Federal Power Commission (FPC), and Federal Trade Commission (FTC) as "captured" bureaucracies—institutions that had failed to make effective public policy because they had been too busy serving the economic interests of their regulatory clientele.[8] The reform agenda generated at the intersection of liberal political activism and skeptical intellectual criticism of federal bureaucratic performance included, therefore, two elements: the need to move the federal government forcefully into new areas of activity; and the need to provide this federal action in new organizational forms that would avoid the lethargy of the past.

There were many diagnoses of the structural problems of the "old" agencies. The vagueness of their statutory mandates, their collegiate form, their broad prosecutorial discretion, their imperviousness to the interests that they were designed to protect, their independence from executive direction, their ponderous and inefficient adjudicatory techniques were all indicted as contributing to their ineffectiveness.[9] The new agencies were to be different: their mandates more specific; their power more concentrated in a single administrator; their enforcement discretion more circumscribed; their processes more open to the participation of putative beneficiaries; and their powers more focused on the establishment of mandatory policy by general rule.

This last change, indeed, was the most significant legal innovation of the new era of regulation. From the perspective of the legal reformers of the late 1960s and early 1970s, rulemaking was vastly superior to adjudication as a regulatory technique. General rules could be made through informal, and presumably more expeditious, procedures. Policy would apply immediately to whole areas of regulated activity. Any person or organization, not just the "regulated interests," could participate in informal rulemaking proceedings. General rulemaking would also foster comprehensive planning (at least broadly informed policymaking) rather than ad hoc policy formation in the context of particular adjudications. Agency initiatives, or lack of initiatives, would be transparent and, therefore, subject to political debate and direction. Judicial review, presumably, would afford regulators wide latitude in shaping policies while avoiding the courts' preoccupation with adjudicatory formalities that had often paralyzed individualized enforcement and licensing proceedings. Judicial review of rules could easily be structured to include review of an agency's failure to act; hence potential beneficiaries would be able to back their demands for action with credible threats of legal recourse. The virtues of regulation by rulemaking seemed endless.

Operating at the forefront of the public health and regulatory reform movements that would later revolutionize environmental protection, occupational safety and health, and consumer product safety legislation, the Motor Vehicle Safety Act of 1966 defined the regulators' central task quite simply. The National Highway Traffic Safety Bureau (NHTSB), later Administration (NHTSA), was to promulgate rules that would force manufacturers to build vehicles that better protected their occupants in case of a crash. The agency's mandate was not confined exclusively to the protection of vehicle occupants by rules addressed to postaccident energy transfer (the "second collision"). The agency also could exercise its rulemaking authority to promote crash-avoidance technologies, and it had adjudicatory authority to force manufacturers to recall and repair automobiles containing defects relating to vehicle safety. In addition, the National Highway Safety Act, passed in the same year, gave the new bureau authority to attempt to coordinate and improve state programs aimed largely at control of driver behavior. But the big safety payoffs were thought to lie in the agency's central mission of "forcing" the development of technology that protected vehicle occupants. Indeed, the scientists, engineers, and public activists who supported the 1966 act foresaw public health benefits from redesigning the automobile that rivaled the most significant public health breakthroughs of the past, including such staggering successes as the protection and treatment of public water supplies.

From today's vantage point, the optimism of 1966 seems rather quaint. The leaders of the 1960s regulatory reform movement believed in the social efficacy of federal power expressed through law. Their central political heuristic was the development of civil rights law from *Brown v. Board of Education*[10] to the Civil Rights Act of 1964.[11] Surely other social ills, from poverty to pollution to the carnage on the roads, would respond to appropriate forms of national legal intervention. The proponents of the new science of accidents were equally sanguine. They often drew their supporting political images from the technological and managerial accomplishments of the space program.[12] With a NASA-like combination of political will and technical sophistication, success in the battle against vehicle injury and death seemed inevitable.

The combination of these political symbols proved extraordinarily powerful in the legislative debate over the act. Safety partisans characterized the vehicle safety problem as a problem of social irresponsibility.[13] Fixated on styling and power, the manufacturers were said to have failed to provide the public with the safer vehicles that were technologically feasible.[14] Regulation, therefore, was thought essential to shift the industry's design priorities from tail fins to passenger protection. Acting out a consensus that rarely attends legislative programs more controversial than the declaration of National Crocus Week, Congress passed the National Traffic and Motor Vehicle Safety Act—directly regulating the largest industry in the United States for the first time—without a single negative vote in either house.[15]

Today expectations have been lowered. The central images of political debates are Watergate and Vietnam. The moral force of *Brown v. Board of Education* has been blunted by the ambivalence of *Bakke*.[16] Neil Armstrong's "giant step for mankind" is remembered less vividly than the cloud that engulfed the space shuttle *Challenger* seventy-two seconds after takeoff. When we say that the vehicle safety program has not fulfilled its sponsors' dreams—that it has virtually abandoned its safety goals—there may be no surprise at this report of yet another "government failure."

Yet there are many explanations for NHTSA's failure to redesign and socialize the automobile in the ways that safety activists imagined in 1966. None need be intepreted as making failure inevitable. Each regulatory problem has, or had, a remedy. The failure to use the available remedies suggests that there is a deeper, more interesting, and less easily resolved issue concerning motor vehicle safety regulation. In fact NHTSA has succeeded politically by failing programmatically; it has legitimated and preserved its existence by abandoning its statutory mandate. The legislative revolution of 1996 confronted a broader legal culture that remained structured in terms of the ancien régime. It had to adapt or die.

Explaining Regulation

The analysis of regulatory systems—why they emerge, how they operate, why they succeed or fail, who gains or loses from their operation—

has been a thriving academic cottage industry for nearly two decades. This burgeoning interest is not difficult to explain. Not only is regulation a ubiquitous feature of late twentieth-century social, economic, and political life, but there has been enormous ferment in the regulatory arena. Regulation and deregulation both have been "in" and "out" as political ideas; regulatory and deregulatory statutes have emerged, sometimes in waves, sometimes in trickles, from Congress and from state legislatures. The individual and the social stakes in regulation are high.

At the risk of oversimplification, we may assign prior analyses of regulation to two general categories. One is a policy analytic, or "public welfare," tradition with roots stretching back at least to the Progressive era. In that tradition the basic reference point is the "public interest." Inquiry concerns how best to design and operate regulatory agencies to serve that interest. This tradition is both normative and reformist in orientation. It seeks to distinguish good regulatory design from bad, explain why some systems succeed while others fail, and teach lessons about appropriate norms and techniques of regulatory administration.

A second approach, with even older roots, is the tradition of political economy. In its more modern forms it is sometimes known as "interest group theory" or "capture theory." This is a tradition more positive than normative in its focus. The central inquiry is why a particular regulatory regime takes the form that it takes or operates in a particular fashion. Explanation is sought through attention not to the public welfare but to the underlying private interests that are affected by regulation. And although there are surely normative overtones to analyses that describe regulatory systems as, for example, designs to create government-sanctioned cartels for privileged interests, the explicit focus of most analyses is on explanation, not evaluation.

These two traditions have much in common. Both assume that regulatory institutions, as well as the other political and legal institutions that make up the regulatory environment, are highly malleable. Both assume that contemporary political actors have a relatively free hand in designing and operating regulatory institutions to accommodate either public or private demands. Indeed, unless institutions are highly malleable, neither the design activities of the policy analysts nor the strategic maneuverings described by interest group aficionados have much point.

To put the idea somewhat differently, both sets of analysts make easy transitions from motivations to behaviors. Policy analysts see institutional design and operation as an attempt by critical actors to realize some vision of the public interest. There may be mistakes, false starts, and failures, but this generally suggests only that the institutional designer should repair to the drawing board (or computer screen) to see in what respects the regulatory situation was misanalyzed. Political economists similarly view dominant coalitions as having the power, through selective political rewards and sanctions, to mold regulatory structures to suit their purposes. If regulatory institutions do not benefit their creators, it is usually because some other powerful political actor has made strategic moves that thwart the original coalition.

In both traditions one finds complex analyses that try to take account of other factors. Some theorists give significant explanatory force to the power of new ideas and to external events or shocks that alter or redefine regulatory direction. Nor is personality, leadership, or entrepreneurship always absent from regulatory explanation.

Yet both approaches tend to ignore a critical, often dominant, dimension of regulatory dynamics. Most accounts of regulatory behavior miss the inertial force of the general political and legal culture within which any regulatory regime must be constructed and operated. The dominant legal culture defines the repertoire of institutional techniques available to either policy-analytic planners or strategists concerned with political economy. Both must make their plans (or play their games) within the constraints that are established by broader institutions that elaborate and preserve the culture. Legal culture, as expressed through the operation of judicial review, the separation of powers, "federalism," and associated "checks and balances," provides a powerful, perhaps the most powerful, explanation for the particular form taken by regulatory regimes and for their ultimate success or failure.

This is both a strong and a controversial claim. Do we really mean to argue that people, new ideas, external shocks, concentrations of economic power, and a host of other variables do not matter? Of course not. The legal culture is not the motive force for regulatory activity. It provides only broad models for and constraints on behavior. These models are subject both to situation-specific avoidance and long-term adaptation.

Yet we do claim that viewed over the medium range—not a year or a century, but a few decades—legal convention exerts continuous and surprisingly sharp pressures on regulatory structures and regulatory behavior. Where regulatory policy goes and how it gets there can be traced in general, and sometimes in quite specific, terms to the way in which the regulatory regime reflects or challenges the conventional assumptions of the legal order. Substantively, regulation triumphs or fails to the degree that it can or cannot adapt to or transform the legal culture of which it is a part. The form that regulation takes is even more highly contingent on the means of legal implementation that the culture deems appropriate. Regulatory form and substantive regulatory accomplishment are often closely connected, as we shall see.

But what "regulation" are we talking about? What is the regulatory form, process, or product to be explained? Federal motor vehicle safety regulation in the period from 1966 to roughly the present, but concentrating particularly on the first fifteen years of regulatory activity, is the short answer. Thus, although the theoretical claim here is a broad one, it is made primarily through close attention to a particular regulatory regime. Given our thesis the choice of a case-study format is necessary: in cultural explanation the details matter.

A study of this particular regulatory experience, nonetheless, teaches important general lessons. The new motor vehicle safety regulation promised a dramatically more effective legal form for addressing an old regulatory problem—a form that was then copied, at least in part, by later legislation in fields ranging from environmental protection to occupational safety and health to consumer product safety generally. The Motor Vehicle Safety Act signaled a sort of regulatory paradigm shift. It is a watershed between "old" and "new" federal regulatory regimes, and it contributes to our understanding of both. An analysis of motor vehicle safety regulation, thus, tells us much about other, perhaps all other, regulatory domains as well.

What Happened

NHTSA's regulatory behavior can be described concisely. Established as a rulemaking agency to force the technology of automobile safety design, NHTSA indeed functioned in a predominantly rulemaking mode until about 1974. NHTSA's promulgated rules, however, have had extremely modest effects in forcing the development of innovative safety technology.[17] The rules that have become operational have required already-developed technologies, many of which were already in widespread, if not universal, use in the automobile industry at the time of the standards' promulgation. Since the mid-1970s, NHTSA has instead concentrated on its statutory power to force the recall of motor vehicles that contain defects related to safety performance. It has retreated to the old, and from the reformist perspective, despised form of legal regulation—case-by-case adjudication—which requires little, if any, technological sophistication and which has no known effects on vehicle safety.

This last, somewhat startling assertion is hardly obvious, but it is surely understood by the agency. The most authoritative studies of the causes of automobile accidents indicate that, at most, 13 percent involve some mechanical failure. Within that 13 percent most failures result from inadequate maintenance, not from defective design or construction.[18] But even if one ignored the maintenance factor and adopted the highly unrealistic assumptions that every accident-related mechanical failure is due to a defect, every recalled vehicle is defective, and every repair of such a vehicle is faultless, recalls would address only 7 percent of the accident problem. Why? Because on average, only 50 percent of owners respond to recall notices.[19] Recalling "defective" automobiles affects only a minuscule portion of the vehicle safety problem. And for reasons detailed in Chapter 8, it is even possible that recalls *decrease* overall safety levels.

By contrast the best, though very imperfect, studies of the effects of NHTSA's modest vehicle standards suggest an overall improvement in vehicle safety of around 30 percent.[20] If true, that is on the order of fifteen thousand lives saved and one hundred thousand serious injuries prevented per year. That is why we describe the agency's shift from rules to recalls as the virtual abandonment of its safety mission.

Let us be clear also, however, about what we are *not* saying. We are not at this point asserting that any particular estimates of the safety effects of either rules or recalls should be accepted. The evaluation of such claims is a very complex matter, to which we will return in Chapter 10. For now our only claim is that a search of the historical record, both inside and outside NHTSA, makes it impossible to believe that the agency's shift from rules to recalls represented a new *safety* strategy.

It is somewhat more plausible to deny that any change in regulatory strategy took place, at least prior to 1981. Some personnel at NHTSA have, sometimes hotly, contested the existence of the shift this book describes. These officials maintain that NHTSA retained its rulemaking focus at least until the first Reagan Administration, when NHTSA's safety rules, like other automobile regulations, were abandoned in the pursuit of "regulatory relief." But this is demonstrably not the case. Of some fifty general safety regulations adopted under the 1966 act, forty-five (90 percent) were issued prior to 1974. Not one of the fifty was first issued after 1976. By contrast, motor vehicle recalls have increased from about fifteen million motor vehicles between 1966 and 1970 to some thirty-three million vehicles from 1971 to 1975, to over thirty-nine million vehicles between 1976 and 1980. Indeed, during the period 1972–1977, the agency supervised the recall of more American automobiles than were sold new.[21]

"Regulatory relief," moreover, even in the Reagan era, did not include the abandonment of regulation by recall. Recalls did level off somewhat, to a total of about thirty million vehicles between 1981 and 1985. But this figure does not include over ten million Ford vehicles initially determined by NHTSA to have defective transmissions, for which the negotiated remedy was distribution of a dashboard warning label to motorists in 1981. More important, this considerable recall activity came at a time when NHTSA was relaxing, rescinding, or shelving a number of existing and proposed safety standards.[22]

The date of first adoption of general rules may, of course, not be the best indicator of the agency's rulemaking activity. A number of automobile safety standards are quite broad. Federal Motor Vehicle Safety Standard 201, for example, specifies requirements for car interiors to minimize postcrash injuries.[23] It covers a variety of topics, including requirements for instrument panels, seat backs, protrusions, sun visors, and arm rests. Over time, advances in technology or design might well require major amendments to such a rule, perhaps totally transforming the prescriptions contained in the rule at the time of its adoption in 1967. In measuring rulemaking activity, therefore, one must also pay attention to amendments.

It may also be plausible to imagine that the agency could maintain its level of rulemaking effort while not successfully concluding many rulemaking proceedings. After all, in the early years of its operation an agency can borrow standards that are already used elsewhere—by insurance agencies, private standard-setting associations, government procurement offices, and the like—which have a significant history and are relatively noncontroversial. Rulemaking initiatives proposing the use of truly novel technologies may require a much longer gestation period.

These considerations suggest that in measuring rulemaking activity one should take into account not only amendments but also the general level of rulemaking activity, as revealed by all actions related to rules. Later, more technologically advanced activities may also have greater safety effects, such that a smaller number of actions would in fact represent a more aggressive regulatory presence. Finally, one should be attentive to the allocation of agency resources. A small output of important and novel standards may represent an increasing rather than a decreasing investment in rulemaking as a regulatory technique.

Yet from any of these perspectives the general picture of NHTSA activities remains the same. It is surely the case that NHTSA's official rulemaking activity, as evidenced by Federal Register notices, is much more significant after 1976 than its issuance of final rules suggests. But the maintenance and amendment functions those notices reveal are often substantively trivial. Taken together, the trivial and the significant, total rulemaking issuances in NHTSA's second decade are less than half those of its first.

From the standpoint of regulatory effects, counting rulemaking issuances actually overstates the impact of NHTSA's post-1976 rulemaking activity. Although we are unaware of any year-by-year data on the incremental benefits of NHTSA's safety standards,[24] price impact information is available from the Bureau of Labor Statistics (BLS).[25] The bureau's data reveal that 96 percent of all price increases tied to NHTSA safety rules occurred from 1967 to 1976. Only 4 percent of net price increases were imposed during the following decade. There is no evidence that NHTSA discovered, sometime around 1976, a way to get more bang for the regulatory-compliance buck. It seems much more probable to imagine that the pre- and post-1976 cost figures reflect the real effects of NHTSA's regulations on automobile manufacturers in those periods.

Nor does a story of intensified effort stymied by technological barriers square well with the data. As we detail in subsequent chapters, the regulatory record is littered with ideas and proposals that have never found their way into regulatory form. NHTSA also has sponsored considerable research on vehicle safety technology; but it has used very little of what it has learned from any of these research contracts.

NHTSA's shift from rules to recalls is further reflected in its allocation of agency resources. When reasonably full staffing had been achieved, in the early 1970s, the agency employed nearly five times as many rulemaking engineers as "defects investigators." From that time forward there has been a continuous decline in the former and increase in the latter. Parity was achieved in 1982, and since then recall personnel have outnumbered rulemaking officials.

For all these reasons we are persuaded that the motor vehicle safety program really has changed over time and that the changes are very nearly as dramatic as simple statistics on the output of rules and recalls suggest. These changes began long before the Reagan Administration took office. Indeed, the shift from rulemaking to recalls is particularly characteristic of the Carter Administration, during which Joan Claybrook, a longtime associate of Ralph Nader and a vigorous and staunch defender of automobile safety regulation, headed the agency. Something happened at NHTSA to shift its energies from rules to recalls, and whatever it was cannot be explained simply by reference to the pro- or antiregulatory bias of a new administration.

Although the regulation of the safety of the private passenger car involves a consumer good with some claim to a unique hold on the American imagination, the fate of automobile safety regulation in operation has not been unique. Regulatory standard setting has overpromised and underperformed elsewhere as well. Many agencies that flexed rulemaking muscles in the early 1970s have retreated to regulatory techniques more reminiscent of New Deal agencies' adjudicatory processes. To some degree, of course, these retreats have been responsive to general political shifts in regulatory zeal that are too obvious to require explanation. But regulatory retreat is only a part of the story. For the retreat is not, or is seldom, *from* regulation—it is *to* regulation in a different form. OSHA's regulatory lethargy has been offset to some degree by its own use of adjudicatory enforcement and a major increase in civil damages litigation. The CPSC, like NHTSA, has turned from standard setting to recalls. Indeed, in NHTSA's case, recall activity was for a decade so vigorous that "retreat" may not be an apt description of the agency's regulatory posture. The events to be explained, both at NHTSA and elsewhere, are not so much changes in regulatory effort as changes in regulatory technique.

Explaining NHTSA's Regulatory Behavior

How then are we to explain NHTSA's (and by analogy other agencies') history? As we have said, there are two dominant traditions of explanation. We must now say something more about those traditions, their limitations, and our own approach.

The Public Welfare Hypothesis. According to the public welfare hypothesis, legislators adopt regulatory legislation in order to pursue the public interest, or general welfare. Implementing agencies pursue these public welfare goals by applying appropriate, expert judgment to decision-making tasks within their jurisdiction.

The particular form of regulatory legislation is thus explicable through an analysis of the social or economic problem that the legislature intended to address. Natural monopoly conditions bring forth entry and rate regulation; information asymmetries generate a regulatory response in the form of labeling requirements or other methods of information disclosure; the necessity to preserve urban amenities yields planning and zoning requirements. To be sure, the legislature may misanalyze particular social problems and prescribe the wrong solution. But reform, from this perspective, merely entails the correction of cognitive errors.

The public welfare view of regulatory implementation has a similar cast. The problems of implementation largely concern technique or methodology. Bureaucratic behavior is a constant search for appropriate means to implement legislatively prescribed goals. Administrative reform thus entails changes that promise to bring appropriate technical, scientific, or managerial expertise to bear upon the agency's task.[26]

From this perspective, one might explain the course of auto safety regulation by imagining that NHTSA's choice of regulatory technique has been driven by the pursuit of the congressional goal of automobile safety. One would then attempt to determine whether the agency's decisions have indeed produced beneficial results and, if not, where its analysis of the costs and benefits of its two forms of regulation has gone wrong. Of course one might discover that the agency has been trapped into a suboptimal regulatory posture by some flaw in its empowering legislation, perhaps through lack of congressional foresight concerning the legal or other resources that the agency would need to accomplish its mission.

Alternatively, NHTSA's behavior might be explained by taking a more complex and dynamic view of the public interest. Perhaps Congress misestimated the need for design changes in automobiles, and the agency learned over time that the best use of its rulemaking power simply was to let it atrophy. Perhaps Congress had in mind goals other than automobile safety when it passed the 1966 act and its subsequent amendments. Perhaps changing circumstances shifted public priorities and NHTSA's behavior followed these new images of the public interest, notwithstanding the continuance of its formal legislative mandate to "socialize" the automobile through safety standards.

The Private Interest Model. A private interest perspective gives rise to a similarly rich set of accounts and hypotheses about legislative and administrative behavior. Here the search is for *whose* private interest is being served. Candidates abound.

One of the most thoroughly elaborated self-interest models helped to shape the regulatory reform movement of the 1960s—"industry capture." This theory relies on a set of interlocking private interest premises. The first is that industries seek to obtain supracompetitive profits by inducing the government to limit competition. The second is that industries pursue this objective by offering support to reelection-oriented legislators in return for appropriate regulation. Third, legislators are prepared to enter into the bargain because significant benefits can be given to a well-organized industry without arousing much notice on the part of the widely dispersed and unorganized citizenry that will pay in small, per capita amounts for this regulatory largess.

Once in operation the regulatory scheme is maintained in the interest of the regulated industry by bureaucrats who look both to Congress and to the industry for their rewards. These rewards flow from industry in the form of social and business relations and the prospects of further career opportunities in the private sector. Rewards also include the goodwill of oversight and appropriations committees staffed by those legislators who can derive the greatest electoral payoff from the regulation in question.

The capture story has a number of variations. It might be imagined, for example, that the industry does not actually solicit the regulatory legislation and may even oppose it. But once in place the regulatory bureaucracy succumbs to the perennial blandishments of industry coupled with the self-interested preferences of those few legislators who elect to serve on the relevant oversight or appropriations committees. In an even less conspiratorial mode, "capture" comes about simply by virtue of the industry's superior resources and organization in generating and presenting information to the relevant decision makers. Ultimately the industry view of regulation becomes the factual predicate upon which regulators regulate.

Nor need the "capturer" be an industry. A capturer must merely have the organization and resources to deliver rewards to reelection-oriented legislators or career-oriented bureaucrats. The capture story for automobile safety regulation can thus be told with either General Motors or Ralph Nader in the role of captor. Or at least it could if the facts so warranted. And the captors might change identity over time. Perhaps Nader captured Congress in 1966 to get the legislation passed, but by the mid-1970s the system had switched to operating in the interests of industry.

There is also a somewhat less developed literature on the *internal* capture of regulatory systems by particular coalitions of bureaucrats or bureaucrats and legislators. Perhaps the most tantalizing discussion for our purposes concerns the influence of various professional subcultures on agency regulatory activity. The FTC's prosecutorial policy, for example, has been described as the output of negotiations between lawyers and economists within the commission who have quite different professional perspectives and, more important, quite different professional reward structures outside the agency.[27]

NHTSA is also an agency that contains within it several different, and arguably competing, professional cadres. We might imagine policy choice to have been the result of a competition for the heart of the agency's regulatory program among safety engineers, the legal staff, and economists who staff the policy and evaluation office. Perhaps the shift to recalls is the result of internecine professional warfare.

A Critique of Traditional Approaches. Both the public welfare and private interest traditions have provided useful perspectives on the development of regulatory policy. But a satisfactory explanation of regulatory behavior cannot be articulated within either of these traditions. In part this results from the ahistorical stance of both forms of explanation. Within these traditions the power of critical actors to create new worlds is assumed. But there are other difficulties as well. Chief among them is that both theories are sufficiently vague that virtually any outcome can be "explained."

In the most general sense, the idea of the public welfare or public interest in American political life tends to be more a procedural than a substantive notion. In a pluralist democratic polity the policy output of competition among various interests may be precisely what is meant by the "public interest" or "pursuing the public welfare." Pluralist theory, which undergirds our dominant tradition of political analysis, does not hypothesize an overarching general will or unified public interest that can be specified as the aim or goal of the social order. Hence a legislative-administrative policy process in which people both inside and outside government are imagined to be pursuing their own aims may be said to generate "public interest" outcomes, provided that the institutions and procedures that mediate this competition are themselves "fair" or "representative."

At some level, of course, this blending of public and private interest hypotheses in pluralist theory renders the idea of the public interest completely empty. The public interest becomes simply the vector sum or output of the policy process, whatever that output might be. As a behavioral hypothesis this form of public interest theory is nonfalsifiable; as a descriptive heuristic, it is indistinguishable from a private interest perspective.

Private interest notions suffer from similar defects. If a regulatory statute has any effect at all, it necessarily rearranges the legal claims available to various members of the body politic. If rights have values, their redistribution will benefit some more than others. Every regulatory scheme can thus be found to be run in the interest of some group or coalition of groups that obtains special benefits.

Even if some or all of the benefited groups initially fail to recognize the improvement in their positions that the regulatory scheme will bring, it seems likely that they will notice over time. Eventually they will attempt to sustain or even improve these beneficial results. Finding a group or groups who are being benefited and who are working strategically to maintain those benefits is virtually ensured with respect to every regulatory system. The null hypothesis is always rejected. And because no group will ever get all it wants and the rhetorical conventions of political life suppress the expression of simple greed as a basis for public policy, the private interest story is one of complex compromises among groups whose goals all can be, and are, articulated in public interest terms. The statutory or regulatory outcome is thus descriptively indistinguishable from the public interest story.

Mindful of the vagueness, overlaps, and normative loadings of these traditions, others have tended to blend them into what might be called an "environmental hypothesis."[28] This type of explanation might posit, for example, that NHTSA has been struggling to provide the form of regulation that society wants (public welfare) in order to maintain or enhance its own institutional position (private interest). As it engages in this struggle, the agency receives feedback from many sources in its regulatory environment, including Congress (and its component parts), the courts, the Executive Office of the President, the Department of Transportation, the states, interest groups, and general public opinion as expressed in opinion polls and in expert and press commentary. The apparent success or failure of its efforts to satisfy these various constituencies induces adaptations that, over time, profoundly influence the agency's regulatory approach.

This approach is helpful, but it seems to promise only a textured descriptive account, at best. It has little to say about which environmental actors or signals will be most salient or meaningful, or even how the agency might interpret environmental feedback as supportive or threatening. To be more than a history of a particular regulatory regime, however fascinating such a story might be, an account must seek to get behind the story, to illuminate the structure of American regulatory politics.

The analysis that follows, therefore, uses a more specific form of environmental hypothesis, which we call the "legal culture hypothesis." In short form the hypothesis is simple: the legal system makes adopting regulatory standards quite difficult, but tends to facilitate recalling "defective" automobiles. But when applied to a concrete case the result is both textured and complex, combining an appreciation of the structural features and the basic political presuppositions of American law with the highly contingent, sometimes unique, political-administrative history of federal vehicle safety regulation. In the end we argue that although the specific twists and turns of policy and politics were hardly foreseeable, the legal-ideological minefield confronted by NHTSA's standard setting was planted so heavily that safe passage to the goals envisaged in 1966 may well have been impossible.

Demystifying Legal Culture

What do we really mean when we talk about the "legal culture"? Can this idea be given any determinate shape? Does it lead to specific predictions about regulatory form or the operation and experience of regulatory institutions?

Skepticism about cultural explanation is widespread in the intellectual circles usually most interested in regulation. Sociologists and anthropologists may speak confidently of culture, but for most economists and political scientists, to engage in cultural explanation would be a confession of intellectual poverty. Yet aside from well-known disciplinary conceits, there is no persuasive reason for this position. For our purposes a useful and succinct definition of culture is provided by Edgar Schein: "A pattern of basic assumptions—invented, discovered, or developed by a given group as it learns to cope with its problems of external adaptation and internal integration—that has worked well enough to be considered valid and, therefore, to be taught to new members as the correct way to perceive, think and feel in relation to those problems."[29]

The real problem with such a definition, and the place where skeptics generally exclaim "Aha," is the reference to a "pattern of basic assumptions," which is something that cannot be directly observed. Other traditions of explanation, however, have similar difficulties. Neither "the public interest" nor private interests are observable directly. Both entail assumptions about norms and preferences, constructed (usually) by interpreting behaviors. For those interested in legal and political culture, the impossibility of direct observation should be no more (and no less) disabling than it is for public welfare or private interest theorists. Although an outsider to the culture might have some difficulty in interpreting the evidence, for those familiar with a particular legal culture its basic assumptions are reasonably transparent. They are embedded in the persistent norms, institutions, and processes of the legal order.

To describe the legal culture of motor vehicle safety regulation actually requires a discussion on two levels. The first and more abstract level, discussed in the next section, has to do with the general culture of federal regulation. Here the concern is with the underlying assumptions of the legal order concerning the role of the federal government in regulating individual or firm conduct and the means by which that regulation is to be accomplished. At this level "legal culture" and "constitutional culture" are virtual synonyms. The second, more particularistic aspect of the legal culture of vehicle safety regulation might be called "automobile law." It is analyzed in Chapter 2, which focuses on assumptions about the role of law in the control of the automobile and its safe use on roads and highways.

The Legal Culture of Regulation

The American legal culture's approach to federal regulation is a synthesis (or attempted synthesis) of two competing visions. The first is the Madisonian project embodied in the original Constitution and the Bill of Rights. From that perspective governance, including regulation, is preeminently rights-protecting and remedial. The national government's principal purposes are the unification of international affairs, the creation of a free trade area (including the necessary infrastructure to support commerce), and the protection of individual rights. Within this vision national lawgiving is the function of the Congress. But the jurisdiction of the representative assembly is strictly limited by specific conferrals of power and is further restricted by a separation of powers that, first, involves the Chief Executive in approving laws and, second, presumes judicial review of legislation to ensure legality.

The processes of law in this vision are the processes of the constituent assembly for legislation and of judicial trial for the determination of legal rights. Bureaucracies, regulations, and all the other conventional trappings of the modern administrative state are missing from this basic constitutional design. This legal culture, in short, denies the need for or legitimacy of administrative regulation. For at least the first hundred years of U.S. history the legal structure of the federal government might be said to have conformed to this vision, thus conferring effective power largely on courts and political parties. To the extent that there was regulatory activity of a sort that we now would recognize as "regulation," it was the function of states and localities.

This Madisonian vision of governance changed gradually. Major shifts occurred both with the Civil War amendments to the Constitution, which realigned state and national power, and with the triumph of New Deal activism over the constitutionally based resistance of a Supreme Court dedicated to maintaining strict limits on governmental competence. This post–New Deal vision of governance is indeed radically different from its eighteenth- and nineteenth-century predecessor. This is a legal culture more oriented to the accommodation of social interests than to the protection of private property. It imagines a positive government wielding national powers for the solution of national problems. It emphasizes executive leadership and expert policymaking in the place of the older vision of assembly governance. It also demands flexible processes of implementation, free from judicial formalisms that constrain policy in the interest of protecting legal rights.

But it would be going much too far to suggest that the New Deal, revisionist account of our constitutional legal culture wholly displaced the original, Madisonian vision. Americans have not given up their ideals of individual rights, limited government, the separation of powers, assembly lawgiving, judicial protection, and state and local autonomy. We have instead attempted to synthesize these older principles with the new demands of positive governance.

Such a synthesis produces many uneasy compromises, which are impossible to describe or analyze fully here. For the purposes of understanding the legal culture as it applies to federal regulation, three features of the contemporary legal culture are most important. First, the notion that lawmaking should be in the hands of experts rather than in the hands of politically accountable representatives is a source of continuing anxiety. Constitutional scholars, political analysts, lawyers, and Supreme Court justices continue to bemoan the delegation by Congress of broad lawmaking powers to administrative agencies. The response of the legal culture to this sense of unease has been to reinterpret the idea of the rule of law. Government according to law has come to mean not that all lawgiving will be done by the legislature, but that regulatory agency policymaking will be controlled, substantively by judicial review and procedurally by the requirements of the Administrative Procedure Act.

This cultural reinterpretation of the rule of law is the political compromise envisioned during the New Deal era itself. Although the Roosevelt Administration won the substantive battle concerning the reach of national regulatory power, it gave ground steadily on the procedural and legal controls that should be applicable to the exercise of regulatory authority. The Administrative Procedure Act of 1946 was a procedural triumph by those dedicated to older visions of governmental legality and represented by the establishment of the American Bar Association. As we shall see, this particular synthesis of Madisonian and New Deal constitutionalism has had a dramatic impact on the current shape of and prospects for federal regulation. Coping with highly proceduralized decision processes and satisfying courts of the soundness of their regulatory judgments weigh heavily on the shoulders of all federal administrators.

Beyond this basic reinterpretation of the rule of law for a positive, administrative rather than a reactive, legislative state, two other aspects of our synthetic regulatory legal culture require particular mention. But both may be less examples of legal syntheses than of continuing ambivalence concerning the appropriate structure of regulatory regimes. The first involves the continuing struggle between Congress and the President for control over the direction of administrative policymaking. This battle is waged continuously by the Congress and the Chief Executive using their respective weapons of legislation and appropriations on the one hand and appointments, removals, and executive directions on the other. It is an internecine warfare, mediated by the Supreme Court, but with few clear rules for the conduct of hostilities and very little chance of a permanent settlement. It is perhaps fair to say that the best the Court can do is to try to preserve the combatants' constitutional positions by interdicting raids on each other's arsenals of constitutionally conferred armaments. From the regulators' perspective, this state of affairs is menacing. It means that each regulatory system is subject to attempts at, and often effective control and direction by, two political principals. The legal culture presumes that much of this control and direction is entirely legitimate and that administrators must do the best they can with contradictory instructions from their political overseers.

The competitive situation is not entirely fluid, however, for the contest between President and Congress is not entirely disconnected from the post–New Deal synthetic vision of the rule of law. In accordance with that vision's acceptance of the legitimacy of the positive or activist state, substantive judicial review is no longer a search for rationality as judicially constructed—a search that could easily lead to judicial invalidation of regulatory legislation. It is instead a search for instrumental rationality *within* the legislative scheme constructed by the Congress. The culturally sanctioned vision of judicial review of administrative action thus necessarily implies a preeminent place for the Congress in shaping administrative conduct by statute. It also implies a subordinate, interstitial, or coordinating role for presidential direction. But here lies the rub. The culturally approved "dominant" principal (the Congress) is often incapable of framing statutory commands in terms that clearly resolve important, even fundamental, issues of policy. Meanwhile, although the "subordinate" principal's (the President's) directions may be clear enough, they also may be legally insufficient to sustain an exercise of regulatory authority. As a result the administrators' formulation of regulatory policy is cut adrift politically and legally. The dual principals problem is thus not just a problem of conflicting instructions, but also a problem of having no reliable or useful political instructions at all. This situation has a major impact on regulatory behavior.

The third crucial feature of legal culture concerns the appropriate allocation of regulatory authority between the states and the national government. Looking at the judicial opinions concerning the reach of congressional powers, one might imagine that here Civil War and New Deal revisionism had triumphed over all attempts to preserve state prerogative. The powers available to the national government under contemporary conceptions of the commerce clause, the general welfare clause, and Section 5 of the Fourteenth Amendment suggest a constitutional order entirely hospitable to the exercise of national powers that displace state regulatory competence.

The reality of the exercise of federal regulatory power is actually quite different. There has been much displacement over the past five or six decades, but the forms and limits of displacement should not be missed. There has been continuous attention, both legislatively and judicially, to the preservation of state control over private remedial actions. Since these actions are both supplementary to and an alternative form of legal regulation, preserving state power in this domain may have very substantial consequences in defining the forms of regulation available to the national government. In addition, many federal regulatory statutes preserve state autonomy in implementation. These statutes are in fact policy frameworks that both permit and fund state implementation to the extent that states have "approved plans." Framework statutes include not only the so-called grants-in-aid statutes, of which there are hundreds, but also many federal regulatory statutes. Nor do federal regulatory activities in one form necessarily preempt state application of different regulatory regimes to the same topic.

We have thus witnessed a fantastic growth of national power that is nevertheless combined with the preservation of much state prerogative, particularly at the level of direct implementation. The federal government makes many broad policies but leaves states and localities, often energized by federal funds, substantial latitude to adapt implementation of those policies to local conditions and preferences. And as Karl Llewelyn once remarked, the real power in legal regimes flows to those who have the "doing in charge."

From the perspective of federal regulatory systems, continuing attention to federalism and the values of local autonomy creates a host of problems. Chief among them are that federal regulatory legislation may take a suboptimal form in order to preserve state jurisdiction, and that regulatory activity by federal administrators must continually confront the cultural challenge that state regulation is constitutionally preferable to the exercise of federal regulatory power.

The rest of this book explores how these basic legal ideas concerning federal regulation structure the regulatory environment for motor vehicle safety regulation and shape its course. We will content ourselves here, therefore, with a broad generalization about the effects of the synthetic or ambivalent legal culture just described: to the extent that an exercise of regulatory power entails the remedial protection of preexisting rights, is exercised in a judicialized form, and supports or mimics state regulatory activity, the legal culture will tend to view it as essentially nonproblematic. To the extent that regulation is in a legislative form, but not embodied in legislation, is forward-looking and prophylactic in its purpose, and displaces, confronts, or contradicts state and local control, that exercise of regulatory power will be legally problematic indeed.

Moreover, what is culturally problematic is almost always operationally contentious. Problematic exercises of power can be expected to be caught up both in congressional-presidential competition for policy control and in legal contests made available through those forms of judicial review and administrative procedural formalities that have been developed to harmonize the exercise of regulatory authority with our basic constitutional assumptions concerning the rule of law. It is in this much more complex sense that we intend to demonstrate that the legal culture makes rulemaking difficult and recall activity easy. And it is because the complexity of the explanation is generated by attention to fundamental structural features of the legal culture that we believe that its findings have application well beyond the specific arena of motor vehicle safety regulation.

The story we are about to tell is hardly a simple one, but it has a discernible plot. Chapter 2 provides a picture of the particular legal culture of "automobility" as it stood in 1966. It explores what the revolution of 1966 challenged, not just in the regulatory culture generally, but also in what we call the "law of a mobile society."

Chapters 3 through 7 describe motor vehicle safety regulation from 1966 through 1974. Chapter 3 details the legislative process that produced the 1966 act and analyzes the legal product that emerged. Chapters 4 and 5 recount NHTSA's formative experiences in wielding the legal tools the act provided. By 1972 or 1973 basic patterns of behavior had emerged as a result of the agency's encounters with its immediate regulatory environment. Courts, Congress, and the executive branch all seemed in differing ways to be inhibiting rulemaking, but supporting recalls. A counterrevolutionary force of some sort was having significant effects.

By 1974 much had happened to suggest that motor vehicle safety regulation could not go forward in the form envisioned by the revolution of 1966. Chapters 6 and 7 recount Congress's reappraisal of NHTSA's statutory mandate. The amendments that emerged from that legislative reexamination were, however, highly ambiguous. They neither entirely contradicted nor reinforced the basic regulatory mission that the 1966 act seemed to establish. The time had come for agency reassessment. Chapter 8, therefore, steps back to take analytic stock of what the legal environment seemed to be telling the agency about its rulemaking and recall efforts. It also explains why the legal culture had legitimated one regulatory technique while eviscerating the other.

Regulatory agencies are, of course, not people, but collections of people in particular relation to one another. Agencies do not receive and interpret signals from the legal environment or act on that information; the people in them do. Moreover, the people are not fungible ciphers. They have individual careers, plans, ambitions, commitments, ideologies, and preferences. Chapter 9 investigates how repeated signals from the external legal environment empower and disempower internal actors and simultaneously legitimate or delegitimate their ideas and commitments, even their careers. The change in the agency's external product or regulatory strategy is thus mirrored by (or mirrors) the transformation of the agency internally. The external regulatory culture penetrates and, ultimately, reshapes the internal culture of the regulatory bureaucracy. The strength of these cultural determinants is particularly notable in the face of the energetic efforts of a strongly pro-consumer, pro-regulatory agency administrator in the years 1976–1980.

Chapter 10 returns to the themes with which we have begun. It argues on the basis of the evidence already presented, and by close attention to NHTSA's most important, notorious, and hotly contested rule, that neither "private interest" nor "public interest" analyses of this regulatory experience have much explanatory power. Chapter 11 draws together the threads of the cultural explanation of motor vehicle safety regulation. It then reinterprets these lessons as more general lessons for the future design and management of the regulatory environment, both at NHTSA and elsewhere.

TWO

The Law of a Mobile Society

The true ambitions of the authors of the 1966 Motor Vehicle Safety Act can be appreciated only by attending to the legal regime that it sought to replace. And from that perspective, the 1966 act was perhaps even more revolutionary than our prior discussion suggests. With its enactment Congress was engaged in an attempt to shift the social purposes, legal techniques, jurisdictional presuppositions, even the intellectual style, of virtually all of the prior American law related to automobile safety.

The Four Commandments of Automobile Law

Automobiles Are America. In 1893 the Duryea brothers of Springfield, Massachusetts, put an internal combustion engine in a modified horse carriage. Within just three decades the American automobile industry, so modestly begun, had become the largest manufacturing industry in the country. The people were ecstatic about the product. In an article in *Collier's* in 1912 Gouverneur Morris put it this way: "God gave us the automobile that in the short life which is ours we may see a few more hills and valleys, a few more fields of flowers."[1] Less poetically, Joel Eastman explains:

> The American public accepted the motor car as enthusiastically as its early proponents, and the reason for the response is not difficult to discover. The motorized passenger vehicle fitted perfectly into American culture because it appeared to offer inexpensive, individualized transportation to an individualistic, highly mobile people. With the introduction of dependable, low cost motorcars like the Model T Ford in 1908, Americans rapidly

abandoned their horse-powered vehicles for mechanically-powered ones, and the motorized highway system appeared full blown, almost overnight. Once it had arrived, its mere existence became its raison d'être, and it developed a momentum all its own, fired by a growing number of interest groups with a direct economic stake in continuing and expanding the motorized highway transportation system.[2]

From this public demand the first commandment of automobile law follows quite naturally: legal rules should facilitate automotive travel. Indeed, as this manufacturing behemoth came to represent greater and greater shares of national employment and gross national product, it became plausible to assume that the law should also facilitate the growth, or at least the maintenance, of the automobile industry. In the 1950s when Charles Wilson defended his suitability for high public office against charges of industry bias by asserting, "What's good for General Motors is good for America,"[3] only the intellectuals scoffed. For most Americans, one in six of whom worked in jobs connected to automobile production, sales or service, Wilson's remark only asserted the obvious.

Safety Is Job One. Yet fabulous as the growth of automobility has been, when the Duryeas hooked an engine to a buggy it was not entirely clear that the horseless carriage would improve mobility. Frank Duryea and others seemed at first to promote the new device primarily on the basis of the safety benefits of its "horselessness": "The horse is a willful, unreliable brute. The ever recurring accidents due to horses which are daily set forth in the papers prove that the horse is a dangerous motor and not the docile pet of the poet. The mechanical motor is his superior in many respects, and when its superiority has become better known his inferiority will be more apparent."[4]

This rosy picture was short-lived. Although automobiles were getting better and better (faster, stronger, quieter, more attractive, more comfortable, more reliable, and cheaper) during the first decade of the twentieth century, automobile accidents were occurring with startling and increasing frequency. Citizens, particularly nonmotorists, were outraged. Magazine articles complained that it was no longer possible to bicycle or to walk on the roads because of the hazard of automobiles. Elected officials found it prudent to lament the carnage and urge controls over the growing "evil" of automobile fatalities. Life insurance companies, whose actuarial estimates were upset, had an economic interest that eventually funded as well as motivated safety campaigns. Lamenting the "distortions" of this emerging pro-safety, and potentially anti-automobile, movement, James R. Doolittle wrote in 1916: "In the view of some of the press, the automobile is today a juggernaut, a motoring speed-monster, intent on killing and maiming all who stand in its way. The motorist . . . is an intoxicated savage, in charge of a dangerous device."[5] To mobility, therefore, was added safety. The second basic command of automobile law was that the law should make safety a central preoccupation.

The Intelligence in the Machine. When a good product produces bad results the reason is usually obvious—misuse. The automobile was not causing accidents by itself. And since the horse was gone, the driver was the only serious candidate for blame. This was simple common sense—so common that virtually every utterance on motor vehicle safety in the critical early years of its social conceptualization focused on the driver as the problem. Whether one consulted the industry, the popular press, the trade journals, public officials, emerging local and national highway safety groups, or the insurance companies, the prescription was always the same. If drivers could be made to behave properly, there would be no auto safety problem.

The third commandment of automobile law was thus straightforward: legal controls should be designed to promote good driver behavior and discourage bad. Drivers had to be educated to drive carefully, and traffic laws had to be enforced against those who did not. Careless or reckless drivers should be made to compensate for any personal injury or property damage that they caused.

Don't Argue with Success. In the rush to acquire cars, facilitate their use, and regulate their operations, the automobile itself as a focus of safety policy and legal intervention was for the most part overlooked— but not entirely. As early as 1902 the trade magazine *Horseless Age*[6] called for national government standards for motor vehicles. But the social context of this call for action gave it a meaning quite different from the superficially similar demand that emerged sixty years later.

In 1902 the basic structure of the automobile was still up for grabs. It appeared that the French vision of the machine—motor forward, enclosed passenger compartment behind—had overtaken the Duryea-style horseless carriage—a buggy steered by a tiller, with the engine under the buggy's single seat. But scores of design characteristics varied significantly from manufacturer to manufacturer. And there were scores of manufacturers. Within the automobile industry itself there was substantial concern about the basic structural integrity of the products that came from many small producers. If buyers became fearful of the automobile, demand would be stifled. *Horseless Age* thus reflected the views of the major industry participants.

Particular apprehension surrounded the relationship between the hard-edged, high-velocity automobile and the other softer and slower inhabitants of the roadways. Pedestrian injuries (defining "pedestrians" broadly to include all nonmotorists) *were* the accident problem in the early years of automobile use. Safety partisans had numerous solutions. Most—such as a proposal to require that automobiles be preceded on the roadways by a person on foot bearing a flag by day and a lantern by night—sought to limit the automobile's promise of mobility.[7] They were doomed by the first commandment.

One proposed solution, however, was technologically adventurous and focused on the automobile itself. In 1908 John O'Leary patented a "smart" fender; it deployed a net that scooped pedestrians out of harm's way at the slightest impact. Unfortunately, the bulk and configuration of this contraption made it unpopular with automakers. Although later inventors improved substantially on O'Leary's design, they were never able to interest auto producers in the idea. But this is not to say that auto manufacturers were uninterested in a technological approach to safety problems. Henry Ford himself was adamant to the point of eccentricity on the strength of door latches. The electric starter grew out of Cadillac manufacturer Henry Leland's concerns with injuries from crank-starter kickbacks.

Clearly, the automobile itself was recognized as the source of some safety problems. But early suggestions for national standardization of vehicles (like the manufacturers' requests for preemptive federal regulation of driver qualifications, highway speed limits, and vehicle registration) were resisted in Congress on the combined grounds of custom, precedent, and lack of need. Regulating either driver conduct or vehicle design at the national level did not conform to existing political ideas about the appropriate federal division of responsibilities or to contemporary jurisprudential understandings of the federal government's constitutional power to regulate interstate commerce. Automobiles were, after all, a *private* mode of transport operated primarily on state and local roads.

There was also insufficient reason for Congress to focus its energies on regulating vehicle design or performance. To the extent that calls for "federal standards" were meant primarily as a means of avoiding the impediments of conflicting state regulation or the risks associated with technically incompetent small producers, those problems were solving themselves. State legislatures rapidly learned that the populace would not brook much interference with its access to cars. Responding to the first commandment, states rapidly moved to harmonize, if not completely unify, their regulatory requirements. And when Henry Ford introduced the mass-produced Model T in 1908, the days of backyard auto construction were clearly numbered. Multiple small and sometimes technically unsophisticated producers manufacturing strikingly different motorcars was not to be the industry pattern. Private mass production would provide bureaucratic assurance of quality.

By most early accounts the automobile was indeed a technological marvel, one whose performance and affordability were improving dramatically from year to year. A federal attempt to standardize a rapidly developing and rapidly improving technology, whose innovations were enthusiastically received by the populace, looked like an errand for the politically foolish.

The only useful and politically acceptable action Congress might take was to help the states and localities construct more and better roads. Such an effort was thought to have some safety benefit, and its payoff in improved mobility was obvious. Moreover, the states could use federal aid to promote automobility, if, when, and where they wanted. "States' rights" and local control would be maintained. It is therefore hardly surprising that one of the earliest uses of Congress's enhanced power to generate revenue through the personal income tax was to fund a federal aid program for rural roads.[8] Automobile law's fourth basic commandment was confirmed: federal power should be used to support, not challenge, the auto manufacturers' technical mastery of their product and the states' control over motorists and roadways.

The Conventional Structure of Automobile Safety

The law's treatment of automobile safety from the time of the commercial introduction of the automobile to passage of the Motor Vehicle Safety Act of 1966 (and perhaps beyond) has been consistent with this early conceptualization of the automobile safety problem. First, automobility has been promoted. Most regulatory "restrictions" in fact have a largely facilitative character. The most ubiquitous of all automobile regulations—rules of the road for traffic movement—illustrate this fundamental commitment. Common legal requirements, such as stopping at stop signs and traffic signals, driving in one direction only on particular streets and on the right-hand side on others, are surrounded by an aura and rhetoric of safety. They thus follow automobile law's second commandment. Nevertheless, they are all designed primarily to facilitate traffic flow.

This seems an odd claim. But its very oddity demonstrates how thoroughly "safety" and "mobility" have been linked in the law's regulatory commands. To prevent accidents, after all, drivers need only exercise caution. In the absence of all rules of the road motorists would not commit collective suicide; they would drive in a fashion that achieved an acceptable level of risk. Rules of the road simply permit much greater mobility at the same risk levels by making custom instantly transparent. Even traffic rules that seem to work against mobility, such as speed limits, have this characteristic. Virtually all speed limits are set by observing how fast motorists customarily drive and then setting a limit that will, if effective, inhibit only 15 percent of the existing traffic.[9] This rule of thumb is based not on safety considerations (although a safety rationale can be constructed) but on the belief that such limits maximize the carrying capacity of the roadways. The object of the exercise is to optimize traffic flow by maximizing speed subject to drivers' revealed "consensus" on the speed that produces an acceptable level of risk. The first commandment of automobile "safety" law is seldom flouted.

Examples of the second and third commandments are equally ubiquitous. Safety is the constant theme of virtually all official action that inhibits either drivers' access to automobiles or drivers' preferred behavior on the roads. And it is important to note that "safety" here is synonymous with "safe behavior by motorists." Attempts at driver behavior modification have dominated the legal approach to vehicle safety. Enforcement of traffic laws, for example, is universally understood as necessary to increase safety. Similarly, driver training and licensing requirements are designed to educate drivers in correct—meaning safe—driving habits. Even the civil liability system, in assigning liability for accidents, focuses on the reasonableness of the motorists' behavior. The system thus identifies unsafe driver behavior as the cause of injuries and property damage and, presumably, reinforces drivers' incentives to behave reasonably.

The combination of demands for mobility and demands for the reform of bad driving habits shapes the law in a reactive mode. Measures that would prevent access to motor vehicles by high-risk drivers simply because they are high risk have been employed very sparingly. Drivers need only demonstrate modest competence to be licensed, and that often only once in a lifetime. Reform of drivers' behavior is sought largely through criminal punishment or civil sanctions after an accident has occurred or a traffic rule has been violated. From the operational standpoint of the legal system, "bad driving" is largely an individualistic moral judgment about the past performance of particular drivers. Sanctions are applied after the fact in reaction to misbehavior.

The conceptualization of automobile law, both civil and criminal, as promoting access to automobility, limited only by reactive, fault-based behavioral controls in the interests of safety, has achieved quasi-constitutional status. In 1971 the Supreme Court ruled, in *Bell v. Burson*,[10] first that drivers had a constitutionally protected property interest in driving and, second, that the license of an uninsured and impecunious driver could not be suspended pending the outcome of a damage claim against him without first providing that driver a hearing on the issue of whether he had been at fault. Viewing access to an automobile as a necessity, and Georgia state law as designed generally to facilitate that interest in the absence of negligent or reckless *behavior,* the Court found Georgia's claim, that it merely wanted to keep persons who had accidents and were unable to pay compensation off its roads, irrational. Steeped in automobile law's general structure, the Court seemed incapable of viewing Georgia's asserted prophylactic purpose as anything other than incomprehensible. What could it mean to have a policy that limited access to automobility on a basis other than a driver's proven inability or unwillingness to drive sensibly?

Yet in overturning Georgia's statute on the basis of the intellectual structure provided by automobile law's first three commandments, the Court was careful not to violate the fourth. It found automobile law's conceptual structure, not in some overarching federal policy, but in the provisions of Georgia's own licensing, traffic control, and liability law. Nominally, at least, state and local control was maintained.

Imagining a Different World

Neither automobile access as a basic right, nor automobile accidents, injuries, and property damage as a function of drivers' faulty behavior, nor state and local control of motor vehicle use is a logically necessary element of the social conception and legal structure of automobile law. It is certainly possible, for example, to imagine a civil liability system that rejects the negligence standard (unreasonable behavior) as its basic principle for dealing with automobile accidents. In liability suits between motorists, such a legal regime might treat each motorist as "assuming the risk" of his or her chosen mode of transportation. (Some such notion seems to underlie the recent adoption of limited no-fault insurance schemes in some states, under which motorists must insure themselves against their own costs of being involved in an accident.) And with respect to injuries to nonmotorists, the legal system might have taken the position that the use of a motor vehicle, for whatever purpose, was inherently dangerous. On that theory, the owner as well as the driver might be strictly liable, without fault, for injuries to pedestrians or other nonmotoring interests. A common law oriented in this way would not focus attention on the modification of faulty driving behavior as a major purpose or effect of its allocation of legal responsibilities. By further burdening the ownership and use of automobiles with these liability costs, however, this hypothetical legal system would violate automobile law's first commandment; it would fail to promote automobility.

Similarly, we can imagine a social conception of the rules of the road that recognizes their function as enhancing mobility and ignores the safety rhetoric. On this view the failure to provide stop signs and traffic signals, with their attendant enforcement apparatus, would be not unsafe, but merely inefficient. The lack of these legal controls would require elaborate attempts by motorists to gauge and signal their respective intentions, thus perhaps slowing traffic to a standstill. But there need be no unhappy *safety* consequences. Without the facilitation of traffic rules, traffic flow probably would be so slow that damage from accidents would virtually disappear.

Nor would it have been utterly unthinkable, even in 1900, to institute a regime of national vehicle safety regulation oriented toward the design or performance of motor vehicles. As early as 1837[11] Congress had begun to regulate the safety of one increasingly popular mode of transportation—steamships. By 1852,[12] comprehensive federal legislation regulated the allowable working pressure for any boiler; the quality of iron plates required in their fabrication; the number, location, and design of safety valves; and other features of boiler design and performance.[13] This regulation was premised not on the common view that the fault for boiler explosions usually lay with the steamboats' engineers but on the scientific investigations of research engineers, particularly those at the Franklin Institute in Philadelphia.

A vehicle-centered, scientifically based, and national approach to automobile safety thus was conceptually possible during the formative years of American automobile law. Such a regulatory system would almost necessarily have focused on manufacturers', rather than motorists', responsibilities. The demands for "automobility" might have been satisfied by efficient rules of the road and improved highways while demands for pedestrian safety and compensation were honored through appropriate combinations of strict liability and no-fault insurance. What then explains the fabric of the pre-1966 law? Why did the law respond to the "commandments" that we have articulated in the fashion that it did?

A partial answer is implied by the history recounted so far, which is a compound of custom, common sense, intellectual fashion, and specific economic interest. First, custom. States and localities were already in the business of providing, maintaining, and regulating streets and roads. That these jurisdictions would also be the ones responsible for the provision of the "rules of the road" applicable to automobile travel seemed virtually self-evident. Change might have come via demands for national uniformity, but the states met that challenge through harmonization.

Second, common sense. The automobile injury problem, as it gradually emerged, looked different from the steamboat safety problem. Steamboat boilers were blowing up; automobiles were colliding with each other and with other things on the road. The steamboat safety issue looked like a problem of design or manufacture; the automobile accident problem like a problem of driver skill or care. There were claims that steamboats blew up because of operator misuse or poor maintenance, and operator behavior modification was tried first. But when licensing and inspection failed to stem the tide of explosions, the Franklin Institute's technological fix was attractive.

Third, intellectual fashion. The negligence principle, with its behavior modification connotations, was the consensus candidate for adoption by the courts at the time that automobile accidents began to produce substantial litigation. Oliver Wendell Holmes had delivered his famous lectures, "The Common Law," in 1881. Their principal purpose was to give a unifying theme to common law doctrine. And on the question of tort law Holmes was clear—the unifying principle was negligence.[14] So influential were his lectures, and the activities of other proponents of the negligence idea, that by the turn of the century liability based on individual fault, and particularly negligence, was accepted by most lawyers as the unifying principle of American tort law. Even those who today question (and in fact reject) the notion that negligence "explains" what courts were actually doing in tort suits in the late nineteenth century still agree that negligence *was* the principle basis for civil liability in accidents involving strangers.[15] Hence, in the early twentieth century, to premise civil liability for automobile accidents on negligence was simply to use the intellectual structure that was generally thought to fit these cases at the time.

Finally, specific economic interest. It has been argued persuasively[16] that the conceptualization of automobile accident losses as a problem of behavior modification calling for state and local control had the happy consequence of satisfying all the major interests that surrounded the motor vehicle as a mode of transport. For instance, certain professional groups (the police, state vehicle administrators, the bar, and public school educators) were almost necessarily involved in traffic management and driver education. By characterizing their rather mundane efforts as a quest to save lives and prevent injuries, these groups upgraded their otherwise rather low-status activity and mobilized political support for the funding of public programs. Speaking of an era in which automobile accidents were just becoming a public concern, Stephen Merrill concludes:

> There is substantial evidence that the police, motor vehicle, and bar associations opted to reform rather than abandon traffic controls to gain the respect of the public as a whole for tasks including but not limited to traffic enforcement, driver licensing, and traffic adjudication. Educators, on the other hand, responded to client demand by designing a drivers' education program that would obviate colleagues' objections to training students in simple manipulative skills. Claims that reformed traffic controls could prevent accidents and save lives promised to convert public contempt into respect and to advance related goals characteristic of professional reform movements—autonomy and integrity in the exercise of authority, expertise and specialization of practitioners, discretion in the treatment of clients, and uniformity of results in the handling of similar cases.[17]

This intellectual structure was equally congenial to the other interested parties. The "clientele" to whom Merrill refers was the general public. The behavioral problem that the professionals defined (irresponsibility, selfishness, inattention, lack of skill, or poor attitudes) allowed a legal response that was modest in its restrictions and strongly oriented toward exhortation and education as an effective cure. This served the public's basic interest in relatively unlimited use of a highly desired form of personal mobility. Automobile manufacturers too were interested in a well-regulated system of automobile use, one that reduced the perceived threat of automobile travel, facilitated mobility, and maintained the motorists' sense of control over their own destiny. The automakers, having the same perceived interests as motorists, responded by providing financial support for the professional associations that identified and promoted behavior modification as effective public policy.

The behavior modification strategy for automobile safety was comfortable for its proponents and comforting to its audience. It portrayed the automobile as inherently safe. The mobility, privacy, and prosperity that the automobile promised were there to be enjoyed. Safety problems were to be taken seriously, but they would give way before the combined effects of education and enforcement. Belief in the efficacy of public education was and is, after all, a central tenet of American progressive and egalitarian ideology. All individuals can achieve, and individual achievement is at base a process of personal reformation, combining opportunity, effort, and learning. A few must be dissuaded from bad habits by the enforcement of penalties, but even the criminal law has a reformative impulse.

Although safety partisans early adopted the "Three E's" slogan— engineering, education, and enforcement—to identify their strategy for highway safety improvement, the first "E" referred primarily to highway engineering. Vehicle engineering was left to the manufacturers. This was obviously sensible. The automobile manufacturers had been wonderfully successful in improving both the design of the product and the design of the production process. This latter achievement made cars not only cheaper but safer. The buyer no longer needed to rely on the skill of the artisan-builder, a reliance made virtually untenable by the complexity of the motor car. The buyer could instead rely on a rational-bureaucratic production process that required few special skills and produced identical machines in a tightly monitored environment. Any attempt to establish a safety-engineering competence separate from the automobile manufacturers not only would argue with an obvious success, but also might undermine further progress.

There is thus built into the very conception of automobile safety law as driver behavior modification a concomitant delegation of engineering or design judgment to automobile manufacturers. The conventional legal structure of automobile safety presumes that automobile technology may force changes in the law, but that the law does not force changes in automobile technology. Nowhere is this principle clearer than in the two areas of law that have focused directly on the automobile itself—state regulation of automobile equipment and the common law of manufacturers' liability.

State Regulation of Automobile Design

State regulation of vehicle design need not long detain us. This safety strategy has been insignificant in scope and extremely modest in its technological ambition. As of 1961 almost all states had adopted legal requirements for vehicle equipment.[18] But these requirements merely incorporated standard manufacturing practice, such as the provision of dual brakes (regular and emergency), headlamps, rearview mirrors, and windshield wipers. A smaller number of states required such exotics as turn signals, and legislation was under way in some to require seat belts or seat-belt anchorages. At most some of these state standards had, at the time of their adoption, pushed existing optional equipment into the standard equipment category. And state laws almost always contented themselves with the "technological" specification that such equipment be "adequate"—thus delegating all engineering judgments to manufacturers.

The one apparently exceptional and technically sophisticated state regulation, on brake fluids, was not in fact an exception. At the recommendation of the National Committee on Uniform State Traffic Laws, states merely adopted the requirements specified by the Society of Automotive Engineers (SAE). Because there was (and is) virtually no automotive engineering profession outside the automobile industry, state legislation on brake fluids in effect delegated substantive regulatory power to a committee of engineers employed by automobile manufacturers and acting to define an industry consensus. As Moynihan put it: "It has on the whole been the consensus of the American public that the automobile manufacturers are responsible firms which produce reliable products. It has generally been believed that automobiles are not likely to be improved by the interference of legislatures and government agencies which cannot, in the nature of things, know as much about manufacturing automobiles as the manufacturers themselves."[19]

There was a flurry of legislative activity concerning vehicle equipment in New York and California in the early 1960s. And in 1962 a federally promoted interstate Vehicle Equipment Safety Compact came into existence, ostensibly as a means of promoting uniform state laws on vehicle safety equipment. But these "innovations" were not highly significant. The New York laws, requiring emergency flashers and windshield defrosters, mandated off-the-shelf technology already in widespread use; and California's major efforts related to emission controls, not safety. Although signed by virtually all states, the compact had by 1966 produced only one recommendation for state adoption, a standard on tire performance and testing. It appeared to some that the compact was a major obstacle to state regulatory innovation. It was yet another device for maintaining the manufacturers' hegemony over engineering and equipment decisions.[20]

Automobile Safety and Manufacturers' Liability at Common Law, 1899–1966

The second domain of safety law that focuses on the automobile itself is the civil liability system. The automobile, and particularly the structure of automobile production and marketing, created a need for products liability law, a legal regime that did not exist—indeed that conceptually could not exist. That need pushed the common law relentlessly. Time and again the inadequacy of the old law to the new world created by the automobile twisted the logic of the law into the rhetorical analogue of a pile of scap iron, melted down the scrap, and poured it into a new mold. Automobile manufacturers, who in 1916 faced no liability to the users of their products should those products prove defective, were very nearly insurers of the quality of their automobiles when the Motor Vehicle Safety Act was passed in 1966. Almost all states now recognize some form of "strict liability" for product injuries, and nearly half adopted that doctrine for the first time in cases involving automobiles.

This story of consumer triumph, however, like the story of state vehicle equipment regulation, is also a story of industry hegemony. Allegiance to automobile law's third commandment was maintained. The intellectual structure of the law as it emerges from 1899 to 1966 is one in which law follows and responds to manufacturing technology. Technology thus defines both the need for legal reform and its limits. To be sure, manufacturers' control over the technology is not a device to escape liability; rather it is a means by which their own technological aspirations define the standard by which their liability will be judged. As of 1966, the common law of products liability confessed its incompetence to force the technology of the automobile in directions demanded by the new, epidemiological vision of vehicle safety developed outside of the automobile industry. Liability there would be, but based on the manufacturers' own evolving standards of safety engineering as embodied in their products.

Horse and Buggy Law in the Age of the Automobile. The first recorded automobile fatality in the United States occurred in 1899. Had that death resulted from a malfunction of the vehicle, and that malfunction from some defect in its manufacture, a suit by the decedent's survivors against the manufacturer of the car almost certainly would have been dismissed before trial. Unless the manufacturer were also the seller, the decedent had no direct relationship with the manufacturer and was, therefore, owed no duty of care.

This result, startling to the modern legal imagination, was the legacy of *Winterbottom v. Wright,*[21] a famous English case decided in 1842. In *Winterbottom* the defendant manufacturer had contracted with the Postmaster General to supply a mail coach to transport mail from Hartford to Hollyhead. The defendant was also responsible for maintaining the coach in safe repair. The plaintiff, a coachman, drove the coach pursuant to a contract obligating the coachman's employer to supply drivers for the Postmaster's mail coaches. The coachman-plaintiff's vehicle overturned and he was permanently disabled. He sued the manufacturer for damages on the theory that the manufacturer had "improperly and negligently conducted himself" with regard to his duties as either a manufacturer or provider of maintenance services to the Postmaster General.

Judgment was entered for the defendant. In a passage that has become worn by frequent citation, Lord Abinger reasoned:

> We ought not permit a doubt to rest upon this subject, for our doing so might be a means of letting in upon us an infinity of action . . . There is no privity of contract between these parties; and if the plaintiff can sue, every passenger, even any person passing along the road, who was injured by the upsetting of the coach, might bring a similar action. Unless we confine the operation of such contracts as this to the parties who entered into them, the most absurd and outrageous consequences, to which we can see no limit, would ensue . . . by permitting this action . . . we subject [contracts] to be ripped open by this action in tort.[22]

Given the ubiquity of modern products liability litigation, these reflections demonstrate Lord Abinger's prescience. But why were they a reason for denying liability? The puzzle is deeper still. *Winterbottom* was almost universally viewed in subsequent litigation as deciding that manufacturers were not liable, either in contract or in tort, to consumers or users of a product who were not in contractual privity with the manufacturer. And although hardly warranted by the facts of the case, this broad construction of *Winterbottom* largely controlled the scope of manufacturers' liability in the United States well into the twentieth century. Why?

The conventional wisdom among commentators is that, by means of the *Winterbottom* rule, courts sought to shelter the emerging industrial state from the risks of indefinite and enormous liability.[23] Perhaps. But legal development does not generally proceed in such a grand or purposeful fashion. Tort law was, and is, relational. It is therefore dependent upon the sorts of relations that are perceptible to courts at a particular time. In 1842 the idea of the "consumer," the "manufacturer," and their social relations simply did not exist. Coaches were made on contract, as were virtually all other goods in commerce, and not mass produced.

When Lord Abinger said that the consequences he perceived from allowing the plaintiff's action would be "most absurd and outrageous," he may have been speaking of the effects on infant industries. It seems more likely, however, that he should be taken to mean that the idea of social relations and social responsibilities that the plaintiff was espousing were, at that time, essentially unintelligible. Relations between legal actors giving rise to rights and duties were either direct—personal and individual—or imperceptible to the legal imagination. This was a view of social and economic life that reflected, as the law so often does, the social and economic relations of the recent past.

The Influence of Mass Production. The automobile was not the first mass-produced product, of course.[24] Gutenberg's fifteenth-century printing press had interchangeable parts; Venetian war galleys in the same period were outfitted by being inched along by pulley through an arsenal; and continuous-flow techniques were employed in iron-manufacturing plants in the seventeenth century. Still, industrial life before the mid-1700s continued to be dominated by master mechanics employing modest numbers of laborers—journeymen, apprentices, and family members. These small entrepreneurs often combined farming and industry, and they sold their wares personally in local markets. The steam engine, power loom, and spinning machine, along with other advances and inventions, replaced this pastoral system with large-scale factory production. Introduction of mass production techniques moved generally from textiles to medical articles and food stuffs, later to the manufacture of iron and steel, and finally to machinery.

By the mid-1800s the United States was assuming a leading role in this new industrial development. A shortage of skilled labor, the absence of a firmly entrenched artisan class, comparatively high and evenly distributed per capita income, and abundant natural resources were among the principal factors prompting genuine mass production and consumption. Whitney and Colt recognized one such market early on and pioneered the machine production of standardized firearms to satisfy it. Their production methods spread to the manufacture of other goods—clocks, harvesting equipment, sewing machines, locks, and so forth. By the end of the nineteenth century, more efficient production methods were being applied to the manufacture of carriages and bicycles as well.

The manufacturing techniques pioneered by the American automobile manufacturers in the first quarter of the twentieth century thus built upon technological advances and production methods in other industries and other countries. But the automakers' techniques were, nevertheless, radically innovative. For the first time the constituent elements of the mass production process—coordination and synchronization of materials flow, systematic use of main-trunk and back-feed moving assembly lines, the elimination of wasted effort and motion, high-volume production, replacement of skilled craftsmen by highly specialized machinery, the use of interchangeable parts, and the minute division of labor—were synthesized into a comprehensive, rational composition.

The production of automobiles was also radically decentralized and defused throughout the country. Early automobile manufacturers had neither the resources nor the inclination to develop their own retail outlets; the industry's principal preoccupation was production, not marketing. The general perception was that selling cars was easy enough; the problem was how to produce enough of them. In addition, the manufacturers used both distributors and parts fabricators to finance their own expansion. The manufacturers had sufficient leverage to compel independent distributors and dealers to make deposits with their orders and to pay cash on delivery. By 1921, for example, the Ford Motor Company was using the credit of seventeen thousand dealers to maintain its own cash flow. Similarly, in the early decades of production the automobile companies were largely fabricators, who bought most of their parts from independent producers on thirty- or sixty-day credit. Buying on credit and selling for cash produced enormous capital resources for expansion. It also meant that the production and selling of motor cars involved literally thousands of independent companies.[25]

This is hardly the social or economic world envisioned by *Winterbottom v. Wright*. The image of individual contractual relations between a coachmaker and a coach user was being supplanted by an image of complex, distant, and far-flung manufacturing operations in which faceless hordes of fungible workers produced, through processes understood by none of them, products that were marketed, through yet different firms, to another faceless horde of consumers demanding the goods.

Equally important, these changes generated a social need for law to recognize these new forms of commercial relations. While other goods had previously been mass produced, although not on such a grand scale, none of them had either the capacity of the automobile to create mayhem when parts or workmanship were defective or a sufficiently complex character to render quality assurance difficult. Defective hosiery didn't take off your leg and defective clocks seldom produced more than psychological trauma. Automobiles, by contrast, rapidly became the leading source of accidental death, injury, and property damage in the United States. Within twenty-five years of the first known automobile fatality, motor vehicle mishaps became the nation's leading cause of accidental death. And for every person fatally injured in a motor vehicle accident, an additional thirty-five people sustained nonfatal injuries.[26] Most of this carnage was the result of collisions, but some of it was caused by defective products. In short, this was a world in which courts were increasingly asked to consider the damage caused by automobile use and the dramatic changes in the social organization of production that mass consumption of automobiles entailed—a world in which the rule of *Winterbottom v. Wright* could not survive.

The Success and Failure of the Common Law. Through doctrinal twists and turns too numerous to detail here, the no-liability rule of 1899 became the strict liability rule of the modern tort law. By 1966 the combination of mass production and mass mayhem introduced by the manufacture and distribution of automobiles had transformed the law of manufacturers' liability for defective goods. The courts had responded to the need for compensation and risk-spreading by revolutionizing the common law.

Yet for a number of reasons, this laborious and hotly contested transformation of the common law has had an extremely modest impact on the broader social issue of automobile safety. With respect to manufacturers' liability, even perfect performance by the manufacturers (that is, the production of automobiles completely free from defects) would, as noted in Chapter 1, eliminate only a very small percentage of automobile accidents. Although with few exceptions automobile defect litigation has routinely topped the list of product liability suits, product defects are not a major cause of injury and death from automobiles.

But the problem goes deeper than this. Common law litigation seems to have only a limited capacity to alter primary conduct. Thus, though the automobile has had a major impact on the common law, the common law has only minimal influence on the characteristics, use, and effects of the automobile. Much of what is learned in defect litigation is irrelevant to the future. It relates to defective parts or models that are no longer in production. And for automakers, paying insurance premiums or self-insuring to cover product liability claims will often be much cheaper than attempting to reorganize production processes to ferret out and prevent all defects, which are as yet unknown. A production process that ensured the perfection of each automobile would be both wonderful and wonderfully expensive.

In at least one sense the failure of the common law to stem substantially the tide of automobile injuries and fatalities was a function of its reactive legal technique. The common law of manufacturers' responsibilities was certainly *responsive* over the period from the Model T to the Motor Vehicle Safety Act. As the technology of mass production changed economic and social relationships, the law responded by modifying the legal duties consequent upon automobile production. But this responsiveness to technological change is the common law's limitation as well as its strength. The common law has the flexibility to recognize or perceive new relationships requiring new legal doctrine. But in reacting to or responding to technological innovation the law also tends to rely on that same technology for its standards of conduct.

The 1916 case that began the major reform effort in automobile manufacturers' liability for defective products, *MacPhearson v. Buick Motor Co.*,[27] provides a good example of this process. MacPhearson's Buick was defective because the wooden spokes in the wheel collapsed. Collapsing spokes obviously create a dangerous condition, and it is normal to expect that spokes will be designed and constructed to bear the necessary weight. Buick's legal responsibility was premised upon its failure to market an automobile that conformed to general consumer expectations. This is the standard approach of the common law. It takes its normative requirements from the usual run of situations. Articles are defective, unreasonably dangerous, or the like when they fail to live up to the standards implicit in ordinary commerce in those products.

The *MacPhearson* case would have looked quite different had the plaintiff attempted to convince a court that, although manufacturers generally constructed wheels with oak spokes, the Buick Motor Company should have redesigned the wheel to be supported by a pressed steel disk. Such a claim would ask the court not to respond to the standard technology of automobile construction, but to force that technology in a new direction as a means of preventing accidents. The court would, in effect, be asked to design a safer automobile and to impose those design requirements as a standard of care in adjudication. Common law courts are by and large resistant to this sort of claim. When cut loose from the customary, even if technical, standards of existing practice, courts begin to lose their moorings.

An indication of this attitude, as of 1966, can be found in *Evans v. General Motors*.[28] *Evans* was the first judicial opinion to consider whether manufacturers could be held liable for failing to make their vehicles "crashworthy." Plaintiff, the decedent's wife and personal representative, sued on the theory that her husband's death was proximately caused by the negligent design of the family car, a 1961 Chevrolet station wagon. She asserted that decedent was driving across an intersection when he was struck from the left side by another vehicle; that the force of impact caused the station wagon to collapse inward, inflicting fatal injuries; and that the automobile's X-shaped frame was improperly designed and constructed because it included no outer perimeter rails to protect the passengers in side-impact collisions.

The manufacturer's design choice was not asserted to have played any role in causing the accident, only to have aggravated the injuries that resulted. The lower court dismissed the complaint for failure to state a cause of action. The court of appeals was no more hospitable. It affirmed, reasoning:

> Perhaps it would be desirable to require manufacturers to construct automobiles in which it would be safe to collide, but that would be a legislative function, not an aspect of judicial interpretation of existing law.
> The intended purpose of an automobile does not include its participation

in collisions with other objects, despite the manufacturer's ability to foresee the possibility that such collisions may occur. As defendant argues, the defendant also knows that its vehicles may be driven into bodies of water, but it does not suggest that defendant has a duty to equip them with pontoons.

We cannot agree with the plaintiff that the defendant had a duty to equip all its automobiles with side rail perimeter frames, or that such a duty can be inferred from the mere fact that some of its defendant's, or some of its competitors', automobiles are now made with side rails.[29]

This is not to say that courts will never open this Pandora's box, but only that they are resistant to doing so. The law remains, conventionally, in a reactive mode. In short, the common law is unlikely to force technology, however much technology forces the common law.

As the problem of automobile injury and death grew over the decades of this century, many became convinced that forcing the development of safer technology was precisely the remedy required of an effective legal regime to promote automobile safety. The law's other safety strategy, modifying driver behavior, seemed to have reached the limits of its (generally assumed, but little investigated) efficacy. The time had come to challenge all of automobile law's commandments—to adopt prophylactic, technology-forcing, federal regulation of the motor vehicle itself.

THREE

Science, Safety, and
the Politics of Righteousness

As it emerged from Congress in 1966, the Motor Vehicle Safety Act attacked the perceived institutional and intellectual deficiencies of existing law with a vengeance. Safety triumphed over mobility, scientific intelligence over commonsense impressions, federal over state power, and a proactive over a reactive policy stance. Abandoning the institutional model of multi-member, independent commissions and the historic jurisdiction of the Commerce Department in transportation affairs, the act was to be administered by a bureau, with a sole chief administrator, within a new Department of Transportation. And if that were not enough to energize the new safety agency, the statute made regulation mandatory. Regulators were not merely empowered, but required to establish "appropriate federal motor vehicle safety standards" that were to "meet the need for motor vehicle safety."[1] Initial standards were to be in place by January 31, 1967, and new and revised standards by January 31, 1968.

Standards under the act were to be minimum standards of performance, not design; but the criteria for their development seemed to give the agency wide latitude to standardize the safety attributes of the automobile. When prescribing "objective" performance requirements, regulators were required merely to consider relevant data, including the results of research, development, testing, and evaluation conducted pursuant to the act; to consult, to the extent "appropriate," with state officials; and to consider whether proposed standards were "reasonable, practicable and appropriate" for the particular type of motor vehicle or associated equipment for which they were prescribed. The statute made it an offense for manufacturers to offer for sale or introduce into interstate commerce any automobile or automobile equipment not conforming to these standards. Violations were subject to a civil penalty of $1,000 (each vehicle or item of equipment constituting a separate offense) and to injunction by civil action in the United States district courts.

In order to develop the information necessary for this continuous technological revolution, Congress authorized an accident and injury research and test facility. In doing so, it recognized the pioneering work of such institutions as the Cornell Aeronautical Laboratory and sought to ensure that safety research would be carried out on the much larger scale necessary to support federal standard setting. Abandoning exclusive reliance on technological innovation in private industry, the federal government was prepared both to develop and to require the implementation of new technologies of crash avoidance and occupant protection.

The Implausibility of Federal Regulation

Legal innovations of the Motor Vehicle Safety Act's scope and force tend to reflect similarly powerful economic, social, or political upheavals. The act was conceived by its sponsors in precisely these apocalyptic terms. For President Lyndon Johnson and his congressional allies, the act was essential in order to address an issue that was "second only to Vietnam" in social significance.[2] In retrospect this formulation of the problem seems oddly disconnected from the facts. In several respects, it is baffling.

That automobile injuries and fatalities had increased steadily from the moment of the automobile's introduction into American life and that by 1965 fatalities for the first time hovered near the fifty thousand mark had not gone unnoticed. Regulation of automobile safety had been the preoccupation of state and local institutions for roughly sixty years. A vast legal and regulatory bureaucracy centering on rules-of-the-road enforcement, driver training and licensing, vehicle inspection, and a host of other measures had been erected around the culture of self-mobility.

Moreover, the notion that state and local regulation was a failure hardly seemed a fair characterization of the statistical evidence. Although motor vehicle injuries and fatalities had increased in absolute terms, so too had the frequency, speed, and extent of automotive travel. More Americans were driving, more often, more quickly, and for greater distances, than ever before. Fatalities expressed relative to risk exposure, that is, fatalities per vehicle mile, had actually decreased by 37 percent from 1947 to 1960.[3]

The rate had increased moderately in the five years immediately preceding the act's passage—from 5.16 fatalities per 100 million vehicle miles in 1961 to a corresponding rate of 5.70 fatalities in 1966.[4] But this fluctuation was thought to be tied to a population bulge of younger, more "accident-prone" motorists—a problem that arguably would resolve itself in time and that seemed most immediately and directly solvable through driver education and licensing. New automotive safety technology mandated for post-1966 automobiles would require ten years to incorporate into the whole of the nation's fleet.

In any event, the increase in fatalities per mile driven hardly seemed the most pressing topic on the national agenda. Nor is there much evidence that constituents thought the issue an urgent one as Senator Abraham Ribicoff gaveled his auto safety hearings to order in 1965. A poll taken in April of that year indicated that only 18 percent of the population ranked auto safety as a top-priority issue calling for governmental action.[5] Respondents were much more concerned with questions related to crime, disease, unemployment, poverty, environmental pollution, and racial discrimination.

Voters as consumers also seemed satisfied. Although the market for automobiles was highly concentrated, competition for market share remained intense. Opponents of the act urged, therefore, and with some plausibility, that current levels of safety simply reflected consumer preferences. Although safety advocates occasionally advanced a "market-failure" rationale for the legislation, no serious effort was made to justify the act on this basis. The Senate Commerce Committee, after lengthy hearings, reported that it hadn't the foggiest notion whether it was true that "safety does not sell." Committee members unanimously supported the legislation anyway.

Finally, if one takes seriously the private interest explanation for regulatory legislation, the Motor Vehicle Safety Act of 1966 should have had virtually no prospect of passage. The diffuse benefits of regulation— if indeed risk reduction was perceived by motorists as a "benefit"— would be spread over the entire population. Regulatory costs, however, would be borne in the first instance by a highly concentrated industry, and in particular by three manufacturers that accounted for the vast majority of all domestic sales.

These companies wielded immense economic power. The "Big

Three" automakers, General Motors, Ford, and Chrysler, ranked as the first-, second-, and fifth-largest companies in the nation. Automotive retail sales (motor vehicles, accessories, and gasoline) exceeded $80 billion—roughly 11 percent of the gross national product. Some 13.5 million workers—nearly one out of six persons in the labor force—were employed directly or indirectly by highway transport industries. The industry's mass production and marketing operations blanketed the entire political landscape. Approximately thirty-five thousand franchised dealerships were scattered across the fifty states. Assembly plants were located in every region of the country. Politically, every congressional district was dependent to some degree on economic interests that opposed this legislation.[6]

The Motor Vehicle Safety Act thus is a historical oddity. It subjected an unwilling industrial giant to regulation that its putative beneficiaries had not requested in order to address a social problem that had grown progressively less serious under nearly sixty years of uncontroversial state management. And yet passage of the act commanded a political consensus of rare proportions, at least in peacetime. It was adopted by a vote of 371 to 0 in the House and 76 to 0 in the Senate. If the act was a political oddity, it was nonetheless an oddity whose time had come.

The Drama of Legislation

In some sense, the Motor Vehicle Safety Act could be justified by the argument that accidental mortality and morbidity in the United States had grown worse by failing to get better. Purification of water supplies, pasteurization of milk, environmental controls, vaccination programs, and a host of other public health strategies had dramatically reduced death from disease. Accidental death, by contrast, had for many years been a stable proportion of overall mortality. The absolute increase in automobile fatalities and injuries could be portrayed, therefore, as all the more troublesome. Auto safety became a "problem" largely because of changes in context—significant advances in public health—that gave old accident data new political significance.

But this insight was for the most part confined to a handful of epidemiologists, safety specialists, and their followers in Congress. It did not inspire public demand for legislation—or at least it did not do so at first. For these ideas to become serious candidates for political action required a curious combination of Ralph Nader's policy entrepreneurship, the scandal-mongering needs of a free and private press, the institutional competition of certain key members of Congress who were seeking to establish or expand their legislative bases, and one critical industry error.

Ribicoff Takes the Initiative. Most ambitious and effective politicians achieve some portion of their electoral success by becoming identified with a popular issue or reform campaign. For Abraham Ribicoff, governor of Connecticut in the late 1950s before moving on to the Senate, that issue was traffic safety.[7] Yet, although perhaps politically satisfying, the substance of his efforts until the mid-1960s had been, as Moynihan observed, inconclusive at best. Ribicoff, whose efforts had earned him the nickname "Mr. Safety," was, more than most, a substantive politician.

More to the point, Ribicoff had become aware of William Haddon's new epidemiological approach to automobile injury and death. Hence, when he became chairman of the Senate Government Operations Committee's relatively obscure Subcommittee on Executive Reorganization, Ribicoff saw an opportunity to pursue his long-standing interest. He arranged a series of hearings, in 1965, on the federal role in traffic safety.[8]

Much of the testimony at Ribicoff's hearings addressed the structural inadequacy of past federal efforts to promote auto safety. A number of witnesses argued that the government's efforts had been ineffectual because they were diffuse. Sixteen different federal agencies exercised authority in one way or another over auto safety matters; yet government funding for safety research was hardly visible in the federal budget. Other witnesses suggested that federal programs had been quietly controlled by the motor vehicle industry. Federally sponsored research findings were sometimes not publicly disclosed, Ribicoff was told, apparently from concern over possible embarrassment to the manufacturers who had funded the projects jointly with the government. Nor was this the only example given of "industry capture" of traffic safety efforts, ostensibly conducted under governmental auspices. As the hearings progressed, it was disclosed that the President's own Traffic Safety Commission was staffed by individuals who were not on the federal payroll but on the payroll of automobile manufacturers. Suddenly a whiff of scandal was in the air.

The new substantive vision of vehicle safety was introduced by Daniel Patrick Moynihan, then assistant secretary of labor and perhaps the most thoughtful and provocative witness to appear before Ribicoff's committee. Moynihan's interest in automobile safety, like Ribicoff's, sprang from involvement in state activities during the 1950s. Moynihan had served as staff aide and acting secretary to Governor Averell Harriman of New York and had presided as chairman of the New York State Traffic Safety Policy Coordinating Committee. There he had made the acquaintance of Haddon, another committee member. In his testimony before Ribicoff, Moynihan drew specific attention to a book Haddon had recently edited with two colleagues, *Accident Research: Methods and Approaches* (1964), and then bore down relentlessly on the need for a scientific approach. Moynihan decried the lack of accurate and reliable accident data in the automobile safety area, and urged that vehicle design and driver behavior be subjected to systematic scientific inquiry in order to develop appropriate countermeasures. "Spectacular progress" had been made in highway safety design, he reported, largely because "highway design is the one area of traffic safety which is associated with a recognized profession—the highway engineering profession."

Whether these bouquets were tossed to the highway engineers out of belief, hyperbole, or the need for political allies, Moynihan's further testimony certainly suggested that he was no political naïf. While urging strong new federal regulation, he held out the prospect that the overall burden of vehicle safety regulation might be reduced. He even seemed to suggest the possibility of an engineering utopia in which behavior modification would become largely obsolete. Congress should act, he testified,

with the object of freeing the American people from the massive fines, imprisonment, punishment and extortion which have been imposed on it in the name of "traffic safety." Twenty million traffic-court cases a year is an outrage; we have been making a nation of felons of ourselves while so clogging and overwhelming the court system with insoluble accident litigation that it becomes increasingly difficult for the American citizen to obtain justice from the courts in matters of true substance. Suppose, to use an obvious example, an electronic control system were devised and installed that would make it impossible for automobiles to go through a red light or to collide at blind intersections. Would not one of the effects be to free, each year, untold numbers of Americans from the humiliation and guilt of the traffic-court conviction.[9]

Regulation was freedom, not its antithesis.

Other witnesses from the federal government were less than enthusiastic about Ribicoff's and Moynihan's crusade. Secretary Anthony Celebrezze of the Department of Health, Education, and Welfare testified that the automobile industry "has shown rather good interest in putting out a product which is usable and also one with safety features." Paul Joliet, M.D., chief of HEW's Division of Accident Prevention, similarly testified that he had been "impressed with the amount of money [automobile manufacturers] are spending on safety." John T. Connor, secretary of commerce, testified that "we are not advocating at this time any Federal standards for the entire automobile"; his position was based largely on concern about costs and recognition that traffic regulation "heretofore has been really the province of the States." The parade of official naysayers seemed endless. As an exasperated Ribicoff adjourned the hearings in July, the auto safety issue had yet to attract more than modest public attention.

But political help was coming. The release of Ralph Nader's *Unsafe at Any Speed* in November 1965 made vehicle safety an issue of national interest. Nader's research seemed thorough, his story well written, and his message compelling—cars could and should be made safer. This story was, of course, the same one that De Haven, Haddon, and others had been telling for years. But Nader had made a discovery of momentous political significance. He had found a villain, the General Motors Corporation, whom Nader claimed was marketing Corvairs that had a *known* propensity to go out of control on turns. The *New York Times* gave Nader's book front-page coverage, and reviewers around the country greeted it with critical acclaim. As Nader's stock soared, so did auto safety as a political issue.

Can You Hear Me Now? When Ribicoff resumed his hearings in February, 1966, his midsummer frustrations were clearly behind him. The committee room was jammed. Opinion surveys showed that the public considered auto safety one of the top issues of national concern. Testimony in support of the need for motor vehicle safety standards poured in from all sides. Even witnesses who represented organizations that were seen as sympathetic to industry did not vigorously defend the industry's record. Howard Pyle, president of the National Safety Council (which critics denounced as a "flunky organization" that strongly supported state regulation), conceded that he was "dissatisfied with the pace of vehicle design improvement by industry." Pyle's reluctance to endorse federal motor vehicle standards prompted Ribicoff to inquire: "If this is a national problem, how do you solve a national problem without the Federal Government playing a definite role?" The question apparently answered itself.

The star witness was, of course, Ralph Nader. He hammered home the argument of *Unsafe at Any Speed*—that the vehicle, not the driver, was responsible for injuries produced by the "second collision." Nader denounced the automobile industry for "an orgy of expenditure on style." Ribicoff's public health campaign was on the way to becoming a moral crusade.

The President's Program. Momentum for federal action continued to build. On March 2, President Johnson delivered a Message on Transportation to Congress, asking for the creation of a Department of Transportation and support for a related legislative package, including a proposed "Traffic Safety Act of 1966." The President's message portrayed transportation as one of the three great bonds, along with common political values and the English language, uniting the nation. But this system of common carriers and private passenger vehicles was not strong enough, Johnson said. It had become technologically stagnant, inefficient, and worst of all, unsafe. Johnson implied that this was because transportation services had arisen in an uncoordinated and haphazard way without benefit of adequate governmental control and supervision. "The United States is the only major nation in the world," he remarked, "that relies primarily upon privately owned and operated transportation."

The proposed Transportation Department, Johnson reported, would address the asserted inadequacies of private ownership by consolidating and enlarging the activities of the Federal Aviation Administration (FAA), the Coast Guard, the Civil Aeronautics Board, the ICC, and other existing and proposed organizations, including the proposed traffic safety agency. The new department would bring "new technology to a total transportation system, by promoting research and development" and "by encouraging private enterprise to take full and prompt advantage of new technological opportunities."

Johnson's auto safety bill was a key part of the plan to coordinate the transportation system. The bill would increase federal grants to states for highway safety; improve vehicle safety by giving federal regulators authority to set vehicle safety performance standards; and fund a national highway safety research and test center to support standard-setting and other national programs. "Congress has not hesitated to establish rigorous safety standards for other means of transportation when circumstances demanded them," Johnson urged. The time had therefore come for "creative federalism" in the auto safety area, for a new partnership between Washington, the states, and private industry, to "replace suicide with sanity and anarchy with safety."

Although this would have been a bold, perhaps visionary, proposal in July of 1965, seven months later safety proponents complained that Johnson's legislation did not match his rhetoric. Under the administration's bill vehicle standards would be voluntary; mandatory rules would be imposed only if industry compliance were not forthcoming. The President's bill was the toughest safety legislation then before Congress, but Nader rejected the proposal as a "no-law law," and Senator Ribicoff complained on the Senate floor that the bill was too weak. Many other legislators agreed. A battle developed to determine who could produce the strongest auto safety bill.

Magnuson Horns In. Reasserting his committee's dominant jurisdiction, Senator Warren Magnuson opened Commerce Committee hearings on the administration's bill on March 16.[10] He had been advised by aides that a "visibility" problem was developing with constituents back home, and he was eager to seize the initiative from Ribicoff. But events continued to give Ribicoff an edge in the contest for the limelight. Ribicoff called a special hearing[11] before his subcommittee to investigate reports that General Motors had placed Ralph Nader under surveillance. At this hearing, on March 22, the corporation's president, James Roche, admitted that his company had hired a law firm to conduct a "routine investigation" of Nader. Further committee prodding revealed, however, that more had taken place than a "routine investigation." As Ribicoff described it, the investigation "had to do with trying to smear a man, the question of his sex life, whether he belonged to left-wing organizations, whether he was anti-Semitic, whether he was an odd-ball, whether he liked boys instead of girls. The whole investigation was to smear an individual."

An issue that had been slowly heating up boiled over. Representatives and senators tripped over each other in the stampede to express their outrage. The press response was equally powerful. The story of General Motors's pursuit of Nader provided a perfect media melodrama—a sprightly David against an oafish Goliath. A pro-Nader, pro-safety, pro-federal-intervention feeling swept the country. On April 1, *Time* ran one of its periodic editorial essays, entitled "Why Cars Must—And Can— Be Made Safer." Both following and leading the national mood, *Time* continued its campaign for auto safety with articles in each of its next three issues, meticulously reporting the progress of the auto safety bill through Congress.

When Magnuson's hearings resumed on April 4, Nader was again called to testify. Having been transformed from bookish lone crusader to media hero, Nader's expertise and credibility now seemed to be viewed as limitless. He was deferentially invited to expound on issues ranging from windshield safety to the administration of research grants. When he warned that the administration's bill rested on the "shifting sands of discretionary authority," Nader was assured that the final legislation would make standards mandatory.

The hearings swelled with further testimony in support of mandatory vehicle standards. The Teamsters' president, Jimmy Hoffa, for example, joined many other witnesses in supporting the bill, and urged its extension to trucks. The senators absorbed the barrage, and the press reported it. In concluding the hearings on April 5, Senator Vance Hartke declared, "It is time for the slogans to pass away, and for action to take [its] place."

As the Senate moved toward final drafting of the auto safety bill, Nader continued to stir interest wherever an audience on Capitol Hill could be found. As other committees began to construe their jurisdiction broadly, he was seldom without a forum. He appeared before the Subcommittee on Public Roads of the Senate Committee on Public Works, for example, to press the case for motor vehicle standards as *the* solution to the auto safety problem, notwithstanding that subcommittee's historical commitment to highway design as the federal government's technological fix for the mayhem on the roads. Nader was also becoming a political entrepreneur of some skill. He utilized the press particularly well, developing contacts, granting interviews, planting leaks, and building enthusiasm for his cause.

The legislative definition of the auto safety problem was also about to take on a critical new dimension. Nader had been tipped off by contacts in the industry that companies sometimes conducted "secret recalls" of cars with defects. Distributors were said to replace or repair defective parts while doing routine maintenance without telling the owners or notifying others who might have cars with a similar defect. Nader's revelation of this practice—strategically timed to reinvigorate interest in auto safety during a lull in the hearings—produced further outrage. Flush with yet another advance and cognizant of the auto industry's crumbling political stance, the safety activists again decided to raise the stakes. Nader developed a series of amendments, which Senator Hartke introduced, to strengthen the auto safety bill. In particular, recalls of defective automobiles were to be both publicly announced and federally supervised.

The auto industry lobby in Washington was nearing collapse. It had never taken Washington politics very seriously—because motor vehicle production and marketing was essentially unregulated, it had never had to. While other industries had developed sophisticated lobbying operations in Washington, the Automobile Manufacturers Association remained comparatively weak and in Detroit. Elizabeth Drew reported[12] that individual company offices in Washington tended to be staffed by company men who did not exercise great influence on corporate policy. The lines of communication between these offices and the corporate elite in Detroit were insufficient to convey reliable images of the rapidly changing political scene in the capital. When finally forced into the political arena, the auto industry appeared, in Drew's words, to be a "lumbering paper hippopotamus."

Apparently more was involved than a simple failure of political intelligence gathering, analysis, or communication. A 1966 account of the auto safety hearings in *Fortune*[13] asserted that automobile company executives simply were not in touch with large areas of social and political reality. The explanation given for this was that senior company officials were "products of a system that discouraged attention to matters outside the purviews of their jobs"; that they tended to deal professionally and socially only with one another; that they were recruited largely from within the companies themselves; and that this environment reinforced itself by attracting individuals who would find such surroundings congenial. Exposure to politicians, intellectuals, or even outside consultants reportedly was rare. The article depicted an insular corporate culture that was utterly confounded by problems whose nature was sociological and political, rather than technological or economic.

And So to the House. The Senate could not, of course, keep the motor vehicle safety issue as its own. Rumors that the House would "gut" the tough Senate bill provoked Harley Staggers, chairman of the House Commerce Committee, to demonstrate his own commitment to automobile safety. He was supported in this effort by Congressman James MacKay of Georgia, a strong and early advocate of federal auto safety regulation and sponsor of a prior House bill to establish a National Traffic

Safety Agency. Much of the necessary legwork for MacKay was performed by a resourceful and energetic congressional intern named Joan Claybrook, who ten years later would become the administrator of NHTSA itself. From the beginning it was apparent that the House Commerce Committee would not rescue the automobile companies.

The Staggers hearings[14] built upon the pro-regulation record previously developed by Ribicoff and Magnuson. Safety activists impressed representatives with their now well-polished arguments. The list of witnesses and groups seeking to add their names to the sponsorship list had swelled. Dozens of other concerned citizens, professors, doctors, and scientists joined in urging the adoption of safety standards. Representative after representative, Democrat and Republican, proclaimed support of this now seemingly one-sided issue.

John Bugas, representing the Auto Manufacturers Association, appeared before the Staggers committee on April 26. His testimony signaled capitulation. The manufacturers abandoned the stand they had taken only three weeks earlier in hearings before Magnuson. Instead of urging voluntary, industry-established vehicle standards, the auto industry now embraced federally mandated safety requirements.

The Act as Anticlimax. By the time the auto safety bill reached the Senate floor in late June, all opposition had faded. The tough Magnuson committee bill was adopted without opposition.[15] On August 17, the Staggers committee bill also sailed through the House.[16] The relatively minor differences between the two bills were quickly ironed out in conference and the final legislation adopted without dissent on August 31. At the signing ceremoney on September 9, President Johnson remarked:

> For years, we have spent millions of dollars to understand polio and fight other childhood diseases. Yet until now we have tolerated a raging epidemic of highway death which has killed more of our youth than all other diseases combined. Through the Highway Safety Act, we are going to find out more about highway disease—and we aim to cure it.
>
> In this age of space, we are getting plenty if information about how to send men into space and how to bring them home. Yet we don't know for certain whether more auto accidents are caused by faulty brakes, or by soft shoulders, or by drunk drivers, or by deer crossing the highway.
>
> There is nothing new or radical at all about [the Act]. Every other form of transportation is covered by federal safety standards . . . [Safety] is no luxury item, no optional extra: it must be a normal cost of doing business.[17]

The Federalist and Egalitarian Logic of Public Regulation

That Congress was ready to act so quickly and dramatically on an issue that had been around for sixty years can hardly be explained fully by anecdotal events. If the Nader–General Motors morality play was the spark that ignited the tinder, and congressmen and reporters had personal and institutional interests in fanning the flame, what was the composition of the tinder itself? What was the ideological context that made the implausible so compelling? The explanation lies somewhere at the intersection of the civil rights movement and the space program—a wedding in the mid-1960s of egalitarian ethical judgment, scientific enthusiasm, and activist national politics.

The three years leading to the act's passage had been a period of prodigious legislative output.[18] From 1964 to 1966, Congress generated well over 1,000 bills; more dramatically, it enacted 650 of them. The so-called Great Society Congress—the second session of the 88th and both sessions of the 89th Congress—produced law in volume and at a rate matched only in the early years of the New Deal and the first half of the Wilson Administration. Relations between legislators and the President were for the most part all sweetness and light. Their collaboration had not yet been confounded by the war in Vietnam.

President Johnson praised Congress in 1964 for having "enacted more legislation, met more national needs, and dispensed of more national issues than any other session of this century or last."[19] But that was only the beginning. Legislative activity was even more remarkable in 1965, when Ribicoff convened his hearings. There were 469 bills proposed; 323—nearly 70 percent—were enacted. In Congress it was reported that the word frequently passed among the Democratic majority to "approve the bill and worry about perfecting details later."[20] The new legislation consistently provided for a more expansive federal role in American life. The President was exuberant.

In this avalanche of legislation, the Civil Rights Act of 1964[21] nevertheless stood out as a paradigm of Great Society law. First, the act represented a reconception of private behavior as social behavior. Second, it replaced state jurisdiction with federal power. These were the very features of the act that provided the bases for a constitutional attack on the statute. But the states' rights vernacular in which that attack was couched was seen as a proxy for state failure to protect civil rights. It was because state inaction had become intolerable that Congress acted. And the judiciary upheld[22] Congress's intervention via the Civil Rights Act on an expansive reading of the interstate commerce clause of the Constitution—a reading that was highly sensitive to the social consequences of individual decision making.

This same theme was expressed in federal health and safety initiatives of the period, particularly in the environmental area. President Johnson designated the 88th Congress "the Conservation Congress"[23] and identified environmental legislation as one of his administration's highest priorities. Public Law 89–324[24] exemplified the new federal role in environmental regulation. It provided for the formation of a Federal Water Pollution Control Agency to enforce standards issued by the states. If the states did not act, the federal government would issue standards. Henceforth all individuals or companies discharging pollutants would be socially accountable for environmental degradation. Between 1964 and 1966 numerous federal statutes anticipated the even more extensive environmental lawmaking of the early to mid-1970s. These included measures to establish a national wilderness preservation system, to regulate the registration and marketing of pesticides, to beautify the nation's highways, and to control air pollution, in part by limiting motor vehicle emissions.

The Motor Vehicle Safety Act, with its application of federal power in an area previously dominated by private choice and state regulation, appeared relatively nonproblematic in this context. Proponents of the act urged that the automobile was "part of our environment—like the jet airplane, atomic energy, pesticides, and a whole host of new life-saving drugs." Automobile safety was, therefore, a "social problem" requiring federal action.

More pointedly, public regulation of mostly private vehicles was legitimated by conceiving of private passenger vehicles as essentially a medium of public transportation. Safety advocates characterized the proposed traffic agency as just like the ICC and the FAA. The act thus could be depicted as an extension of familiar regulatory precedent rather than as a bold new encroachment upon private choice or states' rights. This was everyday, garden-variety, interstate-commerce-clause type regulation. Auto safety was "definitely a federal responsibility," the act's proponents urged; "if ever there was an interstate instrument it was the motor vehicle."

Second and more important, the Safety Act could borrow the Civil Rights Act's basic rationale—the demand for "equal protection." The President had asked the Congress to recognize that "the very structure of society is founded upon the automobile"; that "we have designed our cities and generally arranged our lives so as to make the use of the automobile indispensable"; and that "a driver's license is close to a necessity of life for many, perhaps most Americans." But all Americans were not equally protected from the hazards of participation in the automobile culture. Senator Ribicoff, for example, listed a series of safety features available only on more expensive models and complained that "there are certain basic things that the person driving a Plymouth, Ford, or Chevrolet is entitled to have, just as much as a person driving a Cadillac." "There is no reason," he continued, "why the collapsible steering wheel should not be on every car . . . [or] why the Ford, Chevrolet, or Plymouth shouldn't have dual brakes."

This egalitarian theme was also played in a number of complementary chords. In 1964 Congress had directed the General Services Administration (GSA) to promulgate safety standards for motor vehicles procured for government use.[25] By 1966, seventeen GSA standards were in effect. The upgrading of automobile safety for public employees was cited as a precedent whose extension to private citizens was a matter of fundamental fairness. "Why are not all 17 safety items available as standard items on all cars purchased by the general public?" safety advocates asked Congress. "Why should only federal employees be offered this added protection when riding in cars?"

The Motor Vehicle Safety Act was of course but one of many legislative initiatives reflecting the strong egalitarian impulse of the Great Society. In programs ranging from housing to legal services to medical care, Congress was busily creating whole new bundles of need-based "rights." The reconceptualization of auto safety followed in large part from this same humanitarian impulse. Proponents of the 1966 act urged that "the average motorist [was] performing near the limits of his potential as a master of the modern automobile," and that motorists were disabled from preventing accidents due to "the complexity of the traffic situation and of the driving task." This disability principle required that there be "a change of philosophy and attitude as to what controls in the building of an automobile." The act mandated the construction of "socially responsible" motor vehicles by requiring that automobile design be reoriented around the principle of motorists' ineluctable failures and shortcomings.

The use of safety standards to force more "humane technology," that is, to require that "the machine [be designed] to the man," would result in the construction of what the safety activists called "more worthy" automobiles. Under competitive pricing conditions manufacturers would squeeze out the many "absolutely useless," "nonsensical" features in automobiles, in order to incorporate the safety devices to which motorists were entitled. But without regulation, it was claimed, manufacturers would continue to build flashy automobiles that were "unforgiving" to their occupants.

The complaint that manufacturers had subordinated style to safety had egalitarian overtones in yet another respect, one that must be placed in historical context. The industry's emphasis on style began with the introduction of yearly models in the 1920s, when replacement sales first dominated the market for motor vehicles. Manufacturers had previously been preoccupied with advances in mass production technology. The relatively low priority given marketing was reflected in a remark, attributed to Henry Ford, that consumers could have any color vehicle they wanted, as long as it was black. Before 1920 there was no problem in selling cars; the problem was building them fast enough.

The automobile became an important symbol of personal status in the United States at roughly the same time that it became an item of mass consumption. Status was conferred not merely by automobile ownership but by the particular type of car owned. By 1966, "prestige" styling was a fundamental strategy for market segmentation, one that safety advocates disdained. At least implicitly, the demand for safer, standardized vehicles reflected an egalitarian contempt for automotive styling as an expression of social differentiation.

Political discourse about safety legislation rapidly took on a moralistic flavor. Automobile styling was labeled "obscene," motorists were depicted as feeble and unable to resist the siren call of automobile advertising, and motor vehicle manufacturers were considered "venal." The corollary of this vision was moral outrage that private industry had shown "profound disregard" for "remedial engineering." When company representatives responded that they were merely "catering to what the public feels it wants and needs," they were indicted for social irresponsibility. "You help create the demand for speed by your advertisements and in many other ways," one congressman lectured the trade association's representatives. "It isn't your only job in life to give people what they want . . . one of your jobs is to give people what they can handle in order that they can be safe on the highways."

Technology Forcing and the Efficacy of Government

As the hearings progressed, a political consensus began to form that "the vast scientific and technical resources of the United States" were not being adequately deployed to foster "humane" automotive technology; that private industry's research and development expenditures on safety were an intolerably small fraction of its profits; that society had been "lax" in applying safety engineering principles; and that the role of law was to compel their application.

Of course, this conception of the Motor Vehicle Safety Act assumed both that engineering solutions were at hand or could be feasibly developed and that government was an effective agent of innovation. Both of these assumptions appeared self-evident to safety activists, because both were consistent with strong, virtually utopian, convictions about the capacity of technology to achieve social objectives. By designing the machine to adapt to the operator, "human factors" engineers and biotechnologists promised a new world in which motorists would be safe in spite of themselves. "A crashworthy vehicle can make failures fail-safe," congressional leaders were told, "by strategically placing a vehicle safety net designed to catch aberrant aspects of the accident episode." The choice was between "eugenics or engineering," safety advocates told Congress. Engineering was the more promising solution because "machines are easier to understand than people—they are more tractable [and] they don't talk back." And the engineering solution was "the cheapest, because it is permanent while education and enforcement must be kept up year after year."

This technical emphasis depersonalized automobile use and diverted attention from the objection that regulation would interfere with individual preferences. "The automobile is not unique," one witness told Congress; "it obeys the basic laws of physics the same as any other moving body." The same was true of motorists. "Automobile drivers [do not] differ from other human beings; they have the same basic responses and reflexes; their body sizes and the ability of their bodies to withstand impact forces are the same." In short, idiosyncrasies among individuals were irrelevant. The automobile, after all, was a medium of public transportation, not self-expression.

This technological solution to automobile safety captured the imagination of a Congress apparently mesmerized by the government's own technological achievements. The space program was a central preoccupation of legislators, the media, and the general public. In the three years immediately preceding the act's passage, the United States had effectively overtaken the Soviets in racing to the moon. The highly publicized Gemini project, which encompassed twelve launches from April 1964 to November 1966, was decisive. It included ten manned flights, designed to perfect rendezvous and docking techniques and to acquire experience in extended operations necessary for a lunar landing. In the same three-year period, the United States launched an additional fourteen Explorer satellites, two Pioneer crafts, four ranger probes, two Mariner spacecraft, an Echo satellite, two lunar orbiters, and two Surveyor probes.

At roughly the same time that Magnuson and Staggers conducted their auto safety hearings, NASA successfully launched the first three Apollo missions. In 1969, Apollo Nine was to carry American astronauts to their first lunar landing. This was astonishing progress for a nation that had only achieved its first manned orbit in 1961, and it was widely interpreted in the auto safety hearings as strong evidence of government's prowess in achieving technological innovation through centralized bureaucratic planning.

Witnesses and sympathetic legislators alike cited the space program in support of auto safety regulation. "If we can send a man to the moon and back," one participant asked, "why can't we design a safe automobile here on Earth?" The success of the space program was taken as proof of the efficacy of technology-forcing regulation; after all, "the most completely regulated form of transportation by the federal government is space flight." The space program imagery not only supported the progressive logic and presumed efficacy of public regulation; it also connected with the egalitarian impulse for safety. "You talk about money," Ribicoff told his colleagues, "but if we spend two billion to protect the [astronauts'] lives, we shouldn't worry about spending a billion dollars to protect the lives of 195 million Americans."

The connection between the space program and the automobile was not only made by legislators and expert witnesses. Listen to the revealing lament of David Wallace, Ford's director of planning for the ill-fated Edsel: "I don't think we yet know the depths of the psychological effect that [Sputnik's] orbiting had on us all. Somebody had beaten us to an important gain in technology, and immediately people started writing articles about how crummy Detroit products were, particularly the heavily ornamented and status-symbolic medium priced cars . . . The

American people . . . put themselves on a self-imposed austerity program. Not buying Edsels was their hair shirt."[26]

Epidemiology and the Rationalization of Accidents

The scientific conceptualization of automobile safety also drew heavily on epidemiology and preventive medicine. Witness after witness urged that automotive safety was a public health problem of gigantic proportions. When the medical establishment promised to deliver the same results in this field that it had in eradicating malaria, polio, and diphtheria, Congress listened.

Public health, of course, was a noncontroversial target of federal action. But this metaphor was more than a rhetorical flourish to legitimate regulation. As noted in Chapter 1, it provided an entirely new way of thinking about accidents and of devising strategies to ameliorate their effects. The application of the standard epidemiological triad—the conception of accidents in terms of host, agent, and environment—provided the basis for a convergence of epidemiology, systems analysis, and biotechnology that inevitably focused attention on modification to automobile design. From the epidemiologists came a preference for "passive measures" that did not require the cooperation of putative beneficiaries. Excluding the driver, the host, from this man-machine-highway system led systems engineers to focus increasingly on the malleability of the machine and the highway. The point was put pungently to the Congress. "Which is easier," safety advocates inquired, "to convince 195 million drivers to habitually refrain from panic application of the brake in emergencies or to design an anti-locking braking system in the vehicle?" The answer was clear to the act's proponents. Automobile design was the most easily manipulated variable because relatively few people were required to implement this solution. "An attraction of this approach," Moynihan testified, "is that it [can] be put into effect by changing the behavior of a tiny population—the forty or fifty executives who run the automobile industry."

The aeronautical and aviation sciences provided the specific countermeasures that could be adapted from airplane to automobile design. Safety advocates claimed that the research of De Haven and his followers in studying the impact of deceleration forces, the transfer of mechanical energy, and corresponding passive measures of protection was obviously transferrable to the automobile. They accordingly called for this new biotechnology to be an organizing principle of federal intervention.

Some members of this brash scientific generation were not insensitive to the complexities of human behavior or to the limits of their new science of accidents. One commentator, for example, expressed concern about the possibility that nothing could be done about automobile safety and that "something more basic is wrong with us." It was a well-known finding, he wrote, in 1961, that "improvement of road safety has gone hand in hand with an increase of road speeds which counteracts to some extent the reduction of accident mortality brought about by the improvement. This is an indication that the degree of risk-taking tends to be maintained at a certain level. In an extreme case, the risk-taking could even increase sufficiently to completely offset the safety improvement. In that case, the fatality rate would be kept at a constant level and conjectures related to aggression, the death wish, etc., will have to be taken more seriously."[27] Representatives of the engineering community expressed similar reservations about the efficacy of technological solutions, and sought to distinguish the space program's definite goals and very limited effects on ordinary citizens from an open-ended program of motor vehicle regulation touching the lives of all citizens.

Haddon himself asserted that the forces acting against regulation were not limited to economic interests and that safety itself was a social value of uncertain significance. In his writings he explicitly recognized that risk taking is "culturally prized"; that safety countermeasures might deprive individuals of gratifying their appetite for danger; that regulation could be perceived as an encroachment upon personal freedom; and that motorists "might lose considerable psychic reward if [their] activities were curbed by scrupulously enforced accident prevention measures."[28] But these somber insights were eclipsed by the exhilaration of seeing the world in a new light. Politicians, flush with the successes of space exploration, upped their demands for technological innovations in "the vital concerns of everyday life." Scientists like Haddon and his colleagues could hardly resist staking new claims to expertise in managing social problems.

At the heart of safety ideology was a belief, perhaps a conceit, that science and law together could fashion solutions to problems that would transcend human failure. Previous approaches to accidents, Haddon reported, were "redolent of the extranatural, supernatural, and the pre-scientific," and were reminiscent of "Malinowski's natives in their ap-

proaches to the hazards outside the reef which they did not understand."
The new epidemiology of accidents at last promised approaches that
were "more rational and scientific." "We can no longer afford to deal in
the terms and concepts of the past, with their vague emphasis on
threatening forces," Haddon wrote shortly after becoming NHTSA's first
administrator, for that is "an approach more appropriate to primitive
tribes than modern society."[29]

Understanding the Motor Vehicle Safety Act

The emergence of the Safety Act of 1966 was almost comically over-
determined. The recipe for the legislation read: take a persistent social
evil; confront it with new technological and institutional solutions, pains-
takingly developed by creative scientists and reformist lawyers over
several decades; place problem and solution in the heady atmosphere of
an activist polity, apparently determined to rid the country (if not the
world) of virtually all ignorance, vice, poverty, and danger through the
application of national political power; add the drama of corporate villainy
and heroic individual commitment; wrap in the rhetoric of both scientific
rationality and justice; stir by political competition and by skillful use of
the media; and presto! This is the essence of the revolution of 1966.

And yet for the story of the implementation of the act that is to come,
issues that were ignored or submerged in this drama are as important as
the main plot line. The first is the persistent association in American life
of automobility and freedom. Access to a car is for a youthful America a
crucial element of both self-definition and social status. And although
family, wealth, institutional position, and nonautomotive "toys" may with
age steadily decrease the importance of the automobile as evidence of an
individual's power and status, there are few for whom the personal car
does not remain an important cultural artifact. Imagining motor vehicles
as a public health hazard provides a very partial picture of the object that
was putatively being subjected to stringent social control. The attempt
was nothing less than implicit repeal of the first commandment of automobile law.

Second, over time, interest and resources matter. The automobile
industry may have been a "paper hippopotamus" in 1966, but it was
nevertheless a very big animal with at least the usual instincts for self-
preservation. If that animal was to be bent to the collective will, its
keepers would have to be both vigilant and powerful. Such a posture is

particularly difficult to maintain, however, in a democratic polity committed to limited government. As the President and committee chairs competed to strengthen the 1966 act, the system of checks and balances may well have looked more like a system of ratchets and amplifiers. But American institutions do not routinely operate that way. In designing our particular zoological garden the architects seem to have been more intent on avoiding the criticisms of the SPCA than on keeping the animals restrained. The preference for private or decentralized state and federal control of most social decision making is a structural feature of the American polity generally, not just a peculiarity of preexisting automobile law.

Third, notwithstanding the principal players' understanding that regulatory agencies left without clear legislative direction were subject to capture, stagnation, or both, the Congress failed to give NHTSA a clear target toward which to aim its regulatory activities. The agency was told to "meet the need for automobile safety" and to guard the public against "unreasonable risks." What did these vague directions mean? They had no determinate content, scientifically, professionally, or otherwise. Operationally they meant that the agency was in the business of exercising political judgment—of either creating or following a political will that would surely not remain a static expression of the Zeitgeist of 1966. After all, much of the old automobile law was wrapped in the rhetoric of safety. Had Congress really ensured that vehicle safety regulation in this new mode would pass beyond rhetorical flourish to substantive achievement—that safety would be more than the "second" commandment of motor vehicle law?

Fourth, the legislative debates devoted inadequate attention to the question of how good the new science of accidents was and whether its insights could be translated effectively into engineering solutions. The extent of Congress's ignorance is reflected, of course, in the emptiness of its directions to the administrators. Beyond demanding adaption of some existing GSA and Society of Automotive Engineers (SAE) standards, Congress did not know what to tell the agency to do. Nor did it instruct NHTSA to reduce annual highway fatalities by X percent, or to Y deaths per Z million miles traveled. No one at the time had any idea what numerical goal represented a reasonable expectation. Faith was simply placed in the inexorability of scientific advance, in the superiority of professionalism over intuition. It was the arrogant faith of which tragedies are born.

FOUR

Promise and Performance

At first glance NHTSA's rulemaking activities from 1966 to 1974 suggest extraordinary ferment and creativity. Forty-five of the agency's fifty standards, 90 percent of its mid-1980s inventory, were issued during that period. Virtually no aspect of motor vehicle safety was ignored. From brakes, windshield wipers, and seat belts to fuel tanks, rearview mirrors, and energy-absorbing steering assemblies, NHTSA cast an intricate net of minutely detailed regulatory requirements over a vast array of motor vehicle components and equipment. At the same time, the agency steadily extended its reach over the types of vehicles coming off production lines. Focusing first on passenger cars, NHTSA in the late 1960s and early 1970s gradually revised existing standards and drafted new ones to cover trucks, buses, trailers, and an assortment of "multipurpose vehicles." The law's aspiration was "uniformity." The original act, and NHTSA's earliest rules, allowed no exemptions.

On closer examination, this heyday of rulemaking was largely a testament to modest ambitions. As noted in Chapter 1, the issuance of new rules declined quickly and dramatically: from twenty-nine standards in 1967–1968, to fourteen standards in 1969–1972, to two standards in 1973. No new standards were issued in 1974. Amendments to existing rules told essentially the same story. In 1976 the Senate Commerce Committee concluded an exhaustive study of NHTSA's rulemaking activities over the preceding decade and reported somberly that "What NHTSA has not done speaks louder than the few regulatory actions it has produced in recent years."[1]

The agency's first round of standards took only about three months to prepare. By the mid-1970s, the gestation period for many rulemaking actions had stretched to several years. Lead times, the grace period between announcement of new requirements and the compliance deadline, were doubling and tripling. And much of the agency's rulemaking paperwork was just that—routine technical amendments, dispositions of petitions for reconsideration, and after 1968, grants and denials of requests for exemption.[2]

It was also becoming clear that public regulation had been largely ineffectual in forcing automotive technology. Agency regulators were acutely aware of what study after study later confirmed: NHTSA's rules required modest, incremental improvements in the safety technology of conventional vehicles. A special report prepared in 1970 for the National Commission on Product Safety said of NHTSA's work product, "The safety standards simply set forth legal performance requirements already met by safety features in many or most domestic makes and models when the standards were issued. Thus, the best that may be said for the safety standards issued thus far is that they incorporate some of the best of current practice in the automobile industry."[3] MIT researchers in 1977[4] and a Congressional Office of Technology Assessment report in 1981[5] both agreed.

As the MIT study noted, however, NHTSA had hardly forgotten its technology-forcing mission. The agency's October 1971 "Program Plan for Motor Vehicle Safety Standards" and Federal Register notices of intended actions in the late 1960s and early 1970s described a brave new world of technological wonders, from airbags and automatic radar brakes to speed governors, periscopes, and alcohol interlocks. These innovations, if the engineering estimates accompanying them could be believed, promised drastic reductions in the nation's traffic toll. The October 1971 Plan contemplated rulemaking actions that were predicted to generate benefits of $76 billion, at a cost of only $28 billion. The plan represented itself as a comprehensive blueprint for saving twenty thousand lives each year and halving the auto fatality rate by 1980.[6] Three years later that plan seemed all but abandoned, and NHTSA publicly renounced the goal of cutting fatalities by 50 percent. To understand why, we must go back to the Great Society.

The First Generation of Safety Rules, 1966–1967

The Congress of the United States had placed William Haddon, Jr., M.D., in a difficult position. Less than four months separated the President's appointment of Haddon as the first administrator of the National

Traffic Safety Bureau (later NHTSA) and the January 31, 1967, statutory deadline for issuing "initial" rules. The fledgling agency did not receive its first appropriations until November 15, 1966. Formally, Haddon had seventy-five days to recruit and organize a staff and issue his first batch of rules.

Working without an appropriation and using a staff of eight engineers borrowed from outside consulting firms, the FAA, the ICC, and the Post Office, Haddon rushed to meet the deadline. On October 8, 1966, the Department of Commerce (the agency's temporary home pending establishment of the Department of Transportation on April 1, 1967) published an advance notice of proposed rulemaking (ANPRM), informing the public of its intent to issue standards and inviting proposals and suggestions. The response to that notice established a pattern that was to continue throughout the agency's history. First, the commentary was voluminous. By the November 1 deadline, Haddon had received 3,105 pages of technical comments and data from 172 respondents. Second, the bulk of material was provided by industry; 75 responses from companies, mostly automobile and tire manufacturers, accounted for 2,869 pages of the material. The remaining 236 pages of comments were submitted by 97 respondents, mostly in single-page, exhortatory letters. The agency expressed disappointment that "not more people outside of the industry saw fit to comment."[7]

On December 3, 1966, the agency formalized its proposals in a notice of proposed rulemaking (NPRM) that set forth twenty-three separate standards for possible adoption. As directed by the statute these rules were based on existing standards: primarily GSA rules and SAE standards, but including individual requirements drawm from the Post Office, the National Bureau of Standards, the Uniform Vehicle Code, one state law, and the Swedish National Road Board. By January 3, 1967, the agency had received 4,525 pages of technical comments and data on these proposals. Industry responses again dominated the docket. The fledgling agency somehow coped with this blizzard of paper. On January 31, 1967, the statutory deadline, it issued twenty standards. Twelve did not differ materially from their proposal form. Eight were significantly modified in response to criticisms received during the notice and comment period, and three of the agency's proposals were withdrawn altogether. The first twenty rules were scheduled to take effect January 31, 1968, the maximum lead time provided under the act without a specific finding of "good cause" for further delay.

Sturm und Drang

These initial rulemaking activities precipitated a firestorm of protest. Henry Ford II complained that many of the proposed safety standards were unreasonable, arbitrary, and technically unfeasible and would require higher prices to the consumer for 1968 models. He warned darkly that if relief were not forthcoming, the company would be forced to "close down."[8] Foreign manufacturers and small domestic companies were equally outspoken. Volkswagen, for example, threatened that "unless these proposed standards are modified to the extent indicated in our comments, the importation of Volkswagen vehicles into the United States will not be possible after they go into effect."[9] Checker Motors Corporation declared that compliance was "absolutely impossible."[10]

When the agency revised its proposals in response to these and other concerns, its accommodations were pictured by safety advocates as "surrender." William Steiglitz, an aeronautical engineer from MIT, one of the founding fathers of the new science of accidents and head of the agency's rulemaking team, resigned in protest. Special hearings were held before the Senate Commerce Committee to investigate. Nader and others charged that regulators had caved in to pressure from domestic and foreign manufacturers, and that Haddon, in particular, did not have the stomach for technology-forcing regulation. Nader, adopting a style of criticism that he employed almost weekly in some forum throughout Haddon's tenure, complained that "the Administrator is extremely susceptible to imposing his own self-imposed restraint, rather than coming out, risking a showdown, and losing in court. He has been petrified of a court test ever since early November when representations of such a threat [were] made to him by industry."[11] Nader later complained that Haddon was so sensitive to criticism that he could be "blistered by moonbeams."

The Form-of-Law Problem

Nader's position was both oversimplified and overstated. But the agency did have a problem. Certain features of the legislation, designed to prevent industry capture through special pleading and to force regulatory action, had a paradoxical effect. They made it difficult, given resource constraints, to be both innovative and scientifically responsible. Strong statutory language could actually weaken implementation.

Moreover, the world to be regulated turned out to be much more complex than originally imagined. Consider one aspect of this complexity. The legislative politics of 1966 had pictured the automobile industry as a monolithic entity composed only of the Big Three plus American Motors. These companies were viewed as having virtually unlimited financial and technological capabilities. The statute's action-forcing provisions reflected that vision. Not only were rules to be adopted quickly, they were to be applied uniformly and within short implementation lead times. No exceptions or extended delays were thought necessary for these industrial behemoths.

The comments elicited by the agency's first proposals instead brought into Haddon's field of view a world made up of companies such as Avanti, Duesenberg, John Fitz & Co., SS Automobiles, and Shelby American Corporation. For these and other small producers compliance with the proposed standards, in particular the costs of destructive testing and sophisticated test instrumentation, would work a great financial hardship. The Lilliputians of the industry also had a cogent legal argument. The agency was required to do more than issue standards. It was directed by statute to issue rules that were "practicable" and "reasonable."

Congress had made clear that "vigorous competition in the development and marketing of safety improvements must be maintained." Driving small companies out of business was hardly consistent with this goal, but the tight statutory deadlines gave regulators little time to distinguish genuine difficulties from bluff and bluster. As Haddon reflected on the contents of NHTSA's first rulemaking docket, he determined to harmonize the statute's conflicting demands for "uniformity" and "practicability" by relaxing the proposed rules. This was both an accommodation to small manufacturers and a hedge against technical uncertainty, as we shall see. But whatever the rationale, Haddon set the agency upon a course of conduct that far outlasted its first generation of safety rules.

NHTSA's lowest common denominator approach was reflected both in general modifications applicable to all rules, such as stretched-out lead times, and in the substantive requirements of individual rules, particularly destructive-testing requirements. On their face, these relaxations of the original proposals seemed neither remarkable nor worrisome. An extension of lead time from the originally proposed eight months to one year was insignificant in the overall scheme of things, and nondestructive test procedures were required to be "equivalent" in their reliability to destructive ones. Even so, safety advocates properly grasped that the agency's approach had disturbing implications for the future of auto safety rulemaking. The relaxation of compliance deadlines and test procedures was based on cost and production feasibility concerns that could only grow more troublesome as NHTSA moved toward bolder initiatives. The initial rules, after all, did little more than codify existing practices at the major manufacturers. How much could be expected of the agency if its regulatory pace was set by the smallest and weakest companies?

Regulatory Restraint and the Science of Accidents

Congress had not expected that NHTSA's initial standards would be technically path-breaking. The Senate Commerce Committee expressly recognized that such standards would be promulgated before regulators were able to "derive substantial benefit from the new research and development activities" authorized by the 1966 act, and Haddon interpreted the requirement that rules be "based on" existing standards as preventing the agency from issuing initial rules for which there was no preexisting regulatory analogue. Even so, "based on" was not necessarily the same as "identical to." Steiglitz and others reporting to Haddon argued that the act empowered them to develop composite standards "based on" the most stringent elements of existing public and private safety rules and practices. In addition, nothing in the statute explicitly prevented the agency from promulgating standards that would phase in increasingly stronger safety requirements. The rulemaking staff urged that NHTSA couple stringent initial rules with additional, phased-in requirements that would gradually raise the lowest common denominator of industry practice. Yet in some respects NHTSA's first rules were even less stringent than the GSA standards on which they were based.

The agency's "self-restraint" in shaping initial rules reflected two phenomena of great significance for the future. First, regulators took upon themselves much of the burden of articulating and justifying the technical means of accomplishing regulatory goals, even though the statutory scheme apparently did not require them to do so. Indeed, the statute's demand that regulators set "performance" rather than "design" criteria seemed to contemplate just the opposite approach. It not only protected manufacturers' design discretion but appeared to leave producers with the burden of research and development on the technical means of achieving compliance. Second, regulators set for themselves a meticulous standard of rulemaking proof. Uncertainty was resolved against regulatory intervention. Standards were not issued unless the underlying rationale was virtually unassailable.

To some degree the acceptance of responsibility for demonstrating technological feasibility was induced by the borrowing technique that the statute mandated. Most existing standards were closer to design than to performance requirement. They covered specific bits of equipment—windshield wipers, head- and tail-lamps, and rearview mirrors, for example—rather than specifying a general visibility criterion that could be satisfied in any fashion that the manufacturers chose. Specification in terms of available equipment clearly was useful also in complying with the act's demand that standards be "reasonable." Manufacturers could hardly claim that NHTSA was being unreasonable when its standards incorporated existing equipment or technologies.

"Reasonableness," nevertheless, is a highly plastic concept. And it would be inappropriate to conclude that the agency was forced into an equipment-specific mode by the statute. Instead, reasonableness seems to have been given content largely by Haddon's own professional commitments. His insistence on scientific rigor in the study of accidental injuries was a major theme of his most important work, *Accident Research.*[12] The caution that resulted from Haddon's fastidious commitment to "scientific method" was the basis for his almost constant conflict with his more aggressive rulemaking chief, Steiglitz. A comparison of their views on particular issues reveals just what was at stake.

As initially proposed, for example, Standard 101 required that headlamp, ignition, windshield wiping, and other controls in passenger cars be located within the comfortable reach of a "fifth percentile adult female restrained by a lap and upper torso restraint seat belt." Purged of jargon, the intent of the proposal was to bring essential controls close enough so that short people with short arms could operate them. It was prompted by concern that automotive designers in the past had "overlooked or ignored the obvious fact that their products are sold to and operated by the general public, not by exceptionally well-trained adult male test track or racing drivers." Many of those responding to the proposal in the rulemaking process, however, were uncertain about the definition of the "fifth percentile female" and complained that any requirement to bring controls within a specified short reach would necessitate instrument panel changes that could not be completed by the proposed deadline.

Upon further examination, the agency learned that the anthropometric data defining the fifth percentile female were derived from studies by the Air Force in 1944 using nurses and female pilots who were of greater than average size. Haddon consulted Albert Damon, a lecturer on anthropology at Harvard and an international authority on the subject of body size and arm reach, as well as Damon's colleague at the Harvard School of Public Health, Ross McFarland. Damon and McFarland confirmed that the pilots and nurses in the Armed Forces sample were on average six-tenths of an inch to two inches taller than the general female population. Since arm reach closely correlates with height, Haddon concluded that the fifth percentile data were not "an adequate basis for requiring extensive design changes at this time with respect to the positioning of some of the instruments and the extensive tooling that this would involve." The standard accordingly was revised to provide that designated controls be placed within the operational reach of "a person." Haddon announced that "this illustrates, I think, the care with which we have been approaching this whole field in making sure that the positions we have taken are based upon the best possible scientific information."[13]

The agency's proposal of Standard 101 provoked ridicule. Newspaper commentary appeared depicting "Miss Fifth Percentile" as a woman of "unknown arm length" and critics complained that Haddon and his colleagues had swapped safety for pedantry. An exasperated Steiglitz noted that the standard in final form was "utterly meaningless from the standpoint of providing safety." Furthermore, he complained, although the Armed Forces' sample might be unrepresentative in terms of the subjects' height, the corresponding discrepancy in terms of arm reach was trivial, probably no more than two-tenths of an inch. "On the other hand," Steiglitz reported, "the arm reach of a tall man is 9 to 10 inches greater than these values. Thus, in order to avoid a possible discrepancy of a fraction of an inch, the standard permits controls to be 9 or 10 inches beyond that of even a tall woman."[14]

Proposed Standard 105 met a similar fate. As issued, the standard required that passenger cars be equipped with service brakes capable of stopping the vehicle within 342 feet at 80 miles per hour without swerving out of a 12-foot lane. The controversy surrounding the standard centered on requirements for "dual brakes," that is, for residual braking capabilities in the event of primary system failure. The original draft, prepared under Steiglitz's supervision, required that back-up brakes be capable of stopping the vehicle within 160 feet at an initial speed of 60 miles an hour. The proposal was modified over Steiglitz's objections and, as issued on December 3, called for a stopping distance of 194 feet at 60 miles per hour. Based on available data, it appeared that the prescribed stopping distance was actually greater than the stopping distance of most production automobiles.

Even so, a number of manufacturers complained that the braking requirement was an engineering "impossibility" and that brakes built to the standard's specifications would be severely unbalanced during normal operations. After further revision the standard demanded only that residual brakes "stop a car on a clean, dry, Portland cement, concrete pavement." Steiglitz observed contemptuously that no car could fail this test. In neutral it would eventually stop, and even in gear, it would stop when it ran out of gas.

And so it went with proposal after proposal on collapsible steering wheels, head restraints, and other equipment. Some of the agency's most important proposals were withdrawn for further studies that might or might not ever yield the requisite data. The agency itself had little testing capacity, and its lament, as it withdrew its head restraint proposals, reflected what it usually could expect to receive from external participants: "[Several] physicians submitting comments endorsed the proposal, although none provided specific recommendations or information as to the relationship between the geometry and strength of such devices and the prevention of neck injuries."[15] In evaluating the auto industry's claims and resolving its own uncertainty, the safety agency generally was on its own. If a high degree of scientific certainty concerning safety benefits and technical feasibility were required, rulemaking was going to be a very laborious process—particularly as the agency moved on to topics not embodied in existing standards. For Nader, this approach demonstrated the agency's "defective philosophy concerning burdens of proof and types of evidence," a philosophy that "pervades the entire standard-setting process."[16]

The Second Generation of Safety Rules, 1968–1970

Had the weak initial rules reflected only the exigencies of a tight schedule, inadequate start-up resources, and Haddon's professional preoccupations, their long-term significance might not have been a matter of great moment. The statute required regulators to issue new and revised standards no later than January 1, 1968, and "thereafter at least once every two years, as federal safety research and development matures."

More important, once the initial difficulties of setting up shop and meeting statutory deadlines were behind them, regulators could establish broad performance criteria for major vehicle systems and subsystems that would effectively shift much of the research and development burden back to manufacturers. In addition, standards after 1967 were not required to be tied to existing rules; the agency's regulatory agenda was therefore no longer effectively controlled by the very standard-setting bodies whose ineffectual past activities Congress had disparaged when it passed the act.

As a practical matter, however, the "existing standards" requirement of the statute far outlived the initial rules. The point is well illustrated by the second generation of safety standards, issued between November 1967 and December 1970. These thirteen rules were no more innovative than the first generation had been. A study by the National Commission on Product Safety (NCPS) in January 1970[17] found only five of NHTSA's standards of "moderate significance," that is, to require "significant engineering effort" by manufacturers having more than a negligible market share. All the other rules issued in this period were of little or no "significance" as NCPS had defined the term.

A closer look at the five "moderately" significant rules reveals that the commission was surely generous in its characterization. They include Standard 114, on theft protection, whose significance was attributed to its demand that all manufacturers conform to the practices of certain German manufacturers and one domestic manufacturer; and Standard 202, concerning head restraints, which required that a feature offered as optional by some manufacturers be upgraded and made standard equipment throughout industry. Similarly, Standards 203 and 204, governing energy absorption and rearward displacement of the steering assembly, required a number of foreign manufacturers to make changes in order to incorporate features that were prevalent on domestic models; and Standard 208 required lap and shoulder belts that were by then standard on most domestic vehicles.

The Form-of-Law Problem Revisited

About half of the thirteen rules issued by NHTSA between 1968 and 1970 had gestation periods of a year or more, roughly three times as long as the initial standards had taken to prepare. Senator Ribicoff, along with senior agency officials, attributed the slowing pace of rulemaking and the standards' lack of technical innovation to inadequate resources. But NHTSA had not been forgotten in the appropriations process. Approximately eighty-five physical scientists, research analysts, engineers, psychologists, and other professionals were employed in the agency's research and development group in support of motor vehicle rulemaking in 1971. The rulemaking staff totaled approximately seventy, mostly engineers, devoted principally to the task of translating research into standards. Although these staffing levels may have been less than Congress had envisioned in 1966, they were hardly trivial. What made the standard-setting process such a labor-intensive enterprise?

From a number of perspectives, the quasi-design, equipment-specific genre of rulemaking that NHTSA had inherited from the GSA seemed to be the culprit. That technique placed the agency at an overwhelming strategic disadvantage in fulfilling its mandate. It is much more difficult to specify the details of instrument protrusion, safety harness characteristics, padding requirements, side door construction, and roof strengths than to demand more generally that automobile passenger compartments be designed so that their occupants can survive a crash into a fixed barrier at 30 miles per hour. By comparison with broadly articulated systems of performance criteria, component-specific rules greatly magnified the agency's information-gathering burdens; made coordination of regulatory activities complex and cumbersome; and exaggerated the agency's maintenance and housekeeping chores simply to keep rules up to date.

This approach virtually ensured that obstructionist tactics by recalcitrant manufacturers would succeed. Incremental rulemaking at the level of individual equipment items allowed manufacturers to focus attention repeatedly on production feasibility. The manufacturers continuously portrayed equipment-specific rules as inherently disruptive of automobile production.[18] Some form of this complaint was pressed by virtually every manufacturer in every rulemaking proceeding. And though manufacturers made production feasibility and costs a major issue, they refused to produce supporting data. Early in 1968, the agency began a practice of routinely requesting comments on the costs of implementing proposed rules. Industry ignored the requests.

Under this vague, yet threatening and relentless, onslaught the rulemaking process developed a peculiarly defensive tone. The staff of the NCPS found that "the standard-making process is largely a dialogue between the agency and the automobile industry. At every stage, industry actively presents its views. Other groups are not barred from participating, but few do. The agency thus becomes increasingly preoccupied with the potential dislocations to industry's established patterns of design and production and the likely economic consequences."[19] Even when public interest advocates participated in the notice and comment process, they lacked the information to rebut industry's claims on production feasibility, and NHTSA itself was poorly equipped to evaluate such matters.

Things didn't have to be this way. NHTSA might have charged ahead in the face of industry complaints. In 1966 auto manufacturers had pressed hard for the incorporation of statutory language that would have imposed strict cost/benefit and production feasibility tests on rulemaking. Congress, however, had rejected the manufacturers' proposals. The Senate report made clear that cost and production feasibility concerns were at most a secondary consideration. The report recognized that NHTSA would "necessarily consider reasonableness of cost, feasibility and lead-time," but expressed the Commerce Committee's intention that "safety shall be the overriding consideration in the issuances of standards under this bill."[20]

Yet the "overriding consideration" of safety provided only limited solace for an agency that was having grave difficulty developing hard evidence that proposed safety initiatives would indeed substantially promote the act's primary goals. "Secondary considerations" like costs and technological practicability loom large when the degree to which primary considerations are being furthered is also uncertain. And here again equipment-specific standards compounded the information demands of rulemaking.

If all this were not enough, the incremental, quasi-design form of NHTSA's rules created an additional resource drain. Agency energies were increasingly diverted to simple maintenance and upkeep of rules that were already on the books. Rules maintenance was necessary both to ensure that the agency's regulations did not obstruct technological innovation in other areas of vehicle design and performance and to anticipate and prevent conflicts among regulations. Many rules incorporated SAE specifications and other external source material that was subject to continuous revision by its sponsors. Whenever this occurred, regulators had to be attentive to the implications for their existing inventory of rules.

Standard 108, on lamps and other reflective devices, is illustrative of the extraordinary maintenance burden associated with NHTSA's equipment-specific rules. The standard specified original and replacement equipment for signaling and safe operation of vehicles during nighttime driving and covered most motor vehicle lighting equipment. Between 1967, the year of issuance, and 1980, Standard 108 was amended 37 times and was the subject of 122 notices in the Federal Register, ranging from minor typographical corrections to complete restructuring of the standard.

NHTSA officials reported that between 1966 and 1976 three staff professionals were assigned full time to maintaining Standard 108, and that the agency on average had received a petition to revise the standard every month for ten years.[21] In this and other instances, the cumbersome form of the agency's rules was a result both of regulatory traditions within the agency and the demands of outsiders. State enforcement personnel, who used NHTSA's standards as part of state roadworthiness regulation, preferred equipment standards that were easily checked. The industry preferred highly determinate advice on how to comply. Equipment-specific rules satisfied both, but the maintenance costs associated with this form of standard setting bore no relationship to the rules' production costs, safety benefits, or technological sophistication.

The practical difficulties of regulating the automobile piece by piece were, of course, nothing that a generous dollop of additional manpower and money could not solve. But instead of acquiring more rulemaking resources, the agency during the late 1960s and early 1970s actually ended up with substantially less than had been envisioned when the Motor Vehicle Safety Act was passed. The Johnson Administration's resistance to a guns-butter trade-off had given way to the Nixon Administration's determination to stay the course in Vietnam while cutting back on domestic programs enacted by a liberal Democratic Congress. The new administration imposed a series of personnel freezes that brought Haddon's recruiting efforts to a standstill. Many agency sections were staffed by only one or two employees; others were totally vacant. Haddon later estimated that the agency was subject to funding or staff freezes during four-fifths of his tenure there.[22]

Resource shortages could not be attributed wholly to an ideologically hostile executive branch. Congress itself was responsible for the Expenditure Control Act of 1968,[23] which required that federal employment be reduced to levels in effect on June 30, 1966, and that positions in government be filled at the rate of three out of every four vacancies until that level was achieved. An exemption had been sought for NHTSA but was denied by the Johnson Administration.

To be sure, the act did not flatly preclude hiring agency staff, because the 1966 ceiling applied on a government-wide, not agency-specific basis. But each position at NHTSA had to be filled at the expense of another bureau, either within the Transportation Department or elsewhere, and success in that effort in turn required that NHTSA prevail in the inevitable budgetary warfare within the department. The agency, however, was poorly situated for bureaucratic battles. It was slotted into the Federal Highway Administration (FHWA), where it was dwarfed by agencies like the Bureau of Public Roads, with its $4 billion annual budget, and forced to borrow legal, planning, and other staff from other bureaus. Moreover, FHWA was dominated by the old "three E's" highway establishment, which, according to Haddon, immediately set about "sabotaging" NHTSA.[24]

Meanwhile the agency ran into a host of other unexpected difficulties in building an adequate staff to shoulder the heavy burdens of piecemeal rulemaking. The presumption in 1966 was that aeronautical engineers and other qualified scientists were in abundant supply and could be readily tapped for service in the auto safety effort. Sputnik had reshaped the nation's educational curriculum and generated a virtual glut of engineers, technicians, and other scientists, it was thought. Haddon reported to the Congress in 1969, however, that there was only a "small pool of talent available" and that "many potential recruits have remained in other employment or taken more attractive positions elsewhere."

The agency lacked more than personnel. From the standpoint of fulfilling NHTSA's technology-forcing mission, no resource inadequacy was more disabling than the failure to acquire an independent research and development test facility. The 1966 act envisioned that safety rulemaking would be informed by sophisticated research and analysis conducted at independent laboratories administered by the agency. The original act authorized no funds for actual construction, but instead required the agency to study its needs and report back to Congress by December 31, 1967. On October 7, 1968, almost a year late, the agency issued a two-volume report; it concluded that the agency required two major facilities, a vehicle and highway safety proving ground with supporting laboratories, and a driving simulation laboratory. No test facility was funded, however, until 1972, and it did not become operational until

1975. Until then NHTSA borrowed what facilities it could from other federal agencies.

Whither Safety Regulation?

Mired in regulatory trench warfare with the industry; starved for revenues, personnel, and facilities; under constant attack by its putative public interest friends; flanked by protean bureaucratic bedfellows; and trapped, in part by its own sense of professionalism, in a staggeringly laborious regulatory approach, NHTSA faced the decade of the 1970s desperately in need of some new ideas and loyal allies. To some degree it got both. The reinforcements, however, arrived too late.

FIVE

The Great Leap Forward

There was very little that NHTSA could do about many of the problems that beset it—the lack of well-tested safety innovations, the domestic budget squeeze, the perennial problem of attracting technological talent to the government's underfunded regulatory enterprise, the industry's capacity to mount a full-court press against every rule, the tendency of its friends to behave like enemies. If the agency was going to make headway against this sea of troubles it was going to have to alter its mode of operation. To seize and maintain the initiative on auto safety NHTSA would somehow have to make effective strategic use of its apparent power to demand better vehicle safety performance, leaving the means of compliance up to the manufacturers. It needed to devise a legal form for its regulatory actions that would shift the major responsibility for design, testing, and implementation to the people who had the financial and technical resources to get the job done. In the late 1960s and early 1970s this regulatory form began to emerge.

The Promise of Passivity

Amid the many ideas for protecting vehicle passengers from the effects of the "second collision," one general approach stood out—keeping occupants in place during those crucial fractions of a second when the energy from a crash was absorbed and dissipated by the vehicle surrounding them. If the occupants didn't hit anything, the rapid deceleration to which they were exposed would have very modest harmful effects. This was, of course, the basic logic behind seat belts and shoulder harnesses, equipment that by 1970 was available on 75–80 percent of motor vehicles.

But availability was not enough. The agency's studies revealed that only 25–30 percent of motorists wore their seat belts, and that figure was probably inflated. A much smaller proportion wore shoulder belts. As the epidemiologists already knew, when public health measures require the continuous active cooperation of the populace they are likely to fail. NHTSA, therefore, proposed in 1969 that Standard 208 (requiring lap and shoulder belts) be amended to switch from an active to a passive technology. The technology it had in mind was the airbag.

The airbag was at once simple and exotic. Upon the vehicle's deceleration during a collision, a cushion, concealed in the steering column or lower dash and triggered by a sensor, would automatically inflate to absorb the energy transfer and insulate occupants during the "second collision." It would then deflate to permit occupants to exit the vehicle. Simple enough—until one considers that the airbag was expected to sense the impending collision, inflate, and deflate, in less than half a second.

Although an innovative technology, the airbag's origins stretched back for a decade and a half. The first U.S. patent on a "safety cushion for automotive vehicles" was granted on August 18, 1953. The major domestic manufacturers, particularly General Motors, had conducted extensive research, development, and testing on the airbag during the ensuing years, and by the early 1960s, automotive component suppliers, such as Eaton, Yale & Towne, had begun substantial research and development programs. Air cushion restraint systems, or airbags, were hardly an idea cooked up by wild-eyed safety engineers in the basement of the Transportation Department.

In its July 1969 advanced notice of proposed rulemaking NHTSA reported its conviction that the airbag technology was nearing production readiness. More dramatically, the ANPRM predicted that the switch to passive restraints would save ten thousand to twelve thousand lives per year—many more than the agency's prior forty-nine rules combined. But the costs of this technological breakthrough were equally impressive. The stage was set for a regulatory donnybrook that has now lasted nearly two decades and that has virtually come to define the public image of vehicle safety regulation. This extravagant process has finally produced a rule that one might have thought unimaginable under the 1966 act—expressing a preference for driver (and passenger) behavior modification by the state via criminal law enforcement (mandatory belt-use laws).

This complicated story with its ironic denouement was hardly perceptible in 1969, and it is followed in much more detail in Chapter 10. The striking fact in 1969 was a promising *legal* innovation contained in the airbag proposal. The agency was moving toward general performance-based rules. Although the proposed amendments to Standard 208 presumed the existence of a particular type of equipment, the air cushion, the proposal did not mandate its use. Instead it permitted the use of any "passive" technology ("automatic" belts were one alternative) that would meet the standard's performance criteria. And unlike most of NHTSA's other "performance" standards, the performance criteria in amended Standard 208 were not specified in terms of the equipment used. Rather than speaking of airbag inflation times, belt anchor strengths, or the like, the proposal was framed in terms of the effects produced on an anthropomorphic dummy in frontal barrier crashes at 30 miles per hour. In addition, the proposal announced a moving compliance target. Initial compliance might be achieved with improved manual belt systems, but by 1973 protection would have to be completely "passive" and would have to meet injury criteria for rollovers as well as frontal crashes. Steiglitz would have been pleased.

The trench warfare that ensued initially submerged the novelty of revised Standard 208's approach. As usual costs, lead times, and production feasibility took center stage in industry submissions. Indeed, the three-year process to upgrade Standard 208 to provide passive protection generated twenty-four separate rulemaking notices, hundreds of comments and objections, and dozens of petitions for reconsideration, exemption, and revision. The compliance deadline was pushed from January 1, 1972, to January 1, 1973, to July 1, 1974, and finally to August 15, 1975. Ultimately the agency stood fast in its conviction that manufacturers should bear the remaining research and development burdens necessary to implement the standard. A generous grant of lead time, over three years, was provided for them to do so.

The Reformation of Auto Safety Rulemaking

In October 1971, NHTSA issued its updated "Program Plan for Motor Vehicle Safety Standards." The October Plan's introduction highlighted a new approach that was oriented toward both "performance" and "total systems" and that was finally linked to the agency's research and development efforts. According to the plan, the proposed amendments to Standard 208 were but a first step in the process of folding virtually all existing crashworthiness rules into a Super Rule, a superstandard that would set forth comprehensive criteria. The completion of the overall shift to integrated performance-based standards was scheduled for the mid-1970s.

The October Plan also described the new organizational status of the agency. Under pressure from Ribicoff and others, it had been shifted in March 1970 from the Federal Highway Administration to the Office of the Secretary.[1] The secretary in turn had given the agency the status of a separate operating administration, later renamed the National Highway Traffic Safety Administration, reporting directly to him "in recognition of the priority and visibility required to do the job."[2] At last all the pieces seemed to be coming together to produce the forward thrust envisioned in 1966. Perhaps the frustrations of bureaucratic and regulatory trench warfare were a thing of the past.

In one respect, the October Plan was recognized to be a high-risk strategy. Although the plan envisioned that NHTSA would continue to upgrade and tinker with its existing inventory of piecemeal rules, limited agency resources would increasingly be diverted from that effort to the more promising systems-based approach. As a result, rulemaking schedules to upgrade existing standards, which had already slipped significantly, were likely to slip further. NHTSA seemed willing to bear these costs, however, given their benefits. The plan set out a summary estimate of the costs and benefits of its proposed program that made a strong case for the agency's new course.

So Much for Planning

As it turned out, the new performance and systems-based approach was a high-risk legal strategy as well. On December 2, 1972, the U.S. Court of Appeals for the Sixth Circuit enjoined the implementation of Standard 208 in *Chrysler Corp. v. DOT.*[3] The *Chrysler* decision would not be the agency's last loss in court, nor was the opinion as broadly critical of NHTSA's rulemaking efforts as some future decisions would be. Yet its effects on NHTSA's new regulatory strategy were devastating. It was this case, more than any other, that taught the agency how precarious its legal position in rulemaking really was—a lesson that surely was not lost on its perennial antagonists, the vehicle manufacturers.

The plaintiffs' briefs in *Chrysler* threw the book at Standard 208. They urged that NHTSA lacked statutory authority to force technology and that the agency was limited to issuing requirements based on available equipment: that the standard was neither "practicable" nor "reasonably related to the need for motor vehicle safety," in part because seat belts (when worn) were more effective than airbags in some crash modes; that the standard's test procedures were flawed; that dummies meeting the standard's specifications were not readily available; that various procedural errors had been committed; and that many logical, judgmental, and evidentiary failings rendered the standard "arbitrary and capricious."

In peppering the court with reasons for invalidating the standard, *Chrysler* and the other plaintiffs were behaving like any other litigant seeking to overturn an agency's discretionary exercise of broad statutory authority. It was thought to be an uphill fight, and one never knew what line of reasoning the court might find persuasive. The comprehensive, scattershot attack also reflected the automobile manufacturers' customary strategy in attacking NHTSA's rulemaking efforts: to defend the status quo at every point with every available stratagem, and to keep up a relentless pressure via petitions, objections, comments, and criticisms.

The agency, for its part, played the familiar role of passive defendant, meeting the plaintiffs' claims and letting the latter's arguments provide the organizing principle for its brief. Thus were the issues in the *Chrysler* litigation framed. No mention was made of the October Plan, the new systems approach to rulemaking, the strategic impossibility of equipment-specific rules, the research and development and other informational burdens that the agency had shouldered in prior rulemaking efforts, or any of the other considerations that had led NHTSA to reform its rulemaking approach. The *Chrysler* court addressed a specific rule, Standard 208, not rulemaking generally.

After considering the appropriate standard of judicial review, the court turned to the principle issue in the case. Was NHTSA legally empowered to force automotive technology? Unequivocally (or so it seemed) the court resolved the issue in NHTSA's favor. In sweeping language, Judge Peck wrote:

The explicit purpose of the Act, as amplified in its legislative history, is to enable the federal government to impel automobile manufacturers to develop and apply new technology to the task of improving the safety design of automobiles as readily as possible . . . the agency is empowered to issue safety standards which require improvements in existing technology or which require the development of new technology, and it is not limited to issuing standards based solely on devices already fully developed. This is in accord with the Congressional mandate that "safety shall be the overriding consideration in the issuance of standards."[4]

One by one, the court rejected the plaintiffs' other arguments. Standard 208 was "practicable," reasonably related to the need for motor vehicle safety, procedurally irreproachable, and in all other respects legal—save one.

The court believed the testing procedures by which the crashworthiness of vehicles was to be judged were inadequate. Specifically, the court found that the test dummy specified by Standard 208 did not provide an "objective" standard, as required by the Motor Vehicle Safety Act. The dummy criteria were deficient in at least three respects: the flexibility criteria for the dummy's neck, the "dynamic spring rate" for the dummy's thorax region, and the construction criteria for the dummy's head were all said to be incompletely specified. Differently constructed dummies, which met the literal requirements of Standard 208, might thus yield substantially different results in performance tests measuring the forces applied to the dummy in a crash. The court concluded that these possible variations offended the statute: "Objective, in the context of this case, means that tests to determine compliance must be capable of producing *identical* results when test conditions are *exactly* duplicated, that they be *decisively* demonstrable by performing a rational test procedure and that compliance is based upon the readings obtained from measuring instruments as opposed to the subjective opinions of human beings" (emphasis added).[5]

The Sixth Circuit's demands for "objectivity" were carefully articulated in its opinion. Where the court had found the requirement of *identical results* as an element of objectivity, however, was much less clear. The Senate Report on the 1966 act did not elaborate on the statute's requirement that standards be framed in "objective terms," and the House Report merely stated that "in order to ensure that the question of whether there is compliance with the standard can be answered by objective measurement and without recourse to any subjective determination, every standard must be stated in objective terms."[6] The performance criteria of Standard 208 plainly were "objective" in this sense. The court's demand for "repeatability," meaning "identical results," in "exactly duplicated" tests that "decisively demonstrated" their conclusions without the necessity for human judgment was a heavy gloss on the statute.

The court's analysis and its order both took NHTSA almost completely by surprise. The agency had not anticipated that the suit would turn on "objectivity"; it had devoted a scant three pages of its 123-page brief to the issue. This position was understandable. General Motors had expressed no serious reservations about the standard's objectivity and had publicly announced that it could meet the compliance deadline with little difficulty. Airbag suppliers, who arguably had the most to lose if their products did not comply, had also indicated that they could provide airbag systems satisfying Standard 208 by August 1973, as long as purchasing commitments were received by July 1971. Those involved also knew that at the time the suit was filed, three years remained before passive restraints were required. If the dummy were indeed inadequately specified, there was adequate time to iron out the details, without upsetting the implementation schedule.

The delay and disruption of agency rulemaking caused by the holding seemed wholly unnecessary for several additional reasons. At the heart of the court's analysis was a fairness of expectations test: manufacturers could not fairly be subjected to the uncertainty (financial risk and legal liability) that variable test results would create. But in fact the standard would not expose manufacturers to such risks. The requirements for the test dummy were set out in specification SAEJ963 and had been developed by engineering committees composed of the industry's own technical personnel. As the agency explained in its brief, "So long as a manufacturer's dummy complies with the specifications of SAEJ963, he can use any form of dummy he pleases, and if its cars meet the requisite injury criteria, they will not be determined to be out of compliance with Standard 208."[7] It was possible, of course, that manufacturers might exploit the looseness of the dummy's specifications in order to take engineering short cuts, if doing so would cut costs. That might be a questionable regulatory policy, but it was not unfair to the manufacturers. Underspecification actually worked to their advantage. NHTSA's assurance that it would not take enforcement action where variation could be tied to the dummies should have quieted any residual concern. The agency's position could be taken as a binding statement of policy that the court itself could enforce.

Similarly, the plaintiffs' own treatment of the "objectivity" issue should have alerted the court that it was not a serious problem. The manufacturers seemed to concede that airbags would save thousands of lives, and the court in *Chrysler* flatly stated that the agency's predictions of airbag effectiveness were supported by "substantial evidence." If variations in test procedures were in fact material, how had the agency come to make and support these predictions? If based on subjective, nonreproducible tests, the agency's predicted benefits should have been attacked as premised on insubstantial evidence. But the life-saving potential of airbags was challenged by no one.

The court's conclusion that variable test results would make compliance turn on "subjective determinations" seemed to reflect its own technical illiteracy. The court was confusing "objectivity" with mechanical measurement. Qualified engineering personnel reviewing test results could in fact come to a principled ("objective") determination of whether variable results were attributable to dummy differences rather than to the airbag itself. Indeed, a performance test that requires no engineering judgment is an impossibility.

Nor was the Sixth Circuit's attachment to an unachievable level of scientific certainty its only display of technological naiveté. The court also treated it as "axiomatic" that "a manufacturer cannot be required to develop an effective restraint device in the absence of an effective testing device which will assure uniform, repeatable and consistent test results." The realities of automotive manufacturing were just the opposite. Manufacturers routinely proceeded along several parallel paths in developing new technologies. Standard 208 required no different developmental process. Much of the critical work on installing airbags, such as redesign of the dashboard, retooling, perfection of the sensor, quality-control measures to ensure against inadequate deployment, and a host of other technical issues, could proceed in tandem with refinement of the dummy—provided manufacturers had the incentive to do so. And yet, without discussion of schedules or other intricacies of production planning, the court simply declared that "implementation of passive restraints be delayed until a reasonable time after such test specifications are issued."

In practical effect, *Chrysler* cast NHTSA's technology-forcing mission in procedural terms that made it extraordinarily difficult to complete. As the dissenting judge in *Chrysler* stated: "If the statutory concepts of motor vehicle safety standards and compliance testing are not separated, the effect is substantially to undermine the legislative scheme. New testing procedures progress only as they are needed by advancing technology. If the rationale of the majority is adopted, industry is in effect relieved from the responsibility of developing a concomitant part of new automotive safety technology since without a previously developed testing device and procedure the agency is powerless to press industry toward this end."[8]

The *Chrysler* ruling was thus an automobile manufacturer's dream. The decision articulated no limits on how objective the test device had to be, but demanded that the agency withhold regulatory action until every detail had been worked out. Given the nature of the technical task at hand, regulation under these conditions was ideally suited for the manufacturers' full-court press. There were an almost infinite number of characteristics that *might* come into play in the biomechanics of injury. Regulators could not reasonably be expected to specify them all.

It is important, nevertheless, not to overstate the specific problem that *Chrysler* created. The agency was able to reissue dummy specifications nine months later because General Motors had a competitive incentive to come to its rescue. General Motors was ready to produce airbag-equipped cars, while its competitors were not. The delay in Standard 208's compliance deadline directly attributable to the court's decision was little more than a year. The major significance of the decision was more general.

First, timing was crucial. The new deadline for compliance with a passive restraints rule now shifted to September 1976. As will be discussed in greater detail in Chapter 7, intervening events virtually destroyed the agency's political base in Congress and derailed passive restraints for an additional decade. Second, *Chrysler* lent political support to the manufacturers' basic criticism of NHTSA's new performance-based approach—that they were being subjected to the costly interventions of a technically incompetent bureaucracy to no good end. Third, and perhaps most important, *Chrysler*, combined with other judicial opinions, enormously enhanced the perceived burdens of standard setting. Here and elsewhere the courts' demands for technological certainty trapped the agency in its earlier regulatory mold. NHTSA could be certain of satisfying the courts only if it limited itself to requiring the general use of already developed and tested automotive equipment.

The Legislative Significance of Judicial Review. The auto manufacturers adroitly made *Chrysler* a centerpiece of their testimony in 1974 in congressional hearings on the cost, benefits, and technical feasibility of rulemaking. The following colloquy from the 1974 oversight hearings between Senator Hartke and the Chrysler Corporation's representative concerning the newly announced September 1, 1976, deadline for passive protection gives a sense of the strategic regulatory and political avantages *Chrysler* conferred on auto manufacturers.

Senator Hartke. On Monday the NHTSA proposed revised standard 208 calling for the inclusion of passive restraints on all motor vehicles not later than September 1, 1976. Do you at this time anticipate any difficulty in complying with this proposed standard if it is ultimately promulgated?

Mr. Terry. We certainly do.

Senator Hartke. You do?

Mr. Terry. Yes. We don't see how we can possibly have passive restraints for all cars by 1977 model. The whole situation with passive restraints was thrown up in the air [by the *Chrysler* decision.] Since that time, . . . our progress . . . has been very disappointing . . . . [W]e haven't got out first dummy that fully meets the specs that NHTSA sets for it.[9]

In the course of these hearings Senator Hartke, one of the staunchest legislative defenders of vehicle safety regulation, could be found begging the industry to help NHTSA out with its "dummy repeatability" problem.[10] But though General Motors did provide assistance on that narrow issue, the Big Three were unified in attacking the whole notion of performance testing. As the automakers portrayed the technological situation, there was no assurance that "laboratory" performance, even in "repeatable" tests, would replicate real-world accidents.[11] Performance testing of the type the agency contemplated was therefore inherently unreliable. In a creative reading of *Chrysler,* General Motors even attributed the demand for standards supported by real-world data to the Sixth Circuit Court of Appeals itself.

More Trouble in Court. If a demand for "practicability in use" or for real-world testing seemed a strained construction of *Chrysler,* it was hardly an exaggeration of the opinion in *H & H Tire Co. v. DOT,*[12] handed down by the Seventh Circuit on the same day. The issue before that court concerned Standard 117, a rule governing performance requirements for retreaded tires. Many manufacturers complained that they could not meet the criteria. Industry-wide failure rates for the high speed and endurance tests were reported to be 17 percent and 28 percent, respectively. The National Tire Dealers and Retreaders Association, however, stated that 100 percent of its tires met the test, and NHTSA reported that some retreaders had admitted they could redesign tires to meet the standard's specifications.

The Seventh Circuit, nevertheless, struck down the standard on grounds that NHTSA had not shown that Standard 117 was "technologically and economically feasible. The respondents refer us to no analysis of the costs of such design changes nor to determinations of how long it would take the retreading industry to begin production of the redesigned retreads."[13] Standard 117 might nonetheless be permissible, the court continued, if "retreads *unquestionably* were *major* safety hazards *and* if compliance . . . *clearly* enhanced retreads' safety under on-the-road conditions" (emphasis added).[14] NHTSA, however, had failed to adduce the requisite amount of proof.[15] The court took no notice of the fact that manufacturers had never substantiated the cost and production feasibility concerns that they claimed might destroy the industry. As the court conceived the agency's task, regulators carried the burden of demonstrating both real-world safety payoffs and reasonable production costs. This was necessary because otherwise the agency could not be certain that its rule did not *reduce* safety. If consumers responded to high costs by driving on worn-out tires, any safety benefits from better retreads might be overbalanced by increased risks.

From the agency's perspective the *H & H Tire* opinion revealed a thorough misunderstanding both of NHTSA's powers and of the practical necessities of forcing the development of safer technology. If NHTSA needed on-the-road evidence of safety effects before it could regulate, how could it require anything new? Didn't the court understand that imposing new and more costly technologies always extended the useful life of old ones by providing economic incentives for their continued use, and that there was always a safety loss in the transition period as consumers continued to use worn-out equipment? And how was NHTSA to respond to claims of excessive cost? Only manufacturers had the cost data; they refused to disclose it and NHTSA had no statutory power to require disclosure.[16]

If *Chrysler* and *H & H Tire* correctly depicted the legal situation, NHTSA was in even deeper trouble than it had thought when it devised the October Plan. Although the agency had been told that it could force the development of new technology, any "gaps" in its rules might render them nonobjective, at least in the perception of a technically unsophisticated court. The manufacturers' full-court press on every rule was likely to pay handsome dividends. The agency, in contrast, bore the burden of demonstrating somehow that the technology it was forcing was both technically and economically feasible *and* that it would produce real-world benefits. This was perhaps possible in cases in which the requirements merely upgraded optional equipment to the status of "standard." But could it ever be possible when defending a rule that required system or subsystem performance beyond that available in any of the current fleet? The chances surely did not seem good.

The Regulatory Impact of Judicial Review

The *Chrysler* decision, when combined with *H & H Tire*, left the October Plan in a shambles. In House oversight hearings five months later, Nader reported that the plan had been "abandoned," with the "partial exception of the airbag and two or three minor standards." "There is loose talk around the agency," he reported, "that there won't be any really significant standards imposed on motor vehicles until well into the 1980s."[17] The agency readily conceded at the 1973 hearings that the plan's rulemaking schedules had indeed slipped significantly, and it blamed this slippage largely on the massive disruption that *Chrysler* had caused. According to agency testimony the court's invalidation of the test dummy reverberated throughout the proposed systems-based integration of rules. Delay on Standards 201, 202, 203, and 204 were all explained on that basis. Work on new initiatives related to energy management in crashes also had been held in abeyance because "final scheduling depends upon the schedule of standard No. 208." The same was true of work on windshield mounting. The agency's testimony concerning the interconnectedness of its rulemaking plans indicated that it was still committed to the new systems-based approach. But realization of that goal depended on Standard 208's implementation, which was fading into the distant future.

Chrysler was not the only source of slippage in the 1971 rulemaking schedules. Many delays could be traced to the continuing problems of the piecemeal genre of rulemaking that the October Plan had been designed to reform. "Administrative work load" was given as the reason for delay in work on accelerator control systems and warning devices.

Pending proposals on brake systems were delayed due to "extensive and detailed comments received in response to the NPRM." Proposals to strengthen Standard 106 on brake hoses and assemblies were tied to "extensive comments to the docket [that] have been added since the NPRM which require careful study and analysis to resolve controversial issues." A similar rationale was given for delay in work on new truck-camper loading. Other delays were attributed to the familiar compound of difficulties that made piecemeal rulemaking such a painstaking chore—manufacturing production schedules and lead times, the unavailability of validated test procedures, and inconclusive, inadequate, or insufficient technical data.

An agency's suggestion that it was being slowed down by "extensive comments" in rulemaking proceedings might seem unpersuasive, even trivial. After all, the Administrative Procedure Act, which lays down the procedural requirements that agencies must observe, is neither unique to NHTSA nor, on its face, especially cumbersome. The act requires agencies like NHTSA to give interested parties adequate notice of intended regulatory actions and an opportunity to comment. Thereafter the agency is required to explain its decision in a "concise, general statement of basis and purpose." The courts in turn are expected to uphold the decision, as long as it is within the agency's statutory power and is not "arbitrary or capricious." What could be simpler?

As *Chrysler* and *H & H Tire* demonstrate, simplicity can be deceiving. Nor are those cases in any sense radically discontinuous with the "hard look" review that was being developed by appellate courts with respect to other agencies during this same period. The basic framework for judicial scrutiny of NHTSA's rulemaking efforts, as well as those of its fellow "new breed" health and safety agencies, had been established in 1968 in a careful and scholarly opinion by Judge Carl McGowan of the D.C. Circuit Court of Appeals in *Automotive Parts and Accessories Association v. Boyd.*[18] Two aspects of that opinion are of particular interest; both aspects in some sense "proceduralize" the reviewing court's investigation of the reasonableness of the agency's standard setting. Given the dynamics of rulemaking, this proceduralization necessarily reinforces the agency's caution in dealing with notice and comment rulemaking in the face of an aggressive opposition.

Judge McGowan set forth what he perceived to be the basic scope of review under the "arbitrary and capricious" standard under the Administrative Procedure Act. In his words, "The paramount objective is to see whether the agency, given an essentially legislative task to perform, has carried it out in a manner calculated to negate the dangers of arbitrariness and irrationality in the formulation of rules for general application in the future."[19] So stated, whether an agency's rule is deemed arbitrary or capricious may turn as much on the agency's apparent reasoning process as on the good sense of the final judgment under review.

In a similar vein, the court addressed the question of whether NHTSA's "concise general statement of basis and pupose" was sufficient to pass muster under Section 4 of the Administrative Procedure Act. The pertinent NHTSA statement was certainly concise and general. It stated in full: "This standard specifies requirements for head restraints to reduce the frequency and severity of neck injury in rear-end and other collisions." The court viewed this statement as unnecessarily terse:

> [O]n the occasion of this first challenge to the implementation of the new statute it is appropriate for us to remind the Administrator of the ever present possibility of judicial review, and to caution against an overly literal reading of the statutory terms "concise" and "general." These adjectives must be accommodated to the realities of judicial scrutiny, which do not contemplate that the court itself will, by a laborious examination of the record, formulate in the first instances the significant issues faced by the agency and articulate the rationale of their resolution. We do not expect the agency to discuss every item . . . in informal rulemaking. We do expect that, if the judicial review which Congress has thought it important to provide is to be meaningful, the "concise general statement of . . . basis and purpose" mandated by Section 4 will enable us to see what major issues of policy were ventilated by the informal proceedings and why the agency reacted to them as it did.[20]

Although Judge McGowan articulated this requirement in his *Auto Parts* opinion as a necessity of judicial review, the demand for more elaborate discussion of the major issues thrown up by the rulemaking proceeding has the equally important effect of reinforcing the participation of outside parties in an agency's deliberations. The agency's failure to respond to significant issues raised by participants can hardly satisfy the basic standard of reasonableness that the court had set forth: to perform its task in a manner "calculated to negate the dangers of arbitrariness and irrationality." And as the *Chrysler* and *H & H Tire* decisions had shown, any issue might be considered significant. It was clearly in the manfacturers' legal interest to raise any and every issue they could dream up and force the agency to respond. It was also clearly very risky for the agency not to address any issue raised. Who knew what some reviewing court would later determine to be "significant"?

Catch 22. Ironically, responsiveness to participants' comments held its own legal risks, as *Wagner Electric Corp. v. Volpe,*[21] decided the same year as *Chrysler,* demonstrated. In that case the Third Circuit suggested that NHTSA might, in effect, be trapped in endless cycles of notice and comment, renotice and recomment on even trivial amendments to proposed standards in order to avoid unfair surprise to rulemaking participants.

At issue in *Wagner* were Standard 108's provisions governing turn signals and warning flashers. As originally issued, Standard 108 incorporated by reference SAE specifications that defined flasher and signal performance requirements (for example, starting time, voltage drop, flash rate, durability), and testing procedures. The testing procedures provided for selecting a sample of twenty flashers at random from a batch of fifty; if seventeen of the twenty flashers passed the performance specifications and a second random sample did the same, the entire lot was judged to comply with the standard.

In January 1970 the agency decided to amend Standard 108 to reflect updated SAE specifications and to incorporate other modifications. The NPRM it issued did not refer to modifications of the flasher/signal performance criteria or testing procedures. On October 31, 1970, the agency issued a series of amendments that included eliminating the sampling provisions. NHTSA had concluded in the course of its review that sampling was impermissible under the statute. The effect of dropping the sampling procedure was to substitute a 100 percent compliance test, while retaining the original performance criteria.

This was a dramatic upgrading of the standard, and the Wagner Electric Company complained that the January 1970 NPRM had given no notice to affected parties that the agency proposed to eliminate sampling. In the company's view it had been blind-sided. It requested that NHTSA withdraw the amendment and commence new rulemaking proceedings on the subject. NHTSA agreed that Wagner's procedural objection was "important enough to merit notice and comment" and issued a new NPRM to eliminate sampling. No reference was made in this notice to any other proposed changes, but the agency was careful to reserve its presumed right to make appropriate changes without commencing yet another rulemaking proceeding.[22]

A flurry of comments ensued from interested parties, including Wagner Electric. Wagner (and others) urged that the performance criteria should be relaxed if 100 percent compliance was required, and that yet another round of notice and comment rulemaking should be opened. NHTSA refused to issue another NPRM, but consulted its own Office of Operations Systems, which agreed that 100 percent compliance testing was not "reasonable" or "practicable," unless corresponding "adjustments" were made in the performance criteria. Accordingly, on August 28, 1971, the agency issued amendments that eliminated sampling and substantially downgraded the performance criteria.

Wagner Electric sued to overturn the amendments on grounds that NHTSA had violated the Administrative Procedures Act by failing to give adequate notice of its intent to relax the performance specifications. The agency, in turn, argued that its notice was in fact "sufficient to give interested parties an opportunity to comment on the entire subject matter of the standard" and that many commentors, including Wagner, had in fact addressed the performance issue. The court rejected NHTSA's defense: "We cannot accept the Administrator's position. Indeed that position is inconsistent with the agency's earlier concession that the first notice was inadequate. The fact that some knowledgeable manufacturers appreciated the intimate relationship between the permissible failure rate provision and the performance criteria, and so responded, is not relevant. Others possibly not so knowledgeable also were interested persons within the meaning of 5 U.S.C. §553."[23] The court pointed out that the state agencies and consumer interest groups had a plausible interest in the matter but had not commented. "The absence of comment from such groups may well be because the notice of proposed rulemaking never advised of this subject or issue," the court reasoned.

In addition to the Catch-22 aspects of combining these "substantive" and procedural decisions—NHTSA's nonresponsiveness is irrational and its responsiveness is procedurally improper—*Wagner* added further burdens and uncertainties to the rulemaking process. With no reliable method for discerning what issues raised by participants might be treated as important by reviewing courts, or what changes in a proposal would be considered sufficiently substantial to require another round of notice and comment, NHTSA could hardly be faulted for taking a very cautious approach to rejecting either manufacturers' substantive arguments or their requests for further proceedings to explore new or modified issues. The manufacturers' full-court press on rulemaking proposals, which also included constant petitions for amendment, interpretation, or waiver of existing rules, was being reinforced procedurally as well as sustantively by judicial review.

From the NHTSA's perspective the *Wagner* decision was another bombshell. The court seemed completely inattentive to the opportunity costs of repeated cycles of notice and comment. With no apparent recognition of the potential for disruption it was creating, the decision greatly complicated an increasingly unwieldy rulemaking process, legitimized opponents' dilatory tactics, and made information gathering much more difficult for the resource-strapped agency. If new data and suggestions were to be the basis for new rounds of rulemaking, it made sense for opponents to parcel them out over time; with any luck, new rounds of notice and comment could go on for decades. All this in the name of procedural fairness to state agencies and consumer advocacy groups, who were about as common in agency rulemaking proceedings as Quakers at prize fights.

Forward to the Past. Haunted by the specter of judicial invalidation, unable to implement its planned switch to systemic performance criteria, and hence still confronted by the usual frustrations of trying to regulate the automobile piece by piece, NHTSA plodded forward. Twelve new equipment rules were issued from 1971 to 1974. But like their forebears, this third generation of rules was a lackluster bunch. Some covered only specialty items on a narrowly defined class of vehicles; others addressed the reliability of existing automotive components. Even rules that addressed plausible safety concerns (bumper and roof strengths, for example) proved on closer examination to be modestly conceived and to address safety problems of small or no moment.

Amid this uninspiring assortment of new safety initiatives only one stood out as signaling, as had Standard 208 and the October Plan, the agency's new determination to force the development of technology through performance-based standards. Standard 121, governing air brakes on trucks, buses, and trailers, sought to shorten the controlled braking distances of large trucks and buses in order to reduce the incidence of accidents involving a large vehicle and a small vehicle. As might be imagined, such accidents generated appallingly high injury and fatality rates. Because the standard included both minimum stopping distances and lateral stability and antilock criteria, manufacturers were expected to comply through use of a sophisticated antilock device (known as an antilock braking system, or ABS) adapted from aeronautical technology.

Although the standard seemed only to require transferring a well-tested technology from one application to another, the technical complexities of the device led the agency to provide a two-year lead time for implementation.

Had the saga of Standard 121 ended here, the era we have called the heyday of rulemaking (1966–1974) might have been credited with forcing the implementation of at least one substantial bit of technology. But Standard 121 did not survive judicial review. When the ABS technology was moved from limited to mass production, reliability problems surfaced almost immediately. In response to numerous petitions, NHTSA was engaged continuously during the early 1970s in relaxing and reformulating the standard. Even so, the problems persisted. Spot checks by some fleet owners suggested that the failure rate of the systems might exceed 50 percent.

The affected parties did more than complain; they sued, claiming that persistent evidence of unreliability made it essential for NHTSA to study the reliability of the ABS device in use. In *Paccar, Inc. v. NHTSA*[24] the Ninth Circuit Court of Appeals found the agency's data base totally inadequate to support retention of the standard. It enjoined implementation of the stopping-distance requirements until the agency could develop evidence that the antilock braking systems would decrease rather than increase the danger to the public.

In addition the court invalidated Standard 121's testing requirements. The stopping distances specified by the rule were for a road surface with skid coefficient of 75 and 30. The coefficient represents the degree of friction between the tire and the road surface and is therefore a quantitative measure of the slickness of the road. The number 75 represents a dry road; 30 represents a wet road. It is impossible, however, to maintain a road surface at a precise skid number. Manufacturers complained that fluctuations in test conditions would require them to overcompensate by testing their vehicles on substantially slicker roads than the regulations required in order to ensure compliance. The court rejected NHTSA's assurance that it would test trucks on a substantially stickier surface than the regulation required, thus allowing a margin for surface variances. "These informal assurances are not enough," the opinion concluded, in terms reminiscent of *Chrysler.* "Manufacturers are entitled to testing criteria that they can rely upon with certainty."

The Standard 121 embroglio lasted nearly ten years and brought with it an increasing sense of frustration. The agency obviously had not operated with the degree of scientific or engineering precision that, abstractly considered, one would like to expect. But as the reviewing court said, "there is much in the standard that has long been needed for highway safety, and it is undisputed that the antilock device, when perfected, will advance that goal. We are also aware that some manufacturers have expended a great deal of time, energy and money over the last six years, in attempting to produce vehicles to comply, and that they have, to a large degree, been successful."[25]

In short, the agency had been engaged in technology forcing that placed the requirements for innovation and experimentation firmly on the automotive industry. The agency had been partially, perhaps mostly, successful, but had not quite achieved the degree of reliability that was needed. Yet, on judicial review, the agency discovered that its responsiveness over time to new data and industry petitions would be viewed not as a sensible incremental approach but as evidence that it did not know what it was doing. It was also required to demonstrate practicability in use in a legal context that almost certainly detroyed its capacity to do so. After the *Paccar* opinion, when truck manufacturers no longer had any obligations to comply with the standard, how was the agency to develop the comprehensive data on road performance that were necessary to sustain its regulation? Unless truck manufacturers and operators voluntarily cooperated with the agency—by installing and maintaining expensive devices that they obviously wished to avoid—that data could never become available. The court seemed to be demanding data that its own opinion rendered unobtainable.

The court's approach to the testing criteria was equally troublesome. As the *Chrysler* decision made all too clear, the Motor Vehicle Safety Act requires that the agency use "objective" performance criteria, and this objectivity requirement applies to testing criteria as well as to safety standards. The agency, therefore, was virtually forced to adopt the "stickiness coefficient" approach, notwithstanding its known and irremediable difficulty in application. There was no other way to specify an objective performance criterion, and hence NHTSA did the only thing that it could do. It recognized the problem explicitly and gave assurances that it would not test trucks for compliance purposes on a surface whose variance might penalize a conscientious manufacturer. But this promise was held to be an "impracticable" guarantee for manufacturers who are entitled to criteria "that they can rely upon with certainty" in doing their own testing. The agency's effort to make an impossible "objective" test feasible in practice had rendered it "impracticable."

Remembering the October Plan

Against the backdrop of "regulatory achievement" represented by NHTSA's first, second, and third generations of safety rules, consider the deeds that NHTSA had, by the mid-1970s (or, for that matter, by the late 1980s) left undone. Woven into the October Plan was a dazzling array of initiatives that were meant to find their way into law by the mid-1970s. Some of these proposals were mundane. Others were innovative and potentially quite important. The plan contained proposals to revise vehicle exteriors to protect pedestrians; to provide motorcycle rider protection; to improve vehicle handling and stability; to increase truck and bus power to improve uphill performance; to provide warning indicators for low tire pressure; to mandate expanded fields of view approaching 360-degree visibility; to require spray protectors on large vehicles that often impaired the visibility of following traffic in bad weather; to regulate maximum concentrations of toxic gases and noise levels in the passenger compartment; to provide high-speed warning and control devices that would limit vehicle speed and warn others when vehicles reached excessive speeds; to deter drunk driving through use of alcohol interlocks that "sensed the driver's impairment due to alcohol consumption" and prevented engine ignition; and to mandate "radar brakes" that would be triggered automatically in advance of imminent collisions.

A subcommittee of the House Commerce Committee offered a host of explanations in 1976 for NHTSA's slowdown. In a list based on conversations with agency officials, the committee cited[26] "the growing complexity of rulemaking actions," "the narrow base of public support for specific rulemaking actions," "increasing resistance from industry," the "need for additional economic analysis prior to issuing standards," and "political interference." Relatively few of the agency's proposals, however, seem to have been abandoned on the explicit cost-benefit grounds that were becoming increasingly popular as a guide to regulatory reasonableness and that a Democratic Congress suspected a Republican administration of using to engage in "political interference." Nor should they have been, if the rosy cost-benefit predictions contained in the 1971 plan were to be believed. The real culprits seemed to be lack of data and industry resistance, both made more crippling by revealed judicial preferences for bulletproof rules. In the face of scientific and legal uncertainty, proposals simply faded into the regulatory mist.

The Realities of Regulatory Research

Like the October Plan's wish list, NHTSA's most ambitious and most significant research project, the development of an experimental prototype known as the Experimental Safety Vehicle (ESV) had virtually no impact on standard setting. The ESV program was begun in 1968, when contracts were placed to examine possible approaches to applying the "total systems engineering concept to the development of an engineering safety vehicle." In a sense, the ESV program was designed as a demonstration project of the October Plan, and the demonstration was a resounding success. The vehicles delivered by the four contractors who participated in the program were designed, fabricated, and tested against total systems performance specifications for crashworthiness, accident avoidance, postcrash factors, and pedestrian safety that were in many respects state of the art. The experimental research vehicles met or exceeded *all* existing and proposed safety standards issued through mid-1970, especially in the area of highest priority, crashworthiness. Agency officials testified in 1972 that the agency planned to make "a number of changes in our [rulemaking] program based on recent discoveries that have taken place in the ESV program"[27] and that to a large extent the ESV program was "leading" the standard-setting program. But the promise to provide the future today never materialized. The General Accounting Office (GAO) later reported that "MVP [Motor Vehicle Programs] officials confirmed that none of the prototype test results have been used to formulate new or improved safety standards."[28]

Part of the explanation for this nonevent was that the safety success of the prototyes came at the expense of other vehicle characteristics. All prototype designs exceeded the 4,000-pound limit specified by program guidelines. The lightest vehicle weighed over 5,000 pounds and the heaviest over 6,000 pounds. In addition, some of the prototypes used costly materials and would have required changed production methods. The ESVs were safe, but they seemed to be awfully expensive.

In June 1973 the Department of Transportation announced its decision to terminate the ESV program. NHTSA's decision was based on "the trend toward smaller vehicles," which was greatly accentuated by the Arab oil embargo of that year. The ESV program had been overtaken by events. Consumers wanted small, pollution-free, and, especially, fuel efficient vehicles. As Lee Iacocca later put it, the American people wanted an economy car, no matter what it cost.

NHTSA accordingly announced[29] the commencement of a new prototype development program to produce a research safety vehicle (RSV) that would weigh in at no more than 3,000 pounds. The RSV program would also "consider the projected changes in automobile use in the next decade, as well as energy, resource and pollution problems." But the RSV would take nearly five years to build. The information gained from it would not be available to support rulemaking until the 1980s. If the ESV was a prototype of the past, the RSV it seemed, was a harbinger of the distant future. Meanwhile, times were changing.

SIX

The Crumbling Consensus

Between 1966 and 1974 Congress made only minor amendments to the Motor Vehicle Safety Act. Pursuant to its charter NHTSA had issued forty-five standards, mandating safety features that by 1974 had been incorporated into roughly 50 percent of the nation's automobiles. According to a later GAO estimate,[1] NHTSA's standards were keeping motor vehicle deaths and injuries 25–30 percent below the levels that otherwise would have been expected. How this could be true was a mystery, given the modest significance of NHTSA's rules, and the agency itself was dubious about the accuracy of the GAO's projections.[2]

Nevertheless, NHTSA's rulemaking activity was slowing dramatically in the 1970s under the joint pressures of manufacturer resistance, technological uncertainty, and judicial review. This slowdown was of major concern to many of those who assembled for oversight hearings before the Senate Commerce Committee in February and March of 1974. The committee was chaired by Warren Magnuson, who boasted of his support for consumer causes "B.N.—before Nader," and was dominated by a liberal Democratic majority, many of whom (Pastore, Hart, Cannon, Long, Cotton, and Hartke, in addition to Magnuson) had participated in the committee's unanimous approval of the 1966 act. This was a committee with a pro-safety regulatory agenda.

Congress Reassesses Rulemaking

The need to reenergize and redirect the rulemaking process was the explicit or implicit message of a series of witnesses who appeared before the committee. First to take the stand was Patrick M. Miller, head of the structural dynamics section of the transportation safety department at Calspan Corporation, successor to the Cornell Aeronautical Laboratory. Miller testified that significant advances were being made in safety research generally and in occupant protection particularly, but that corresponding improvements in fatalities and injuries almost certainly could not be achieved in the near future. The energy crisis had stimulated consumer demand for small, lighter vehicles, he reported, and the widening range of weight distribution in the nation's fleet was creating unprecedented hazards.

Miller held out some hope for the safety-standard process, on the grounds that standards would tend to make small cars heavier at the same time that fuel economy concerns prompted manufacturers to reduce the weight of heavier vehicles. But the gist of his testimony seemed to be that the world of auto safety was rapidly changing, and that it was doing so in ways that were largely beyond NHTSA's capacity to influence. Significant progress might have to await the emergence of the RSV, on which Calspan was a prime contractor.

NHTSA too saw itself as a beleaguered agency. But it located the major threat in its political and legal, rather than its technological, environment. James Gregory, NHTSA's administrator, testified plaintively: "We are the men in the middle in the adversary situation that has developed. We propose something. We are criticized on the one hand, with some support from the Committee, saying we are going too slow. The industry on the other hand is in there fighting and saying we are going too fast. We are trying to carry out our statutory responsibilities to get safety in these vehicles . . . The only thing is that you and some of the critics say we are going too slow. We say we are going with what the Administrative [Procedure] Act permits us to do."[3] During the course of the hearings, agency officials repeatedly defended the pace of NHTSA's rulemaking activity on the grounds that the agency was likely to be sued on almost every rule and that even greater delay in standard setting would result from judicial determinations that the rulemaking record had been inadequately developed and analyzed.

Public interest advocates selected NHTSA itself as an inviting target for reform. Nader's testimony had a strong Watergate-era flavor. NHTSA, he reported, was controlled by officials who opposed the agency's mission on ideological grounds and were intent upon subverting it. "Unlike so many problems in this country which are looking for solutions," he testified, "there are now far more solutions for automotive engineering safety than there is the will to implement them in the Department of Transportation."[4] Executive branch officials were violating their duty faithfully to execute the laws that Congress had enacted, and the solution, Nader said, was more legislation—"An Employee Rights and Accountability Act" that would "make government officials accountable to the citizens of the United States."[5]

Carl Nash, Nader's colleague at the Public Interest Research Group, followed with an indictment of NHTSA's allocation of resources to the old, discredited technique of behavior modification—particularly the agency's new interest in teenage and drunk driving measures. Such an approach was fruitless, Nash asserted, because American society was unwilling to restrict the travel liberties of the problem drinker or to deal with the intractable problems involved in controlling alcohol and automobiles. Besides, he argued, NHTSA's professed interest was really a sham, a transparent attempt to rationalize regulatory inaction. If NHTSA were truly committed to alcohol countermeasures, he said, it would have acted favorably on his petition to issue an ANPRM on the development of alcohol ignition interlocks.

As testimony of this sort dragged on, Hartke, who chaired the hearings, grew testy. "What I am asking," he told agency officials, "is a question which I suppose you get tired of hearing. In a country that can put a man on the moon and bring him back to earth, why can't we make our highways safe?"[6] Perhaps, he later speculated, the auto safety program was being administered by the wrong agency. There had been discussions among the Commerce Committee staff, he earnestly reported, "as to whether or not the NASA program, in view of the turndown in its space program, could take over this whole operation and do a more effective job utilizing technology."[7]

Was it really necessary to fold NHTSA into the Apollo program in order to force the development of safer automotive technology? Or could more modest administrative and institutional reforms break the impasse over safety standards?

A Peculiar Legislative Response

The stage seemed set for a series of amendments to strengthen NHTSA's rulemaking power pursuant to the 1966 act and perhaps its research capabilities as well. Legislation might have been devised to protect the agency from judicial review by limiting its scope and from hostile administrative superiors by renewed regulatory deadlines. Safety partisans also had argued for increased opportunities to participate in the rulemaking process and for greater power to force agency action by litigation. They wanted to counter the manufacturers' full-court press by getting a better offensive team on the floor. The agency also could have been given a massive increase in its research budget, combined with greater powers to sanction noncooperation in research and development by the automobile manufacturers. If Miller's testimony was correct, a major effort to design small cars for safety was urgently needed. Or perhaps, as Nader and Hartke often suggested, Congress itself should legislate a 50-mile-per-hour barrier crash survivability requirement and let the manufacturers figure out how to meet it. When the dust had settled on the legislative battles of 1974, however, the amendments to the Motor Vehicle Safety Act[8] had taken none of these forms.

Rulemaking Amendments. Instead of protecting NHTSA from judicial review on its most important standard, Congress required that any future passive restraints be subject to a legislative veto as well. The 1974 amendments also eliminated the agency's authority to adopt *any* rule that would require connecting existing seat belts and shoulder harnesses to the automobile's ignition (the so-called ignition interlock) or even require provision of any warning device (light or buzzers) lasting more than eight seconds to encourage belt use. Similarly, instead of empowering safety activists in NHTSA's rulemaking and judicial review proceedings, Congress added a public hearing requirement only for passive restraints proposals—a procedural device that was certain to give the advantage to manufacturers and to delay the rulemaking process.

The legislation did codify one pending standard on fuel system integrity, thus shielding NHTSA from judicial review of that particular rule. And Congress directed NHTSA to adopt standards in eight specific areas. But all of this mandatory rulemaking related exclusively to school bus performance, a subject that NHTSA itself had previously avoided because its cost-benefit studies demonstrated that the costs of school bus regulation vastly exceeded its benefits. The 1974 amendments imposed no new general constraints on rulemaking, and they left the basic standard-setting criteria of the original act intact. But it was difficult not to read an obscure, unsettling, and critical message between the amendments' specific lines.

Some parts of the message were downright puzzling. When Congress demanded that NHTSA adopt school bus standards, for example, the message seemed to be that some safety technologies should be forced on manufacturers, no matter how few lives they saved or how poor the cost-benefit ratios. When Congress banned the interlock's use, however, the message seemed to be that some safety technologies should not be forced, no matter how many lives they saved or how favorable the cost-benefit ratios. The problem for an agency trying to respond to congressional direction was to discern which rulemaking initiatives were like school buses and which were like the interlock. What exactly did Congress want?

Recall Amendments. If the rulemaking provisions of the 1974 legislation seemed poorly tailored to energize a languishing rulemaking effort, the recall provisions seemed designed to send the agency off in a different direction altogether. Whatever its view of safety rules, Congress was determined to do something about automobile defects. This objective was embodied in a host of specific provisions, including, in particular, a clear right to have all safety defects remedied at "no cost." These more stringent and detailed provisions were part of a package of new powers given NHTSA to ensure adequate enforcement. Reporting requirements were strengthened, fines and penalties were doubled, and NHTSA investigators were given both subpoena power and new plant-inspection authority.

The 1974 amendments took a no-nonsense approach toward enforcement in a number of other respects. Manufacturers continued to enjoy the right to resist the agency's determination of a defect until they received a court order, but the new provisions made clear that litigants who exercised this right faced penalties for noncompliance in the event the court confirmed the transportation secretary's demand for a recall. The right to judicial protection thus carried a cost—even for the manufacturer who contested NHTSA's position in good faith.

Nor did Congress forget in the recall amendments about the potential support that a regulatory agency might get from potential beneficiaries. "Any interested party" was given the right to participate in NHTSA's recall proceedings, which had previously involved only the agency and the manufacturers. Indeed, "any interested party" was given the right to attempt to mobilize the agency by petitioning it to determine the existence of a defect or to investigate manufacturers' compliance with their recall obligations. At the same time Congress refused to provide manufacturers with evidentiary administrative hearings prior to the implementation of a recall order. The government was permitted to force manufacturers to provide provisional notification notwithstanding the pendency of a judicial proceeding to enforce the agency's defect determination. Proceduralism was here harnessed to the pursuit of enforcement, not delay.

By preserving the informality of defect determinations, constraining access to judicial review, permitting provisional enforcement, clarifying and upgrading NHTSA's authority, and procedurally empowering safety proponents, Congress gave NHTSA the regulatory muscle for its recall program that it simultaneously denied the agency in rulemaking. Overall, the 1974 amendments looked like a new charter, but the charter of a complaints bureau and prosecutor's office, not of a proactive, technology-forcing regulatory agency. The shift in emphasis from rules to recalls seemed to signal a reorientation of auto safety regulation, from science and planning to crime and punishment.

The New Ballgame

The 1974 amendments reveal that the legislative politics of motor vehicle safety had changed in ways that were poorly reflected by the Commerce Committee's oversight hearings in the early months of that year. In fact much had changed, almost simultaneously. A stagnating economy and an ailing automobile industry called attention to competing, non-safety values that had been suppressed, if not forgotten, in 1966. Changes in technology, vehicle mix, and national politics, along with changed perceptions of the regulatory process itself, generated a host of issues that could not have been anticipated at the time of the original legislation. These competing values and multiplying issues both challenged and fragmented a Congress that had unanimously approved the vehicle safety revolution of 1966.

The Quest for Freedom. The 1966 act was premised on a conviction that, as Nader had put it at the time, "the matter of a motorist's choice of automobile can no longer be simply a personal one. It has to be a social decision."[9] Security was the first commandment. The 1974 amendments, by comparison, asserted that motorists had certain individual rights of both a substantive and a procedural nature; and that government should protect those rights, both by enforcing a corresponding set of obligations on auto manufacturers and by limiting the government's own interventions into the domain of private motor vehicle transportation. Motorists should be entitled to waive their rights, even if the result were hazardous to the public health. In both the rulemaking and recall sections of the 1974 legislation, freedom was the first commandment.

The "private rights" and "individual liberties" orientation of the 1974 legislation was not only different from the "expert social control" flavor of the original act; in some ways, the two perspectives were irreconcilable. Seat belts and shoulder harnesses, for example, were in virtually every car on the roads. Yet no more than 20 percent (and perhaps no more than 10 percent) of motorists used them. NHTSA had engaged in energetic publicity campaigns to increase voluntary belt use, but reported to Congress that its efforts had yielded "exactly zero" percent increases in the buckled-up population. The interlock, in contrast, was quite effective. But the interlock was authoritarian. Congress was so outraged by this "social decision" to invade individual liberty that it not only prohibited the interlock but imposed a potential veto on any non-voluntary restraint system.

Similar liberty interests affected the shape of the recall amendments. In explaining the background and need for legislation, the Senate Commerce Committee stated that it "codifies the right of the American consumer to have an automobile containing a safety related defect made safe by the manufacturer free of charge. The Committee believes that the requirement of remedy at no cost will also serve as an added inducement to consumers to put forth the time and effort to have an unsafe motor vehicle or item of motor equipment made safe."[10] The 1974 amendments thus entitled, but did not require, motorists to have defective vehicles repaired.

This particular form of "right," which might serve as an "inducement," was not chosen inadvertently. Congress considered proposals that motorists be required to return defective vehicles for repair in order to pass state inspection. But in the political environment of 1974, motor vehicle use was not a "social decision." The recall provisions spoke the language of individual rights and liberties. If the rulemaking amendments suggested that motorists had a negative right to be free from the ignition interlock and continuous lights and buzzers (and perhaps all "passive restraints"), the recall amendments suggested that they had a positive right to the vehicle that they thought they had purchased, a vehicle free from defects. Of course motorists would be permitted to have buzzers or interlocks installed for themselves, or to drive defective vehicles, if they preferred. Both the negative and the positive entitlements of the

1974 amendments were grounded in the "right to choose." In 1966 safety may have been the overriding concern; in 1974 it was freedom.

This is not to say that the recall amendments thoroughly rejected all the values of 1966. As interpreted by both the press and public advocates, entitlement to free repairs was a matter of social justice, as was the right of schoolchildren to be as safe as "Greyhound passengers." Yet the rhetoric of political mobilization surrounding the amendments deemphasized major components of the safety vision of 1966. In particular the image of the "accident epidemic" as a threat to "public health" had faded. The model of the public as a collective patient requiring preventive intervention had been replaced by the model of the individual motorist-consumer locked in a frustrating battle with unresponsive public and private bureaucracies.

"Consumerism" as a political force had been growing for decades. But in the early 1970s consumers' dissatisfactions were being fueled by inflation. Car prices and vehicle operating costs were being driven sharply higher by an inflationary spiral that produced "sticker shock" in the showroom and fist fights at the gas pump. The President's wage-price freeze announced on August 15, 1971, and terminated April 30, 1974, had no significant effect on car or gasoline prices.

For regulatory technique the political significance of higher costs can hardly be overstated. NHTSA officials reported that consumer complaints concerning safety defects and demand for recalls increased steadily in step with higher car prices. As cash outlays for automobiles swelled, consumers grew more intolerant of defects and they increasingly sought the agency's help in forcing manufacturers to stand behind their products.

The effects on rulemaking were precisely the opposite. In 1966 Ribicoff and other safety partisans brushed aside concern about the costs of regulation. Ribicoff reasoned that safety was imperative; that "if it costs more money, the public should pay the extra cost to save their lives"; and that Congress must "reject out of hand the argument from Detroit that safety doesn't pay."[11] Besides, Ribicoff argued, many safety advances could be achieved at nominal expense, and competitive market conditions would further dampen the cost impact. Manufacturers dared not price themselves out of the market and would therefore substitute mandatory safety features for the "absolutely nonsensical, useless junk" on automobiles that "has nothing to do with the needs of the car," he reasoned.[12]

By 1974 many of Ribicoff's colleagues were not so sure. Reports began to emerge that safety rules were a cause of significant consumer expenditure. In 1972, for example, a White House Office of Science and Technology report on the regulatory effects on the costs of automotive transportation found that regulatory compliance would add a whopping $873 to the price of an average car by 1976—$350 for emission controls and $523 for safety.[13] The industry's estimate was $1,389. The White House report concluded that the "reservoir of cheap and easy beneficial changes [in the safety area] appears to be running dry"[14] and recommended more comprehensive use of cost-benefit analysis.

The costs of motor vehicle safety standards were also the subject of highly publicized press releases by the Bureau of Labor Statistics. Price hikes attributable to safety rules were treated as a "quality improvement" that the bureau "backed out" of its annual computation of increases in the consumer price index. After averaging less than $20.00 per year through the 1972 model year, the bureau reported a $91.60 price increase due to safety rules for model year 1973, and a $107.60 increase for model year 1974 (mostly attributable to the bumper "damageability" standard, not safety rules). The trend seemed to be up. Viewed as a percentage of total car prices, this increase was trivial. But safety rules, which were within the power of Congress to control, magnified the price effects of inflation and Middle East politics, which were not. As inflation mounted, pressure for more attention to the costs and benefits of proposed safety rules grew intense.

By comparison with rules, the costs of recall campaigns were invisible. The Office of Management and Budget (OMB) did not apply its "quality of life review" to recalls, nor did the Bureau of Labor Statistics break them out in its computation of inflation. The Senate Commerce Committee's title for its principal hearings on the proposed 1974 amendments—"Auto Safety Repairs at No Cost"—told the story.[15] Who, other than the automobile manufacturers,[16] could oppose entitling consumers to "free" repairs, particularly at a time of growing consumer unrest over shoddy automotive workmanship?

Neither NHTSA, Congress, nor anyone else had the faintest idea whether the benefits of auto safety recalls were worth their invisible costs. The political context suppressed the agency's proposal to find out. At the principal Senate hearings on the subject, NHTSA urged the adoption of statutory criteria that would introduce cost-benefit analysis into the defect determination process. The agency's proposals included provisions that required weighing the seriousness of defects and the probability of ensuing accidents and injuries against "the potential economic impact of the remedy upon the manufacturer and owners." Agency officials also recommended that the free repair requirement not apply to vehicles over six years old, for by then only a small proportion of any model year would remain on the road and the owner response rates to recalls of older vehicles were very low. Pursuing seven-year-old vehicles was not likely to be a good use of the agency's or the manufacturers' resources.

Congress flatly refused. Senator Adlai Stevenson III's response was illustrative: "I don't understand what difference the age of the motor vehicle makes. If the defect presents a danger to health and safety, it should be remedied. Why should those who happen to drive older cars— traditionally the young and poor—be forced to weather safety related defects to any greater degree than the rich? Since when was economic impact on the manufacturer a factor to consider when recalling a motor vehicle? . . . The purpose of the act is to protect all motorists from unsafe cars."[17] The most the agency could extract was an eight year cutoff of the no-cost repair requirement. The remaining cost-benefit proposals were rejected as an affront to the act's egalitarian principles. Private property rights, individual liberty, cost-containment, consumer sovereignty—these were the values expressed and implied by the amendments of 1974. They were hardly the value matrix of 1966.

Issue Babel. The multiple values expressed in the 1974 amendments were, of course, congressional answers to multiple questions. When asked for a motor vehicle safety policy in 1966, Congress could give a single-minded answer—promote safety—in part because it was allowed to address a single issue. Indeed by comparison with 1974's melange of topics and questions, 1966 was simplicity itself. In highly stylized language, the 1966 dialogue went something like this: *Question:* Is automobile safety a problem? *Answer:* You must be kidding. *Question:* Are there ways to limit the carnage? *Answer:* You bet. *Question:* Will the market do it for us? *Answer:* In the hands of people like GM? *Question:* Can federal law really make improved technology available to all Americans? *Answer:* Look at the successes of the civil rights movement and the space program.

By 1974 specific issues of safety technology, government and industry competence, regulatory priorities, and regulatory costs, only dimly perceived in 1966, had emerged and multiplied. And in the atmosphere of

Vietnam, Watergate, and stagflation, the response to these and perhaps to all issues was much less confident. There emerged a sort of "issues chaos" that seemed to overwhelm the capacity of all the actors to make conceptual or strategic sense of what was happening.

The oversight hearings before the Senate Commerce Committee in February and March 1974 reflected the fragmentation of issues and advocates. Senator Hartke was an impatient partisan—pushing, berating, probing, and interrupting—all in a self-conscious effort to instill a sense of "urgency" in the auto safety program. But Hartke was not the committee, and industry representatives probably doubted his ability to deliver on repeated threats to legislate specific safety standards, beginning with an omnibus 50-mile-an-hour crashworthiness requirement. As the hearings progressed it became clear that 1974 would not be a rerun of 1966, when committee members jostled with one another in a packed hearing room for the attention of reporters and television crews.

The "drama of legislation" had given way to the tedium of enforcement. Chairman Magnuson did not attend the hearings, even to make a symbolic appearance. Hartke not only presided but conducted the oversight hearings virtually alone. Even when his colleagues Stevenson and Griffin made brief appearances, it was for the purpose of questioning NHTSA regulations that they thought might weaken the domestic auto industry and reduce domestic employment.

Detroit Redux. As Stevenson's and Griffin's contributions suggested, the social and economic context of NHTSA's mission had changed dramatically since 1966. The auto manufacturers and their congressional allies constantly urged that safety rules should take into account such matters as the foreign trade balance, national security, the environment, and macroeconomic policy. This position in a sense reflected the manufacturers' post-1966 adaptation to the new multiple-issue policy context that was causing major problems for both NHTSA and Congress.

The domestic manufacturers were represented at the hearings by Sydney L. Terry, vice president for environmental and safety relations, Chrysler; Ernest Starkman, vice president for environmental activities, General Motors; Herbert L. Misch, vice president for safety and environmental affairs, Ford; and Frederick A. Stewart, vice president for safety and reliability, American Motors. Hartke complained that the companies had not dispatched their chief executive officers to the hearings and charged that "their failure to attend . . . demonstrates that they do not have [a] feeling of responsibility to the Congress of the United

States."[18] But Hartke's pique largely missed the point; the witnesses' job titles reflected a reformation of corporate structure in response to the regulatory developments of the early 1970s. The manufacturers in 1966 had only shadow offices devoted to safety regulation and were represented at the principal hearings and related negotiations by their trade association and Washington counsel. By 1974 each company was devoting substantial resources to the maintenance of "regulatory affairs" offices, which coordinated safety, environmental, occupational health, and related matters. This corporate reorganization reflected the fact that the industry was now subject to a host of new regulatory statutes[19] that crossed the jurisdictional lines separating federal agencies, as well as congressional oversight committees. The witnesses' regulatory affairs offices oversaw corporate activities in all of these areas; NHTSA and Hartke's committee did not. The companies' witnesses were better prepared than they had been in 1966—even better prepared, perhaps, than federal officials for the complex state of affairs that presented itself in 1974.

The auto industry may have been better organized to cope with government regulation than in 1966, but it was also financially weakened. As the hearings were called to order, domestic manufacturers were rapidly losing market share to foreign competitors, especially the Japanese. Between 1972 and 1975, over 108,000 employees fell from the industry's payroll. Domestic new car sales actually decreased from 1965 (8,763,000 units) to 1974 (7,449,000 units). Imports during the same period more than doubled, from 569,000 to 1,413,000 units. The manufacturers did not have to dwell on these embarrassing matters at the hearings; Senator Griffin was there to submit the alarming statistics as he questioned agency officials.[20] Instead, industry witnesses hammered away at three central themes: that the marginal benefits of new safety regulations were increasingly doubtful; that the marginal costs were growing prohibitive; and that the automobile industry was being squeezed by conflicting regulations and social expectations arising from the energy shortage, environmental policy, and the quest for safety.

Industry representatives made clear their belief that it was Congress who had been irresponsible—or at least misguided. Their collective testimony asserted that Congress had enacted a plethora of statutes in the preceding ten years without making any genuine effort to fit the new obligations and duties imposed on automakers into a rational composition; that many statutes, in particular those on safety and emissions, conflicted with other goals, particularly fuel economy; and that in effect the industry's "public responsibility" as defined in these conflicting demands was incoherent and impossible to fulfill.[21] The manufacturers cast themselves as victims of uncoordinated federal oversight. Many observers seemed persuaded. In weakness there was strength.

The Safety Fraternity Speaks. The safety advocates who appeared in the hearings had much less cohesive views. The belief that NHTSA, with White House and OMB prodding, was attempting to take account of these broader issues, is of course another way of describing the behavior that Nader excoriated as a "dismantling" of the safety program. But beyond urging the oversight committee to build a fire under the agency, safety advocates had no well-focused program to suggest.

Lowell Dodge, director of the Center for Auto Safety (CFAS), presented perhaps the most comprehensive of the public advocates' statements.[22] He tied NHTSA's slackening rulemaking pace to several causes, some identified in prior testimony, others not. Dodge reported that "disturbing tremors" of a change in "philosophy" had been detected at NHTSA; that the agency's "emphasis of the past seven years on vehicle-related safety countermeasures [was] being downgraded"; and that "NHTSA is placing new emphasis on efforts aimed at improving driver performance." The conceptual core of the revolution of 1966 was being eroded. In Dodge's view the agency was misusing its research budget, botching its systems-oriented RSV program by undertaking redundant studies, and settling for a rulemaking payoff that would not materialize until the distant future.

While Dodge and his associates Nader and Nash vigorously defended the original understanding of the 1966 act, other safety activists seemed to be telling the committee that the safety game had changed. Miller had testified that the critical emerging issue was weight differentials as cars were made smaller in response to the energy crisis. It was clear from his testimony that smaller cars made NHTSA's job harder, but he never addressed precisely how existing regulatory authority could be used to cope with the issue or whether and what type of new legislative initiatives might be required.

The medical fraternity took yet another tack. Seymour Charles, president of Physicians for Auto Safety, focused on the need for school bus safety and child restraint standards on the grounds that "there has been incredible neglect by the administration of the crash protection of new infants and children, the most hapless victims."[23] Why? Charles offered two answers: first, NHTSA had become "an obstructive administrative bureaucracy"; second, regulators were inordinately preoccupied with weighing the costs against the benefits of regulation. Charles was outraged that a public health agency could conclude, as he claimed NHTSA had, that "few children are killed or injured each year and that costly improvements are not warranted."

Nor did the physicians limit their testimony to child protection. Charles seized the occasion to urge anew the adoption of built-in limits on vehicle speed. He urged that "there is no reason why motor vehicles should be designed to drive at a rate of 120 miles per hour," a position echoed by Paul Gikas, professor of pathology at the University of Michigan, who found "no redeeming social value in such high-powered vehicles."[24] Gikas urged that the maximum speed of motor vehicles (other than police and emergency vehicles) be limited technologically to no more than 80 miles per hour.

The safety partisans' testimony was not only eclectic; some of it was odd, even ironic. William Haddon,[25] president of the Insurance Institute for Highway Safety (IIHS), testified at great length and in minute detail solely about IIHS's careful examination of variations in the damageability of automobiles. At a time of deepening crisis in the safety standards enterprise, Haddon, the founder of the public health subspecialty devoted to the epidemiology of accidents, was addressing the consequences of accidents not for public health but for private property.

It was true that the companies underwriting Haddon's institute had a compelling interest in the subject, and Congress itself only two years before had empowered NHTSA to reduce vehicle damageability. But these are merely alternate forms of the observation that public interest advocacy itself responds to change in the political market. Haddon's agenda for automobile regulation in 1974 would have been unimaginable in 1966.

The View from Downtown. The diagnoses of the situation from agency witnesses told yet another story. Hartke was determined to get to the bottom of the safety advocates' claim that policy at NHTSA was being redirected from vehicle design to modifying motorists' behavior. He therefore summoned Secretary of Transportation Claude S. Brinegar for an interrogation directed at the secretary's recent public pronouncements that increased emphasis would be placed on driver problems, especially those of the drinking and young drivers who are responsible for a high percentage of all fatalities.

Brinegar had little difficulty wriggling free from Hartke's cross-examination. No, the secretary testified, NHTSA had not abandoned its rulemaking mission: forty-five standards had been issued; eighteen were undergoing revision; seven new rules had been proposed. Yes, the agency had sufficient funds to administer its programs, including programs "to improve the driver's abilities to either avoid an accident or . . . to survive one." Such efforts were based on the discouraging but demonstrable fact that "something in the order of 80 percent of all automobile accidents are the result of driver error," he said. No, his office was not ignoring NHTSA. He himself had "devoted a great deal of personal effort to [NHTSA's] programs" and planned "to continue to do so in the months ahead." Among other matters, he had been directly involved in evaluating the new dummy regulations issued after the *Chrysler* decision, and in reproposing Standard 208. The involvement seemed to be on an intimate, one-to-one basis:

Senator Hartke. Do you have anyone in your office assigned to oversee the activities of the agency?

Secretary Brinegar. I assigned myself that job.

Senator Hartke. And it's a direct line? There is no intermediary?

Secretary Brinegar. He [NHTSA's administrator] walks in my office quite regularly.

Senator Hartke. How many hours a week do you think you devote to the motor vehicle safety program?

Secretary Brinegar. It depends what other crises have to be performed. It isn't a matter of hours. In one sentence I can do a great deal.[26]

After further questioning that elicited similar testimony from the secretary, Hartke pronounced himself "delighted with the response we have had from you and I compliment you for it. I don't want you to rest on your laurels, though. I want you to pull hard."[27]

Hartke had failed utterly to appreciate the significance of what Brinegar had told him. Brinegar presided over a sprawling, crisis-ridden bureaucracy embracing six separate administrations plus the Coast Guard, the Maritime Commission, and the Saint Lawrence Seaway Development Corporation. The department had 75,035 employees (then the sixth-largest executive branch department), budget authority exceeding $17 billion annually, and day-to-day responsibility for administering scores of statutes—the Federal Aviation Act, the Interstate Commerce Act, the Federal-Aid Highways Act, the Federal Railroad Safety and Hazardous Materials Transportation Control Act of 1970, the Minerals Leasing Act, the Dangerous Cargo Act, and the Urban Mass Transportation Act, to name but a few. How much could be expected of the auto safety program if its individual rules had to be personally reviewed by the top administrator?

NHTSA itself was also represented at the hearings. As the conversation between Hartke and the agency's senior staff wore on, it increasingly appeared that NHTSA was a bureaucracy hovering somewhere between high anxiety and deep fatigue. Its staff reported that the agency was pressing ahead on all fronts, including the RSV, passive restraints, the dummy respecifications, motorcycle helmets, fuel system integrity, infant and child seats, school bus integrity, and a host of other rulemaking and related regulatory actions. But life with Nader and General Motors as constant companions was not easy, and if Hartke failed to grasp the point—indeed, if he insisted upon behaving like any other interest group—all well and good, but he would have to wait in line with the others clamoring for NHTSA's attention. Exhortation was not regulation.

In connection with the agency's work on Standard 208, Administrator Gregory elaborated,

> We have not rushed into decisionmaking because, despite the charges of certain critics, the key factors are not all known. There is a difference between advocacy, which pushes to achieve some action desired by the advocate, and the final action of the statutorily responsible public official. The public official must understand all the key data and the various points of view, make his decision and then accept responsibility for his action. The same does not hold true for the advocate. Dispute is probably inevitable when one is dealing with an issue like passive restraints.
>
> We want to insure, insofar as possible, since the industry took us to court before on this standard, that further delay will not be occasioned by new court challenges.[28]

The agency's hypersensitivity to judicial review in the aftermath of the *Chrysler* decision came up repeatedly and in different contexts, often in tart exchanges between Hartke and NHTSA's chief counsel:

Senator Hartke. Can you push the state of the art forward by proposing a rule for 50 miles an hour, or does that run into the legal question?

Mr. Schneider. It turns into the legal question when you issue it, if you cannot support it.

Senator Hartke. Isn't it a lot better to get knocked down by the court than to concede before you start?

Mr. Schneider. No.

Senator Hartke. No? Give us an example.

Mr. Schneider. . . . Standard 208 . . .[29]

Again, in relation to the agency's effort to promulgate school bus safety standards with all deliberate speed, the chief counsel testified:

> Mr. Chairman, what people say before the committee is fine and good; but you as a lawyer know full well that it is what is in the rulemaking record which we lawyers have to take when we are challenged in court. Everything we do say today, it seems, results in being challenged in court. We have to have support in the record. What they say to you privately, the schoolbus manufacturers are not saying in the rulemaking record.[30]

And again, in relation to NHTSA's overall schedule for rulemaking actions, Gregory stated,

> Mr. Chairman, I too share your concern in what often appears to be unnecessary delays in rulemaking actions. In establishing these dates, however, I think it must be recognized that should we move without a strong engineering position; without proper considerations for cost and lead time; or, without adequate benefit cost information, we are vulnerable to court actions which would result in longer delays relevant to effective dates.[31]

As testimony of this kind was repeated, it began to sound as if Hartke at long last had an answer to the question he had asked early in the hearings. Why could we send people to the moon, but not to the grocery store, in safety? It seemed that NASA had made it to the moon and back because its engineering judgments were not subject to judicial review.

Bangs and Whimpers. The failure of the participants to focus the issues, establish priorities, or reach common ground was deeply frustrating to the senator chairing the hearing. Midway through Hartke complained, "Every time we have oversight hearings, we go over the same questions and roughly we hear the same answers. The bumpers don't meet; the safety belts won't work; the airbags are not developed; the state of the art is not developed. Let me reiterate that it is essential that we get moving on this thing."[32] In a more composed moment at the conclusion of the hearings, he mused: "In retrospect, I suppose I have manifested a frustration at the lethargy with which the whole subject of automobile safety is approached. The program seems to lack the sense of urgency which accompanies many other governmental programs seeking a solution. Perhaps the best way to put it is that safety—a matter which should be approached from a point of commonality—has become in reality, an adversary process."[33]

He had indeed received one clear message: the 1966 safety consensus had crumbled. But amid the clamor it was difficult to discern what issues were firmly on automobile safety's legislative-regulatory agenda for the mid-1970s. Should Congress seek to limit executive branch oversight of NHTSA, or should it increase the executive's capacity for regulatory coordination? Was rulemaking going too slow or too fast? Was NHTSA missing technological opportunities, or was it imposing untested, costly, and potentially useless requirements on manufacturers and consumers alike? Should Congress legislate standards itself, restrain NHTSA's rulemaking enthusiasm, or perhaps do both? Should NHTSA continue to focus on the passenger car or attend to other types of vehicles? Should NHTSA do more cost-benefit analysis or less?

As we know, the 1974 amendments answered these questions in a fragmented, elliptical, and often contradictory fashion. Discerning the "legislative will" after 1974 was to be no easy task. The overall political climate had clearly changed. "Deregulation" rather than "regulation" was now in vogue. "Social consciousness" was rapidly being replaced by "cost consciousness," and visions of "market failure" by visions of "government failure." Yet there had been no substantial cutback in NHTSA's powers; in fact it had been given new regulatory authority. Since they left the provisions of the 1966 act largely intact, the 1974 amendments suggested no general distaste for NHTSA's original regulatory mission. The agency's new powers, however, seemed to proceed from different premises and to respond to different political demands. How was the agency meant to understand this more specific legislative intent—these multiple and more particularized visions of the political will?

In institutional terms, NHTSA was confronted not only with new, partial, and potentially contradictory prescriptions for the "public health problem" in its charge but also with a fragmented political-legislative process. The crumbled consensus that was reflected in the chaos over the issues at the hearings and in perplexing trade-offs of freedom and security in the amendments also marked the demise of the 1966 safety coalition. Control over the legislative, indeed the broader political, conceptualization of motor vehicle safety regulation seemed to be up for grabs— a lesson that emerges more clearly from an analysis of the quite different politics of the three principal segments of the 1974 amendments.

SEVEN

Legislating Liberty

The amendments to the Motor Vehicle Safety Act that emerged in 1974 were simultaneously unified and divided. They were unified in their ideological commitment to "liberty" or "freedom to choose" (at least for adults); fragmented in addressing multiple issues with multiple and apparently conflicting policy prescriptions.

On the One Hand—On the Other Hand

Nowhere is unity and fragmentation better illustrated than on the question of the use of cost-benefit analysis in motor vehicle safety regulation. Concern with regulatory costs was one of the unifying themes of the legislative discussion surrounding the 1974 amendments. That concern was often a proxy for concern with the consumer's freedom to choose. If freedom was to be curtailed, it had better be in the interests of a good safety bargain.

But the use of cost-benefit analysis also had institutional implications. Combined with congressional concern that the agency might be insensitive to costs was suspicion that the executive branch might be interfering with the agency's safety mandate in the name of efficiency. These two ways of framing the cost-benefit question pushed Congress in different directions.

When confronting specific policy problems, moreover, Congress seemed quite prepared to ignore cost control, benefit maximization, and threats of executive dominance. The agency's proposal to require cost-benefit analysis of recalls was rejected, as was its cost-benefit rationale for "benign neglect" of school bus standards. The apparently highly cost-beneficial interlock rule was also overturned. Cost-benefit considerations were not allowed to block regulation thought desirable on other grounds; nor would favorable cost-benefit ratios justify regulation otherwise thought undesirable. Yet consideration of costs and benefits was not to be abandoned: the 1974 legislation did nothing to protect the agency from executive requirements for regulatory cost analyses. On the contrary, Congress extracted promises from the agency[1] that it would devote additional resources to cost and lead time analyses in rulemaking, and it authorized increased funds for that purpose.[2]

The Babel-like quality of these legislative pronouncements on cost-benefit analysis reflected more than cross-cutting pressures and distinct policy contexts. The 1974 amendments were not the product of a single political process. They reflected instead at least three political processes with quite different principal actors and modes of operation. NHTSA thus emerged with more than a revised charter of operation. It would thereafter be engaged in a new, and in many ways bewildering and threatening, form of bureaucratic-legislative politics; one in which the standard forms of agency-subcommittee contact would be inadequate to inform the agency of legislative preferences or to protect it from political attack.

Some such shift in the political landscape is suggested, of course, by the discontinuity between the oversight hearings in early 1974 and the legislative amendments that emerged a few months later. The Senate Commerce Committee was preoccupied with getting the rulemaking process back on the steep upward trajectory imagined in 1966. The amendments, by contrast, seemed to confirm the worst fears of safety partisans—that technology-forcing regulation might be over before it had really begun. Those fears were surely further excited by the 1974 legislative process as it unfolded. In only one of the three major areas of congressional action was the safety coalition of 1966 still firmly in control.

Recalls: The Politics of the Free Lunch

The legislative emphasis on recalls in 1974 may have contradicted the substantive ideological commitments of the original act, but the legislative process was highly reminiscent of 1966. The 1974 recall legislation was conceived in Senate chambers and was nurtured by the same safety partisans, Magnuson, Hartke, and Ribicoff, who had been instrumental in the original act's passage.

Ralph Nader as an Institution. The 1974 recall amendments were no less a testimonial to the entrepreneurial politics of Nader and his colleagues than the original legislation had been. But by 1974, the Nader of 1966 had become an institutionalized presence who in part acted out organizational needs. The famous surveillance episode in 1966 had provoked Nader to sue General Motors. Nader used his $425,000 settlement for "invasion of privacy," along with other funds raised in more conventional ways, to institutionalize and diversify the consumer movement.

The Center for Auto Safety flourished after the original act's passage, and key legislators grew ever more dependent on public interest activists to monitor both NHTSA's and the automobile manufacturers' behavior and to identify issues of concern. Nader, Ditlow, Nash, and others briefed congressional staff, drafted committee reports, planted questions, laid the groundwork for hearings, and mapped strategy to such an extent that it was sometimes difficult to tell where congressional oversight left off and public interest advocacy began. By the early 1970s the Senate Commerce Committee, in particular, had become the alter ego of Nader's Public Interest Research Group and the Center for Auto Safety.

This was the work of which public interest legends are made. But the Nader groups' unremitting pressure to strengthen and energize the recall process at NHTSA was also an expression of the institutional necessities confronting public interest advocacy. Nader's groups were modestly funded and staffed, no match for the large technical operations available to automobile manufacturers—particularly in rulemaking proceedings where proponents of regulation were carrying the burden of justifying the technical coherence, cost-effectiveness, and production feasibility of proposed rules. The "right" to participate in rulemaking was labor-intensive and resource-straining. As we have seen, the auto manufacturers quickly learned that the agency and its allies could be pinned down by extensive rulemaking comments, requests for reconsideration, petitions for exemption, and the like. Refuting industry's claims that proposed safety rules were technically ill-conceived and economically burdensome was exhausting the Naderites as well as NHTSA.

Recalls were a different matter. Safety advocates did not have to generate recall data, but merely obtain and use it. The ammunition was already partially available. Manufacturers were required under the original legislation to disclose to NHTSA copies of all notices, bulletins, and other communications to dealers regarding safety defects. A significant amount of this information was available, openly or otherwise, to safety entrepreneurs, who used it to embarrass both the agency and the manufacturers. When Nader and his colleagues lobbied for amendments in 1974 to strengthen the agency's investigative powers and give "consumers," meaning "consumer advocates," increased rights of information, access, and participation in the defects determination process, they surely were not unmindful that such statutory reforms would in effect subsidize their own operations.

The public advocates' information costs were also subsidized by other sources directly related to NHTSA's recall activity: frustrated consumers, product liability litigants, and their attorneys. Media coverage of the 1966 hearings and the best-seller status of *Unsafe at Any Speed* had long since made Nader a household name. He continued to maintain a high visibility in the press as the consumer movement matured. Consumers might not know the whereabouts, names, or purposes of the various groups that Nader created, but they remembered him. Letters addressed simply "Ralph Nader, D.C.," found their way to his office. The great bulk of Nader's correspondence complained of defects in vehicles owned by the correspondents. Relatively few complained of inadequate safety standards or lack of progress in NHTSA's rulemaking activities.

The flood of "Dear Mr. Nader" mail provided a cheap and virtually inexhaustible supply of issues and empowered the Public Interest Research Group and the Center for Auto Safety as shadow regulatory agencies. The public advocates forwarded copies of complaints or summarized them in detailed, poignant accounts to the presidents of affected companies and senior regulatory officials, including the secretary of transportation. In each case the safety activists' inquiry was largely the same. The manufacturers and regulators had access to the same information; why had they not already acted?

The safety entrepreneurs were also learning that consumer correspondence could be turned into working capital. Acting as an intermediary between the agency and disgruntled consumers, the Center for Auto Safety began a product liability service for litigants. The center provided technical data on specific defects, listings of attorneys and expert witnesses involved in related or similar litigation, accident statistics, investigation reports, and "IMPACT," a monthly newsletter that chronicled the center's activities. The center's promotional literature indicated that "our service is used by attorneys across the country who are leaders in product liability litigation" and asked members' permission to use information contained in their inquiries to "stimulate investigations of vehicle defects." An energized and open recall process would further strengthen these operations. In short, recalls produced synergy between NHTSA and private safety advocates. Rules drained the reserves of both.

The Manufacturers as Heavies. The manufacturers' handling of the amendments strengthening recalls was reminiscent of their ineffectual opposition to the original legislation. But the reasons underlying their political failure in 1974 were much different from those that prevailed in 1966. Public relations and product liability considerations, not political inexperience and ineptitude, accounted for industry's inability to defeat the recall amendments. The prospect of catastrophic publicity deterred manufacturers from vigorously opposing mandatory no-cost repairs. The proposed legislation merely codified traditional industry commitments—commitments that could not be revoked without undercutting the manufacturers' own advertising and warranty representations and attracting media criticism. The manufacturers had learned their lesson from the General Motors–Nader caper in 1966. One public relations debacle a decade was enough. If the companies were going to have to play the villain again, they could at least keep their role small.

The manufacturers' impact on the legislative process was weakened by their failure to dispatch witnesses to testify in person at the hearings. Seeking to insulate themselves from interrogation on sensitive defect-related matters affecting product liability litigation, they elected to submit written statements for the record. But by failing to make personal appearances, the manufacturers conveyed the impression early in deliberations that they were fearful of open debate and unwilling to join the issues on their merits. Later appearances came after momentum for passage had gathered, and they failed to dispel the notion that industry did not take the legislation seriously.

The rationale for manufacturers' passive resistance went even deeper, to the paradox of recall legislation itself. Although the 1974 amendments were born in large measure out of safety partisans' conviction that the industry systematically subordinated consumer protection to profits, the recall mechanism implicitly affirmed industry control over the manufacture and design of automobiles. As a practical matter, the standard of defectiveness for recalls was set by the industry. "Defective" vehicles were identified by their disproportionate failure in comparison with other models produced by the same manufacturer or by its competitors. NHTSA had never challenged the manufacturers' control over the definition of the state of the art by attempting an industry-wide recall. Nothing in the proposed legislation suggested that it would do so. Indeed, in a key case decided shortly before the adoption of the amendments, the agency expressly declined to call vehicles "defective" that conformed with industry-wide standards, even though the vehicles were shown to place heavy demands on the average motorist's competence and driving skill.

By giving new emphasis to recalls, the 1974 amendments thus diverted regulatory attention and scarce resources away from the effort to establish exogenous standards through rulemaking. They emphasized the historically reactive posture of civil liability law, the posture that had been challenged by the revolution of 1966. To be sure, the concept of "defectiveness" was elastic, and regulators might exploit its vagaries by asserting jurisdiction over age-related malfunctions in older vehicles. But those were marginal cases. Most defects were noncontroversial and were caught within a year or two of production. The 1974 legislation thus largely codified manufacturers' practice of making repairs within the warranty period. It challenged the manufacturers neither ideologically nor economically.

General Motors Does It Again. As in 1966, the "bad" behavior of General Motors was the focus of congressional and press attention. And once again the identification of a villain stimulated the demand for further legal controls. The proposal for no-cost repair of recalled vehicles was strongly influenced by two highly publicized defect disputes, both involving General Motors. The first involved another familiar "actor" from 1966—the Corvair. But instead of instability complaints, this time the focus was on Corvair heaters, which were found to leak carbon monoxide into the passenger compartment. The second dispute involved Chevrolet engine mounts, which were determined to be susceptible to sudden breakage, creating unsettling secondary effects such as accelerator jamming, gear shift lockage, and power brake failure.

The industry had stubbornly resisted admission of any problem, and NHTSA had been prodded into action only by the extensive lobbying of safety activists and by strongly negative press reports. Safety activists drew heavily on these episodes to document their claims that industry was contemptuous of its commitments to Congress and to consumers and that NHTSA had been lulled, trapped, or cowed into lax enforcement of the act's overriding safety purposes, in part by defects in the statute itself.

When the Senate Commerce Committee got down to business on the recall amendments in 1973, it was clear that the legislation would be shaped in important ways by the Corvair heater and Chevrolet engine mounts episodes. Substituting for Hartke in the chair, Senator Stevenson stated that legislation was necessary because auto manufacturers had gone back on their word and had misled the American people. The Corvair heater case, in particular, was evidence of industry's breach of its promise to make repairs at no charge. Experience had shown, Stevenson continued, that consumers were "extremely sensitive to the matter of who bears the burden of paying for the repair of defective products" and that "auto safety is severely compromised when the manufacturer does not assume the burden of repairing a defect without charge." When repairs are offered at no cost, Stevenson reported, consumer response rates averaged 75 percent. By comparison, only 7.6 percent of Corvair owners brought their vehicles in for heater repair. Eliminating charges for safety-related repairs was, therefore, "one of the most [important] contributions that Congress can make to the cause of motor vehicle safety in 1973."[3]

Stevenson had no data that recalls either prevented accidents or saved lives—no one did. Nevertheless, from this point on, the legislation progressed in the Senate, the House, and in conference much in the spirit of 1966. Virtually all discussion was within the relevant committees, and passage was noncontroversial. Hearings and mark-up sessions were employed primarily to "perfect" or strengthen the bill. The automobile manufacturers took it in the neck from everyone. Even automobile distributors, who claimed that they were actually bearing much of the manufacturers' costs for defects repair, testified against them.

A Crucial Contrast. We must note, however, an important contrast between the 1974 amendment process and the legislative process in 1966. Although still firmly in the control of safety partisans, the 1974 recall process was informed, as well as motivated, by a populist impulse. The aeronautical engineers and epidemiologists—the experts who populated the 1966 hearings and who instructed the congressmen from the heights of their technical learning—were not involved. The Nader of *Unsafe at Any Speed*—a technical exposé of engineering flaws—had been replaced by "Citizen Nader," the consumers' friend.

When responding to this populist impulse the safety barons may not have reflected on the difficulty of stuffing populist genies, once released, back into legislative bottles. Grassroots unrest can overwhelm legislators and legislative jurisdictions as well as democratize "expert" regulatory processes. As the 1974 amendments proceeded, this lesson was soon to be learned.

Revolt on the Floor

If the recall amendments emerged from the 1974 analogue of the 1966 legislative process, the repeal of the seat-belt interlock rule and the attachment of a legislative veto to all future passive restraints initiatives were products of its antithesis. These proposals were introduced in the House, developed outside the standing committee structure and were opposed, unsuccessfully, by the traditional motor vehicle safety coalition. If the 1966 act was the product of earnest attention to social responsibility and systems analysis of public health needs, the 1974 interlock-veto package was the product of visceral reactions to an inconvenient technology—legislative emotions articulated as two parts rage and one part ridicule.

These changes in legislative procedure and legislative rhetoric had a profound impact on the vehicle safety program. Although the interlock and veto amendments affected only passive restraints, the rule they attacked was, in public health terms, the agency's most significant. More important, as a symbol, Standard 208 was the embodiment both of the epidemiological approach to vehicle accidents and of the agency's overall strategy for moving to systems-oriented and performance-based rules. Automatic intervention to prevent or ameliorate the effects of the second collision was the heart of the vehicle safety revolution of 1966. In 1974 the fruits of that effort were not only being rejected; they were being rejected by a grassroots counterrevolution that pictured NHTSA's passive restraints rule as both un-American and ridiculous. Nader, Haddon, and their legislative allies were being symbolically ridden out of town on a rail.

There is great irony in the safety partisans' discomfiture. The particular form of protection rejected by the Congress—the ignition interlock—was not only *not* of the agency's choosing but it was in some sense a product of the *Chrysler* decision. In the extensive rulemaking proceeding leading up to the rule that was invalidated in *Chrysler*, NHTSA had rejected a Ford petition for a declaration that the passive restraints requirement could be satisfied by forcing seat-belt use through an ignition interlock. The agency argued that "forced action" was not the "no action" required for a truly passive system. The industry, therefore, would not be permitted to substitute $40 interlocks for $400 airbags.

The agency, however, soon reversed its position. On April 27, 1971, Henry Ford II and Lee Iacocca met in the Oval Office with President Richard Nixon and Domestic Affairs Advisor John Ehrlichman. Although Nixon promised that the auto executives' remarks would be held in complete confidence, his secret office tape system was running.[4]

The conversation was in fact pretty tame. In typically garbled fashion Nixon made perfectly clear at the outset that he was one of the boys: "[Our] views are, are, are frankly, uh, whether it's the environment or pollution or Naderism or Consumerism, we are extremely pro-business." That was certainly encouraging to Ford and Iacocca, who had come to ask for help. Their pitch was essentially the same as the industry's testimony would be before Hartke's oversight committee in 1973. Uncoordinated regulatory burdens were adding frightful costs to car prices. The regulators threatened to cripple the domestic auto industry. Ford and Iacocca claimed that compliance with some of the proposed regulatory requirements, particularly the airbag, was simply beyond the industry's technical capacity within the deadlines specified. They needed time to phase in new technology in an orderly fashion. If they didn't get it, they were in trouble.

At times the president and chairman of one of the world's largest corporations sounded pathetic. "We're not only frustrated," said Iacocca, "but, uh, we've reached the despair point. We don't know what to do anymore." And again, "[W]e are on a downhill slide, the likes of which we have never seen in our business. And the Japs are in the wings ready to eat us up alive." Nixon's intervention with the Department of Transportation was apparently their only hope. They wanted relief from environmental requirements too (fuel economy regulation was yet to come), but they knew that was impossible. They had already talked to William Ruckelshaus at the Environmental Protection Agency (EPA) and had been given a lesson in statutorily mandated regulation. The Congress had put EPA emission control criteria under a strict statutory timetable that neither agency nor industry could evade for long. Under that statute manufacturers might get a year's relief, but only if they could demonstrate their own failure in a good faith effort at compliance.

Nixon was ideologically sympathetic. "It's true in, in the environmentalists and it's true of the consumerism people. They're . . . [not] one really damn bit interested in safety or clean air. What they're interested in is destroying the system. They're enemies of the system." But he was also ignorant of the issues and cautious in his promises. At the very end of the meeting, after apparently agreeing with everything Ford and Iacocca had said, Nixon warned them not to expect too much—or perhaps anything. "[U]h, particularly with regard to this, uh, this airbag thing. I, I don't know, I, I, may be wrong. I will not judge it until I hear the other side."

What transpired at the White House and the Transportation Department after this exchange is not known in detail by anyone who is willing to talk for the record. In a Los Angeles television interview,[5] Ehrlichman stated that he and Peter Flanagan ordered the department to go along with the ignition interlock. Indeed, Ralph Nader has charged[6] that Nixon, Ehrlichman, Iacocca, and Ford, perhaps plus Flanagan, concocted a devilishly clever plan to defeat passive restraints by requiring a mechanism (the interlock) so obnoxious to the American people that Congress would rise up and rescind the rule entirely.

If so, the strategy was not developed on April 27, 1971. No one at the meeting in the Oval Office mentioned the interlock. But that a memorandum went to the Transportation Department is not seriously disputed. Authors of a Senate Commerce Committee investigative report in 1976 describe John Volpe, then secretary of transportation, returning dejectedly from White House meetings at which he had failed to save the airbag. The Commerce Committee staff further reported that the "notorious [but never revealed] memorandum" demanded delay on passive restraints *and* adoption of the interlock.[7]

In any event, the department complied. In October 1971 it issued a notice delaying passive protection until August 15, 1975. In the interim, compliance with Standard 208 was made available in the form of an ignition interlock system. That choice then became the single option available when the *Chrysler* decision enjoined enforcement of Standard 208's passive restraints timetable on December 5, 1972. Because the interlock system was attached to normal belts, interlocks were not subject to the injury criteria in Standard 208 that were invalidated in *Chrysler*. Interlocks were an enforceable technology even though all other passive techniques had to be delayed. It was thus the interlock that found its way into new cars for model year 1974.

Although with the interlock NHTSA had an enforceable rule, evidence quickly mounted that the public's opinion of it was at least as low as NHTSA's. In reissuing Standard 208 in March 1974, with the dummy now "fully" specified, the agency noted that the interlock had improved belt usage enormously in model year 1974. But storm clouds were on the horizon. NHTSA's investigations found that usage rates of lap and shoulder belts in 1974 models equipped with interlock were below 60 percent.[8] Over 40 percent of those who had bought 1974 cars presumably had disabled the interlock equipment.

Motorists interested in defeating the interlock were about to get some help. If the 1966 act marked a legislative revolution in legal control of automobile safety, the counterrevolution might be said to have erupted on the floor of the House, August 12, 1974. During the course of the one-hour open debate on the rule and the subsequent voice vote approving H.R. 5529, the House's version of the recall and school bus safety amendments, Congressman Louis Wyman rose to introduce his "citizens' rights amendment," which would repeal the interlock, outlaw any continuous light and buzzer system to "remind" motorists to buckle up, and make any subsquent passive restraints system only an "option." Wyman explained: "All this amendment does is to provide that in the future automobiles can have seat belts and harnesses, but they are not going to be tied to any sequential warning system with lights and buzzers. They can have a red warning light on the dash which says, "seat belts are not fastened," but that is all they can have. Anyone who wants to buy a car in America can have a car with seat belts and harnesses. That is his privilege. He will not have to buy the interlock."[9]

Wyman, it seemed, spoke for many. NHTSA's ignition interlock was "universally despised," as one press account put it, and thousands of letters from constituents attested to the fact. As representatives skimmed their mail, it was obvious something was up. This was no orchestrated letter-writing campaign by a trade association or other pressure groups. It looked more like the firestorm that had followed Nixon's dismissal of the special prosecutor a few months before. One congressman reported that 85 percent of those responding to a questionnaire circulated in his district opposed "compulsory" seat belts.[10] Senator Thomas Eagleton had a similar impression.

In a survey conducted by the Chicago Motor Club, only 15.7 percent of respondents approved of the interlock.[11] A study by Robertson and Haddon at IIHS indicated that at least 41 percent of drivers had completely defeated the device.[12] *Motor Trend* reported that 76 percent of drivers polled were opposed, and promptly published an article instructing its readers how to disconnect the system.[13] Hertz officials indicated that between six and seven of every ten 1974 models in their fleet no longer had interlocks; enraged customers had ripped them out.[14] Chrysler representatives reported that consumer concern over the interlock exceeded concern about gasoline mileage.[15]

The Wyman amendment caught safety activists by surprise. Some hurriedly returned from long-planned August vacations to heed the call to arms; all were perhaps still bleary-eyed from the long television vigil that had culminated only three days earlier in the President's resignation. But there was reason to believe that the skirmish would be short-lived. A compromise amendment requiring that motorists have the option of purchasing a seat-belt ignition interlock system or a combination light and buzzer "reminder" had already been hammered out by Congressman John Dingell and safety partisans on the House Commerce Committee when it reported H.R. 5529 on July 11. Perhaps Congressman Wyman, who was a newcomer to vehicle safety matters, had failed to recognize that he had already received satisfaction on the interlock, light, and buzzer issues.

The committee's concession in the Dingell amendment, however, was not responsive to Wyman's core concerns. Wyman was not interested in the "option" to buy one of two obnoxious systems. He was in favor of motorists' freedom to buy exactly as much safety equipment as they wanted. He preferred safety rules that mandated only that buyers be given options—including the option of buying no additional safety equipment.

As floor debate raged on, the safety activists steadily lost ground to Wyman's army. The rhetoric of prudent paternalism was no match for visions of technology and "big brotherism" gone mad. The leadership decided to offer Wyman half a loaf, an amendment introduced by Congressman Frank Moss that eliminated the interlock and "sequential warnings" in exchange for no legislative restrictions on other passive restraint options. But neither Wyman nor the House would accept the compromise. Within minutes of Moss's last gasp the electronic device on the chamber wall recorded the members' vote on Wyman's *original* provision: 339 ayes, 40 nays, 2 present, 44 not voting. The House had spoken: it would not require the American people to restrain themselves, passively or otherwise. Nor would it permit NHTSA to do so.

The debate now shifted to the Senate. Well before the outbreak of hostilities in the House, in fact, Senator James Buckley had resolved to banish the interlock, which he considered "an arrogant invasion of privacy."[16] On January 21, 1974, Buckley introduced a bill (S. 2863) that would make the interlock optional. But S. 2863 was in some sense both premature and an orphan. Public outrage had not yet reached crisis proportions, and S. 355, the Senate's version of the recall amendments, had long ago sailed smoothly through the committee and the full Senate. S. 2863 therefore languished while Buckley waited for public sentiment to ripen and looked for a parliamentary device to secure Senate attention.

On July 30 he introduced essentially the same bill, now numbered S. 3840, with the cosponsorship of Senator Eagleton. As the House drama unfolded, and public outrage over the interlock mounted, Buckley and Eagleton decided both to strengthen their proposal and to speed its consideration by their colleagues. The two senators' gaze fell on S. 3934, the Federal-Aid Highway Amendments of 1974.

On September 9, 1974, Buckley rose to introduce Amendment 1851, to the highway amendments bill. He called his provision "simply a more comprehensive version of S. 3840," but in fact, Amendment 1851 went much further. It proposed not only to repeal NHTSA's requirements for interlocks and devices other than warning lights but also to require that the agency hold a public hearing and obtain approval of both the Senate and House commerce committees before acting upon the pending Standard 208 proposal or any other general passive restraint requirement.

In their joint remarks, Eagleton and Buckley explained the relationship between the interlock prohibition and the public hearing and legislative veto requirements. The two senators feared that prohibition of the interlock device would quickly drive NHTSA to require passive restraints. But how different were such restraints from the universally despised interlock? As Eagleton explained: "Our amendment seeks to avoid the pitfall of trying to write standards which are highly technical and better left to the experts. Instead, it provides for final congressional review and approval for such regulations before they can take effect and I think we owe that much to the American people."[17]

The following day, September 10, the safety coalition counterattacked. Senators Magnuson, Hartke, and other members of the Senate Commerce Committee introduced Resolution 398. Magnuson alluded to Wyman's floor rebellion and paused briefly to eulogize the congressional committee system, which, he noted sadly, had played no role in shaping the House's actions: "I think it was unfortunate that the House chose to proceed in this manner without the benefit of hearings or committee consideration. Rather, the amendment surfaced on the floor of the House and it did not receive the studied deliberation to which matters of this magnitude are accustomed."[18] To make matters worse, Magnuson continued, it now appeared that the Eagleton-Buckley amendment might follow the same path. The legislation chosen by Eagleton and Buckley as a vehicle for their amendment fell within the jurisdiction of the Public Works Committee, not the Commerce Committee. That meant Public Works would be taking it up in conference. But to confuse the issue further, the conference committee of jurisdiction, Commerce, would in any event be discussing the matter now that the House had agreed to Wyman's amendment. Resolution 398 would untangle these procedural snarls and, though Magnuson did not say so, ensure that he and his Commerce Committee colleagues would play a major role in managing the floor debate.

What followed left all but the most ardent safety partisans completely unmoved. Hartke described the substantive provisions of Resolution 398. He proposed to retain the interlock, but to require NHTSA to provide consumers, at their option, a "button" that would enable them to override it. Safety and freedom were to be technologically fused by legislative fiat. Nor was the old guard prepared to live with Buckley and Eagleton's legislative veto provision. Getting vehicle safety under the control of a technologically sophisticated regulatory agency had been, after all, a major purpose of the revolution of 1966.

But Resolution 398 was dead on arrival. No one discussed the resolution in subsequent floor debate and no vote was ever taken on it. The following day, September 11, Buckley announced that several new sponsors had signed on to Amendment 1851. Momentum was building.

Magnuson and Hartke did not give up. If Eagleton and Buckley persisted in their caper of tying auto safety to public works, the committee chairman and subcommittee chairman made it clear that they would raise parliamentary hell. Amendment 1851 could be portrayed as a "trespass" upon the oversight committee's jurisdiction, one that would result in overlapping and potentially contradictory conference deliberations. Moreover, it was an end run around normal processes, bad manners, and a personal affront to Magnuson and Hartke.

The prospect of prolonged procedural wrangling over Amendment 1851 produced a remarkable compromise. Magnuson and Hartke would interpose no objection to either a debate or a vote on Amendment 1851, provided Buckley and Eagleton agreed to withdraw their amendment immediately after its passage. In other words, the Senate would enact the law, and immediately rescind it. On September 11, a recorded vote was taken on the Buckley-Eagleton amendment: 64 ayes, 21 nays, 15 not voting. The Senate had spoken. It then spoke again, rescinding its pronouncement. Magnuson and Hartke now knew the substantive view of the Senate as a whole, but procedurally their committee's jurisdiction had been maintained.

Neither in the Senate vote on Amendment 1851 nor in the House had the oversight committee chairmen been able to deliver their committees. In the Senate, Pastore, Moss, and Stevens joined Magnuson and Hartke in voting against the Eagleton amendment; Hart, Cannon, Long, Hollins, Tunney, Stevenson, Cotton, Pierson, Griffin, and Beall voted for it; members Inouye, Baker, and Cook did not vote. In the House, Moss's subcommittee opposed the Wyman amendment, 5–3 (1 not voting). The full committee, however, voted with Wyman, 28–7 (6 not voting; 2 not accounted for). This was a legislative process almost completely outside the institutional control of the 1966 safety coalition. Committee jurisdiction may have been maintained, but committee discipline had evaporated in the heat of a grassroots rebellion.

On Liberty. Although the proposals surrounding the interlock, buzzer, and other passive restraints were technologically and procedurally complex, the rhetoric was sweeping and impassioned, as can be seen in the following statements of various participants:

Senator Buckley, on the rationale for his amendment: "I view such coercive measures as the interlock as an intolerable usurpation by Government of an individual's rights in the guise of self-protection."[19]

Congressman Wyman, in opposition to the oversight committee's proposal: "This is a most extraordinary, most unfounded, most unreasonable, and most irrational position. Actually it is un-American."[20]

Congressman Abraham Kazen, supporting Wyman: "That is wrong. That is wrong to tell the individual what is good for him because they are going to rebel . . . Give them the equipment if they so desire, and if they do not, let them do whatever they want."[21]

Congressman John Rousselot, also in support of Wyman: "We are merely saying in this amendment that it is voluntary. What is wrong with that?

That is what our whole country is supposed to be about, a matter of free choice."[22]

The Defense Team. As member after member rose to condemn the interlock as an affront to "freedom of choice," the safety coalition leadership defended it as best it could. Congressman James Broyhill, a safety partisan on the House oversight committee, rose to quote a letter from Secretary Brinegar asserting that the warning systems in 1972 and 1973 cars and the interlock in 1974 cars had "brought about a dramatic increase in the usage of current belt systems," and that 50 percent of occupants in 1974 models were using their seat belts.[23] Increased usage meant lives saved. Was it not ironic, Broyhill wondered aloud, that the interlock should be prohibited under these circumstances. In the Senate, Magnuson made the same case: "With the advantage of 20–20 hindsight, I think we are willing to admit that mistakes have been made. But the simple fact remains that the various restraint systems required by the Department of Transportation have saved and can continue to save many thousands of lives. The Department of Transportation estimates that the interlock system alone would save 7,000 lives per year and prevent 340,000 injuries."[24]

But this sober and "socially responsible" position crumbled before the freedom fighters' fusillade. The interlock had generated a powerful arsenal of political images. An estimated three hundred thousand vehicles in the 1974 production run had an interlock malfunction of some sort. Senator Collins took to the floor to predict that "in ten years three million cars are going to have this electrical problem."[25]

Malfunction horror stories became the order of the day. Ignition interlocks had stranded (or could strand) a motorist in the path of an oncoming train. Women were unable to flee rapists. Parking attendants, who had to buckle up no matter how short the trip, were going nuts. Housewives were buckling in their groceries. Hertz could not obtain sufficient towing services to retrieve malfunctioning vehicles. And in account after account, the family pet, usually a dog, set lights blinking, buzzers buzzing, and interlocks locking.[26]

Senator Cotten: The other day, I spent a half hour trying to get my car started simply because I had laid a pound of cheese and a loaf of bread on the seat next to me. [Laughter.][27]

Senator Eagleton: The cases are legion, Mr. President, of how nonsensical this system is. The distinguished Senator from Vermont (Mr. Stafford) and

I exchanged some experiences on this subject on the Senate floor a few weeks ago. He told me of a personal experience of a rental car in his home state on a weekend visit. When he put his hand on the seat next to the driver's seat, the thing went berserk, and he had difficulty stopping it.

I responded by telling him about my hapless constituent who, on instructions of his wife, was sent to the supermarket to buy a turkey. He then had to strap in the turkey to drive home. As the poor constituent observed, it was the safest ride a turkey ever had on the way to the oven.

Then the distinguished Senator from Texas (Mr. Tower) happened into the Chamber. He has a dachshund. He puts his dachshund on the seat. It is hard to strap in a human being, Mr. President, but a dachshund is damnably hard to strap into one of those seat belts.[28]

There was merriment in the chambers. The members rocked with laughter. The United States Congress was about to enact legislation that experts told them would send seven thousand citizens each year to an early grave. Hartke was both indignant and bewildered:

All the gaiety that we have heard on this floor about people who have had annoyance disappears very rapidly when you consider what we are talking about. What we are talking about here is some way to try to reduce that death toll.

Truthfully, you can talk about "big brotherism." But "big brotherism," as this is called, is not unique to this situation. Look at any type of effective disease immunization program. Whether we are right or wrong and whether human nature should be that way, we have to make it mandatory.

That is what we did about smallpox. That is what we did about the various childhood diseases, such as diphtheria. And that is also what we do in a manufacturing plant. We require a man to put both hands on a machine now, with a safety device, so he cannot operate the machine with only one hand.

In other words, in the whole field of safety human nature seems to require something to force us to do what is safe.

What everyone is saying here is that seat belts are a good idea, but we ought not have them.

It is a paradox.[29]

The paradox could be explained, perhaps, by attention to context. Safety was important, but it did not always trump liberty. And in Hartke's examples the freedom fighters saw precisely the dangerous, progressive logic of regulation that they abhorred. The private passenger car was not a disease or a workplace, nor was it a common carrier. For Congress in 1974, it was a private space.

Costs, Benefits, and Busing

The recall and interlock amendments emerged from legislative processes that lie near opposite ends of a procedural continuum ranging from autocratic control to populist uprising. In the first, committees or subcommittees having traditional jurisdiction over the subject matter consult with directly affected interest groups and work out a comprehensive legislative package that is passed by Congress with virtually no debate. Although the public may demand change, policy experts shape, enact, and implement it. In the second, dissenting committees with jurisdictional authority are circumvented by new players who use general public sentiment to move a Congress acting as a committee of the whole. Public demand is neither suppressed nor mediated by expertise.

From the agency perspective the first legislative process, though not always comfortable for an agency looking to Congress for guidance, is clearly preferable to the second. Committees protect as well as goad, and the preferences of their dominant actors can be learned and accommodated. Outside conventional jurisdictional arrangements, in contrast, almost anything is possible. Indeed, when acting outside conventional legislative allocations of power, agencies have few political resources to deploy and little capacity for anticipatory accommodation beyond their own talent for reading the public and congressional mood. If the interlock-veto amendments signaled a shift in motor vehicle politics from the "autocratic-expert" toward the "populist-sentimental" end of the legislative process continuum, this was surely bad news for those at NHTSA who viewed safety regulation as a technocratic enterprise for public health–oriented professionals.

The third major domain of action in 1974, the school bus safety amendments, suggested that the legislative process that generated the interlock-veto provisions was not unique. Although the school bus amendments were "pro-safety" and proceeded through Congress with neither the jurisdictional sniping nor the florid rhetoric of the interlock ban, they could only confirm NHTSA's suspicions that the 1966 safety coalition, embedded institutionally in the Senate and House commerce committees, was no longer in charge. At the very least the process leading to these amendments provided additional evidence for the view that the agency could no longer rely on the considered judgments of safety professionals and their congressional and interest group counterparts to validate agency policies. For instead of protecting and rewarding expert judgment, the committees ultimately embraced the passions of legislative and administrative outsiders and credited their flimsy rhetoric in the face of the agency's own careful analysis. Once again broad "political" considerations were exalted over "rational" regulation, but this time by the very committees that in 1966 had embraced a "scientific" approach to motor vehicle safety.

The story of the school bus amendments is of great anecdotal interest, but need not be recounted here in great detail. Requiring NHTSA to do more about school bus safety emerged on the congressional agenda through the efforts of congressmen whose districts had witnessed school bus tragedies, the desire of the National Transportation Safety Board (whose bureaucratic mission is the criticism of other transportation safety agencies) for more publicity, and the continuous prodding of various public interest groups, such as the Physicians for Motor Vehicle Safety, Action for Child Transportation Safety (ACTS), and Ban Unsafe Schoolbuses Which Regularly Endanger Children (BUSWREC) (the last consisting of three George Washington University law students carrying out a clinical project). This "movement" had the usual emotional appeal of any group seeking to protect children and armed with descriptions of gruesome accidents.

The activists, however, confronted a problem. NHTSA had studied the issue of school bus safety very carefully, and from a dispassionate view of the data it seemed relatively clear that the proposed amendments made no sense. Motor vehicle accidents had reached an all-time high in 1972 and 1973; accidents in those years claimed 54,589 and 54,052 lives, respectively. But of these, only 150 fatalities (and 4,600 injuries) resulted from school bus accidents. And 60 of the 150 fatalities, plus some indeterminate number of injuries, were adults who had the misfortune of finding themselves, as pedestrians or motor vehicle occupants, in the path of an oncoming bus. Of the remaining 90 fatalities, moreover, 60 were children who perished *after* they had disembarked. The children were run over either by the bus itself or by another vehicle. Yet the school bus amendments, ignoring 80 percent of the fatalities, did not mention pedestrian protection as one of the eight areas for mandatory rulemaking. The rules that Congress wanted NHTSA to promulgate would, therefore, only address the remaining 30 fatalities, plus some fraction of associated injuries.

The cost side of the equation reinforced regulatory caution. The average purchase price of a school bus was then $8,000. The vehicles' useful life was nine to ten years. The manufacturers' data indicated that improvements in seats, body structure, and frontal barriers would add approximately 2,000 pounds in weight and $1,500 in cost. The added weight, in turn, would require other improvements—a larger chassis, heavier front and rear axles, and larger tires—that would further magnify weight and cost increases. The total tab could come to 2,430 pounds in increased weight and $2,070 in added costs, roughly 25 percent of the vehicle's base price, not including extras. Work on emergency exits, windows, and windshields, for example, would cost an additional $112. And the economics of retrofitting buses were even more unappealing. Vehicles depreciated 15 percent the first year, and 10 percent annually thereafter. The resale value of a nine-year-old bus was $600. Retrofit costs would probably exceed $4,000, more than twice the amount required to incorporate safety features in new buses.

Committee members seemed to think that the price tag might be less, about $1,000, and the president of Ward Manufacturing testified that "the cost will not be as great as many suggest."[30] But whatever figures were used, it was obvious the costs were so substantial that further measures might actually reduce school bus safety. At the Senate oversight hearings in 1974, before the provisions were enacted, the agency's chief rulemaking engineer conceded that regulators could "make a schoolbus as safe as a Greyhound bus" but that doing so would drive up procurement costs by 41 percent. "If you increase the cost by 40 percent, these people will have to drive the buses at least 10 to 12 years," he cautioned. "If we are not careful," the engineer continued, "if we try to put too much safety into a new bus, we will be counter-productive in that older, unsafe buses will be on the road for a much greater period of time."[31]

This sort of careful attention to costs, benefits, and priorities was, of course, exactly what the courts, the executive branch, and Congress itself had been urging on the agency. Yet on the school bus issue, Representative Les Aspin apparently spoke for a majority in both houses when he complained that "Given the comparatively low accident rates on schoolbuses, the Department of Transportation—DOT—argues that schoolbus safety regulation is an extremely low priority item. DOT maintains that in terms of a cost-benefit analysis, it is worth neither the time nor the effort of DOT to protect our school children from shoddily constructed schoolbuses. DOT is misusing the concept of cost-benefit analysis."[32] Other members were far less charitable. Senator Lowell Weicker charged that the situation amounted to a "national disgrace,"[33] and on

March 27, 1973, Senator Charles Percy warned that "if DOT does not reorder priorities and act shortly, I plan to call for an investigation in the very near future within the Senate Permanent Investigations Subcommittee, on which I serve as the ranking minority member."[34] As Congress lurched toward adoption of the amendments, it was obvious that regulatory officials had badly botched their assessment of the costs and benefits of school bus safety. They had confused economics with politics. In the political process and in the media, sober cost-benefit calculations are about as popular as rich, absentee slumlords.

At the 1973 oversight hearings, for example, Senator Percy asked that he be permitted to

> put this factor in some perspective, as I believe Harry Reasoner did in his excellent treatment of the issue of schoolbus safety in a special ABC-TV report a few weeks ago. Using the high figure of $1,000 added cost to produce a stronger, safer, and more secure schoolbus, the price would work out to $100 a year over the vehicle's 10-year life and recognizing there are some 180 days in the school year, the added cost per day of the safer bus could amount to 56 cents. But, of course, most schoolbuses are used for at least two runs each morning and afternoon, carrying at least 120 children each day. Thus, the added cost per pupil per day of a far safer schoolbus would be ½ cent.[35]

An "investigative" report by Metromedia News produced similar revelations of NHTSA's "cavalier attitude." Only one of the Department of Transportation's 72,000 employees, for example, worked full time on school bus safety matters.

The media's "cost-benefit analysis" of school bus safety was supplemented by similar "analyses" from the politicians themselves. The mayor of Lomita, California, testified: "[Senator Percy] mentioned the millions of dollars that were rightfully spent to create a better safety situation for the astronauts—many millions of dollars. I know it's pretty far up there. As he said, don't we owe our children the same protection as we owe these astronauts? They are all American lives, human lives, and we do owe them the same protection."[36] This "revised" cost-benefit approach found a receptive audience in the chairman of the House Commerce Subcommittee. Congressman Moss observed that:

> To comment on costs—today we are going to be voting on a supplemental appropriation bill in the House. An amendment will be offered to deal with the cost of the Cambodian bombing from now until the end of June. It is

almost the same figure as the cost of the 275 million dollar recommendation made yesterday for improving schoolbuses . . .

So this brings into focus a serious question of values and judgment on priorities. We have over a decade of spending on many things while we have permitted the real needs of many of our children and our school districts to go totally unmet. I think the question really is, can we afford not to provide the safety which is technologically feasible at this time?[37]

Even under these circumstances, the demand for regulation might have sputtered out. After all, rhetoric of this general sort was a daily staple of political life and there was no end to the domestic programs that might be justified by reference to Vietnam and the moon. As the school bus safety amendments leapfrogged over thousands of other legislative proposals on Congress's crowded agenda, however, it was obvious that some deep resource of political will was being tapped.

In some sense, the demand for more protection in school buses appears to have been tied to the national furor surrounding "forced" busing to achieve school integration. In an article in the *Washington Post* on April 14, 1972, entitled "The Other Schoolbus Problem," the reporter Coleman McCarthy alluded to the connection: "As if schoolbuses weren't getting enough national attention already—on school integration—the recent crash in Valley Cottage, New York, suggests there is another kind of attention schoolbuses ought to be getting, on safety." Busing was not upheld definitively as a means of school desegregation until the Supreme Court's decision in *Swann v. Charlotte-Mecklenburg Board of Education*[38] in 1971. The decision was not popular. A 1971 poll found that 77 percent of the nation opposed busing.[39] Antibusing pressures peaked in Congress in 1972, when they reached the proportions of a "national uproar," as the Congressional Quarterly put it.[40]

But in the Congress, majorities do not always prevail. On August 18, 1972, the House, by a vote of 283 to 102, adopted H.R. 13915, which would have banned busing except to the school closest or next-closest to the students' homes. In the Senate, however, pro-busing forces filibustered the measure and withstood three votes to invoke cloture. The bill died on the Senate floor. Looking back, the Congressional Quarterly called busing "one of the most bitterly fought congressional battles in 1972."[41] And although the controversy quieted in 1973, the politicians' torment continued. The Senate held hearings on a proposed constitutional amendment to prohibit busing, but took no action.

The "involuntariness" of school bus ridership may explain, in part, the distinctive perspective on costs and benefits that the school bus amendments generated. School bus safety could tap reservoirs of concern about equality and freedom simultaneously. If the state was responsible for children being in buses, it surely had the responsibility to compensate their loss of freedom by providing the safest possible involuntary trip. It was essential to "fairness" that these involuntary riders be as safe as those who freely chose to ride commercial buses. A Congress that had participated vigorously in civil rights lawmaking, which in turn had led to a vast increase in involuntary school bus ridership, and that had refused to deny the courts busing as a remedy, could at least try to make the ride safe. It could do something about "busing," even if "safe busing" was at best a distant second on the busing agenda of angry parents around the nation.

It is also true that the vision of protecting children gives any measure that can be so characterized a considerable degree of political appeal. But the overall motor vehicle safety problem would very nearly bear that characterization. The epidemic that Haddon and his colleagues had described was largely the health problem of children and youth. If Congress wanted to protect the lives of children, it would have done better to reenergize NHTSA's lagging standard-setting enterprise as it applied to the passenger car. Even modest safety enhancement there would decrease the risk of death or serious injury for tens of thousands of children who were involved in motor vehicle accidents each year.

But that sort of analysis of the problem is more reminiscent of the legislative agenda of 1966. The 1974 amendments gave a new and highly "political" twist to the conception of federal motor vehicle safety regulation. Henceforth, it seemed, NHTSA's information needs would run at least as much to political intelligence as to scientific data and analysis. If NHTSA was to understand its own regulatory mandate, it would have to understand the political mood of the country. But more than that, it would have to understand how that mood refracted through the political or moral lens appropriate to the different types of issues within its regulatory domain. The legislative politics of 1974 gave dramatic new meaning to the nostrum that, for public health purposes, the community, rather than the individual, is the appropriate unit of analysis. The community itself, it seemed, could conceive of its health as demanding precisely the opposite approach—as demanding a focus on individual rights and on the inestimable value of each individual's freedom to exercise these rights.

EIGHT

Regulation as Recalls

There is a classic *New Yorker* cartoon that depicts two prisoners in a concrete cell. They are manacled hand and foot not just *to* the wall, but *on* it; hopelessly immobilized, their feet hang well above the floor. A window beckons some distance from them, heavily barred and apparently too small for the exit of anything larger than the every-present dungeon rats. One of the prisoners is looking up at the window and saying something to his cell mate. The caption reads, "I have a plan."

Imagine that the cell is the NHTSA administrator's office in 1975. The prisoner's bizarrely optimistic statement has just been made to the administrator by one of his closest advisors. Stranger yet, the speaker is the agency's chief counsel. What could this optimistic counsel possibly mean? Has he found some way to avoid the crippling effects of judicial review? Does he believe that the Congress that legislated the 1974 amendments was about to multiply the agency's regulatory budget by a factor that would make it a match for the industry's full-court press in rulemaking proceedings?

Were the latter what the chief counsel had in mind, the administrator would certainly have been justified in treating his advice as the ravings of a stir-crazy inmate. Congressional funding for NHTSA had never been generous, and appropriations after 1975 hardly revealed a Congress eager to support bold new regulatory initiatives. And the crucial funding for motor vehicle safety research that might have supported further initiatives declined steadily in real terms from 1972 on. A budget that had never been healthy was by 1980 truly anemic. If the Congress that began the auto safety regulation program in 1966 had visions of the space program dancing in its head, it was never willing to support that vision with NASA-like appropriations.

It would have been equally silly to predict that the agency could somehow take advantage of the broad mandate for forcing the development of new technology that the *Chrysler* opinion's superficial rhetoric proclaimed. As we saw in Chapter 5, NHTSA's most ambitious technology-forcing regulation apart from its passive restraints rule, the attempt to require antilock braking systems on large trucks, ended up seven years later in the legal dustbin, along with the original passive restraints rule.

The likelihood of judicial invalidation also derailed a second, much bolder, step that had been previewed in NHTSA's 1971 October Plan. The agency at that time was contemplating a rulemaking approach similar to the simple 50-mile-an-hour crash test that Hartke inquired about in the 1974 Senate Commerce Committee hearings. The idea was to abandon all equipment- or design-specific crashworthiness criteria in favor of a simple demand for "survivability" of occupants in a barrier crash at a predetermined speed. Manufacturers would be allowed to achieve compliance in any fashion they chose. The burden of technological innovation would be theirs. The agency's need to defend itself against industry objection to every detail of equipment-specific rules would be over.

NHTSA's experience in court, however, strongly suggested the incompatibility of this strategy with judicial demands for demonstrably rational decision making. Even if NHTSA would point to a prototype safety car that would meet the 50-mile-per-hour standard, which indeed seemed within reach, it would be unable to demonstrate that its safety car was economically practicable to produce and market, or that the manufacturers could duplicate the safety car's performance in vehicles that were. Forcing the development of technology on a grand scale seemed legally impossible in an environment that had rejected less ambitious standard setting.

Paccar, the antilock braking rule case, later seemed to confirm the pessimistic predictions made on the basis of *Chrysler* and *H & H Tire*. In a bit of sardonic understatement following the *Paccar* decision and the Supreme Court's refusal to hear the case, Joan Claybrook, then NHTSA's administrator, testified to congressional overseers: "It is a litte bit hard to assess the effectiveness of the standard before you issue it, if you have to have the testing done afterwards."[1] But without recourse to a general performance standard, the rulemaking staff had no managerial plan for breaking through the industry's relentless defense.

It cannot be claimed that there was *no* legal means by which the grand design of the October Plan could have been implemented. Audacious standard setting in the face of technological uncertainty can sometimes garner approval, when the judiciary can be convinced that Congress has demanded that such regulatory risks be accepted. But no chief counsel should have believed that the chances were good. NHTSA's chief counsel must have had a different plan. Indeed, he did. Yet strangely, given the story to this point, his plan relied on the courts.

The Adjudicatory Way Out

Congress's behavior in 1974 suggested at least two things. First, NHTSA's rulemaking was in political trouble. Rational attention to the big safety payoffs combined with careful assessment of costs and benefits clearly did not ensure that Congress would be content. A glance at NHTSA's school bus and interlock experiences revealed at least that much. Second, there seemed no diminution in congressional fervor for recalls of defective motor vehicles. In that domain it seemed that NHTSA's only fault lay in its failure to move more aggressively. For an agency politically on the defensive, recalls were a regulatory technique made in heaven. No one but the manufacturers objected, and even they could hardly be strident in their opposition to repairing defects.

Renewed fervor in identifying defects and forcing manufacturers to recall and repair vehicles was certain to meet resistance at some point, of course. As the auto companies struggled in the mid-1970s to cut costs and improve quality, they increasingly relied on parts and systems that were interchangeable across models. Recalls would grow increasingly expensive as a defect in a single part or system came to affect greater and greater proportions of a manufacturer's fleet. And as product liability claims mounted pursuant to liberalized substantive and procedural rules, defect determinations by NHTSA had an ever greater capacity to impose costs beyond statutory repair obligations and loss of goodwill. The manufacturers could be expected to resist a beefed-up recall program. Would the courts give them legal tools for resistance similar to those that afflicted NHTSA's rulemaking effort?

By the mid-1970s this question could be answered with considerable confidence; the answer was a resounding no. *United States v. General Motors Corp. (wheels)*[2] is a good example of the degree to which the judiciary, far from providing manufacturers with effective defenses, had instead eased NHTSA's enforcement burden in recall cases. NHTSA had ordered General Motors to recall a number of its 1960 through 1965 model year, three-quarter ton Chevrolet and GMC pickup trucks because of failures in a particular type of wheel used on those models. General Motors did not deny that a significant number of failures had occurred, but claimed that they would not have happened if the vehicles had been operated in accordance with the owners' manual. General Motors contended that the wheel failures were the direct result of vehicle overloading by owners who added campers or other special bodies to the trucks. More important, NHTSA had not demonstrated the cause of the reported failures. In General Motors's view, there simply was no evidence that a "defect" existed.

NHTSA argued for the chief counsel's "plan," what it had labeled internally the *per se* theory of defects. According to this theory, if the government could establish the existence of a significant number of failures in a safety-related component, it had established a "defect" for purposes of the Motor Vehicles Safety Act even without any showing of their cause or that any accidents or injuries had resulted. And most automotive components were safety-related, in some sense. The D.C. Circuit Court of Appeals agreed with the government. In the court's view, evidence of a number of failures was enough. The government had no obligation to explain or demonstrate the mechanism of failure. The opinion did leave open the possibility that the manufacturer could avoid a finding of a defect by demonstrating that the failures had resulted from owner abuse or neglect, but only if such behavior was not foreseeable by the manufacturer.

This relaxed recall standard was further elaborated in another General Motors case, *United States v. General Motors Corp. (pitman arms)*.[3] The government introduced evidence in the district court that a part of the steering linkage (the pitman arm) had failed on some 1959 Cadillacs in a ninety-degree turn at 10 to 15 miles per hour; that the arms were made of metal somewhat softer than that usually employed to withstand the stresses of low-speed turns; and that General Motors had sold six times as many pitman arm replacement units for its 1959 and 1960 Cadillacs as for the immediately preceding and succeeding years.

General Motors did not deny the facts as described in NHTSA's complaint. It claimed that, notwithstanding these proofs, the government had failed to demonstrate the existence of a defect creating an "unreasonable risk of injury or death," as the statute required. There had been no reported injuries from pitman arm failures, and General Motors had received no complaints about the defect from any of its customers. Moreover, the stress necessary to break the arms could only be applied at very low speeds (as when parallel parking). A sophisticated risk analysis, supplied by the manufacturer, suggested that failures of pitman arms in the 1959 and 1960 Cadillacs left on the road might produce, at most, two injuries before that model disappeared.

On the basis of these uncontested submissions the trial judge awarded summary judgment[4] to General Motors. The court ruled that the government had failed to demonstrate an unreasonable risk of injury from failure of the pitman arms and, therefore, had failed to demonstrate a defect. NHTSA appealed. The court of appeals not only reversed the award of summary judgment for General Motors, but rather than sending the case back for further factual development, directed that summary judgment be granted to the government. The opinion required that NHTSA demonstrate only (1) that there had been failures in the equipment in apparently excessive numbers and (2) that this failure could produce loss of steering control. These facts were uncontested. And because General Motors could not disprove the *possibility* of failure in a driving situation, its pitman arms created an "unreasonable risk." Summary judgment for the government was therefore appropriate.

Similarly, in *United States v. Ford Motor Co.,*[5] the government again was permitted to find that a defect in Ford windshield wipers related to automobile safety even though no reported accidents or injuries had resulted from the defect. The simple fact that the windshield wipers might break off due to metal fatigue sometime during the life of the automobile was sufficient to establish that the automobiles contained a defect relating to automobile safety. Notwithstanding the lack of any accidents or injuries, the court concluded (on the basis of "expert" evidence) that a windshield wiper breaking off during a heavy downpour would create a dangerous situation or "unreasonable risk" within the meaning of the act. The *per se* theory had triumphed.

Understanding Recalls in Court

The posture of the courts in the recall cases contrasted strikingly with the judicial posture assumed in proceedings to review NHTSA's regulations. To put it mildly, the courts gave the agency a very modest responsibility to demonstrate that a significant problem related to automobile safety is involved in a recall campaign. One did not here find the courts asking whether the safety problem underlying the recall was sufficiently serious to justify the expense of repair or replacement, or whether the agency really knew enough to determine that the recall would promote safety. General Motors was required to offer to replace the pitman arms in forty thousand seven-year-old Cadillacs in the face of an uncontradicted projection that this replacement would prevent two injuries. NHTSA was able to force the recall of General Motors trucks without any knowledge of the cause of their failure and in the face of evidence suggesting that the trucks' wheels do not fail when used in accordance with the owner's manual. If offered to justify a regulatory wheel strength requirement or a standard requiring increased durability in steering arms, this sort of data and analysis would have been laughed out of court.[6]

The judiciary's practice of giving the agency a hard time when reviewing its rules and an easy time when enforcing its recall orders is puzzling; in a sense, it is perverse. NHTSA, like most federal administrative agencies, appears before courts both as a plaintiff and as a defendant. It is a defendant in proceedings attacking the validity of its rules. It is a plaintiff in proceedings seeking to force the recall of "defective" vehicles. As is generally true in civil litigation, NHTSA has the burden of proof as a plaintiff and is entitled to the "benefit of the doubt" as a defendant. The agency therefore should have an easier time in court defending its rules than proving its defect cases.

Nor is this assessment altered by any special aspects of administrative law governing the "deference" that courts should pay to administrative judgments. Quite the contrary. Arcane quibbles about the appropriate scope of judicial review aside, courts are supposed to uphold NHTSA's rules as long as they are not arbitrary. The courts exercise a limited scope of review. By contrast, courts should enforce a proposed recall only if they believe the agency is correct, for in a recall proceeding the court technically is not "reviewing" an agency order. The court is making the initial decision itself in a proceeding in which the agency is merely a special prosecutor. Even if the defects determination were viewed as an "informal" agency decision put at issue by way of defense in the judicial enforcement proceeding, judicial "review" in recall proceedings is said to be "de novo," that is, an independent exercise of judicial discretion. If courts observe the norms of administrative law, then, other things being equal, they should affirm rulemaking decisions more often than defects determinations.

The expectations of administrative lawyers have seldom been subjected to empirical verification of a more than anecdotal sort. But what little evidence there is supports the general expectations that the norms of administrative law express. In one of the rare empirical studies of Supreme Court review of agency action, Martin Shapiro found that "the courts generally let the agencies do what they want."[7] Seven years later Warner Gardner came to a somewhat different, more carefully documented, and less succinctly expressible conclusion.[8] Taking all reported federal appellate court decisions in 1974 as his sample, Gardner found that agencies were affirmed over 60 percent of the time. The courts "let the agencies do what they want" in a majority of cases, but perhaps not "generally."

Refining the analysis further, and shifting to a qualitative appraisal, Gardner's audit also found that informal rulemaking, the type exercised by NHTSA, was treated "deferentially" by reviewing courts 58 percent of the time, while informal adjudication, the category that would include NHTSA defect determinations, received the closest judicial scrutiny of any functional category of agency action. The judical tendency toward serious review of NHTSA's rules may be slightly more pronounced than the "norm," but this is, perhaps, not too surprising. The judicial treatment of recalls, however, seems quite unconventional.

In inquiring what it is about recall activity that elicits such gentle judicial inquiry into the rationality of the agency's case, the right question seems to be not "What does administrative law say about these issues?" but rather "What are the presuppositions of products liability law?" Defects litigation seems to respond not the culture of regulatory enforcement but to the preexisting culture of automobile law, in particular of products liability litigation.

The institutional locus of decision making, and the way a shift in location affects legal perceptions, may thus be the key to understanding NHTSA's recall experience in court. The decisional institutions are Congress and the courts. The posture of the agency in defects enforcement is that of a litigant seeking to enforce a statutory command, and the conventional wisdom of administrative law that an agency in this posture loses some of the customary deference paid to an expert decision maker subjected to judicial review of its decisions is not in dispute. But lesser deference to agency expertise hurts the agency's prospects for success in court *only if* other factors affecting success remain constant. Instead, they shift radically.

NHTSA as a recall litigant ceases to be responsible for important aspects of the policy implied by its actions. The substantive policy to recall defective cars is the legislature's. So, of course, is the general policy to make cars safer by regulatory standards. But there the similarity ends. NHTSA is responsible for and must defend the subsidiary policies adopted by it in its rules. It must justify its own position as an "expert" lawgiver. Congress has adopted no rules. By contrast, when pursuing recalls NHTSA need only be an advocate for the congressional command that defective cars be recalled and repaired. If procedural and evidentiary policies—for example, questions of who bears what burdens of proof and what evidence is essential to present a *prima facie* case—must be developed, those issues are to be decided by the courts. This shift of responsibility for policy development from agency in rulemaking to legislature and court in recall proceedings is crucial. It has several major effects on the psychology of judging—effects that, taken together, tend to explain the remarkable generosity of the defects jurisprudence.

First, any failure to protect automobile passengers from defective automobiles that NHTSA seeks to recall will in some substantial sense be the responsibility of the court denying the agency's recall petition. When denying a recall petition the court cannot console itself with the idea that it is remanding the case to NHTSA for reconsideration, or that the agency, not the court, is deciding the substantive issue. A court that is only slightly averse to risk will in these circumstances want to structure the evidentiary burden to give the plaintiff the benefit of the doubt.

A finding of "insufficient evidence" may, in some cases, "proceduralize" the courts' substantive judgments. It might thus appear not to be deciding the substantive issue at all. But the question that has been asked in defects litigation is really the prior legal/policy question, "What level of proof should be sufficient in recall enforcement proceedings?" This, of course, is precisely the issue faced repeatedly by the courts in products liability litigation. And the judiciary clearly understands that this is the critical issue. Who has to prove what determines who wins.

Second, as discussed in Chapter 2, the common law of products liability instructs courts to be risk averse where product defects are concerned. The current state of the law is quite straightforward: if people are injured because products fail in their intended use (are defective), then the manufacturer is strictly liable. In addition, the development of the common law of strict liability reveals that the ethic undergirding the products liability jurisprudence expresses one of the strongest normative commitments of our legal culture.[9]

The incremental strengthening of manufacturers' responsibilities and lessening of plaintiffs' burdens of proof that shaped the law into its present form demanded extraordinary and continuous conceptual innovation. This sort of lawmaking is undertaken by courts only rarely, and only in the face of social needs that are perceived to be pressing. NHTSA as a defects litigant is in some sense a placeholder for consumers who might appear in products liability cases. It has sought and obtained in defects litigation reductions in its burdens of proof that are reminiscent of those won by injured plaintiffs throughout the twentieth-century development of products injuries litigation.

Third, the defects question is not framed as a technological, scientific, or economic issue. The questions are framed instead very much as they are in products liability cases. Should people expect steering arms to break, wheels to collapse, or windshield wipers to fly off? Obviously not. People expect cars and their components to work. If they don't work, the car is defective. And if one can imagine the relevant failure causing or exacerbating an accident, then that defect surely relates to automobile safety.

Fourth, the court in a defects case is being asked to give a limited remedy in a limited context. The Ford transmission case aside, recalls tend to involve a minuscule percentage of cars on the road at the time of the case. Moreover, the remedy only demands that manufacturers notify owners of the defect and repair cars that are presented. Since owners decide for themselves whether the reported defect is sufficiently serious to warrant the inconvenience of presenting it for repair, the preferences of car owners will ameliorate any excessive caution in the judicial decree.

Defects litigation is thus particularistic and ordinary. It is not perceived to have systemic consequences. The stakes are defined largely by the parties' interests. Like any litigant, the transportation secretary may settle.[10] Like any set of beneficiaries, owners may choose whether or not to avail themselves of their rights. And, as in any private litigation, the judge proceeds to shape the law in the light of authority, history, social need, and the merits of particular cases. This is law in the particularistic, remedial form that our legal culture has always preferred. Embedded in the legal culture of products liability litigation, all these considerations press defects litigation in the direction of modest burdens of proof and expeditious judgment for the plaintiffs.

Compare the psychology of recall litigation from the bench with the psychology of a rulemaking review proceeding from that same perspective. In rulemaking, the responsibility for regulatory implementation is clearly the agency's. It must act and be seen to be acting as the legislature's expert surrogate. The court's function is quite different. Its role is to ensure the rule of law by keeping NHTSA within its statutory mandate. The provision of judicial review is premised on the notion that the judiciary must guard against administrative failure, not product failure.

Remember the portrayal of the constitutional legal culture of regulation in Chapter 1. The teaching of the Madisonian–New Deal synthesis is that although delegation of policy choice to administrators is constitutionally permissible, it is a reluctant necessity. Delegation is justified primarily by the complexity of the regulatory tasks assigned and the need for a high level of expertise. It is hardly remarkable, then, that reviewing courts are on the lookout for agencies operating on the basis of hunches or bromides. NHTSA cannot respond to a judicial demand that it demonstrate the practicability of a rule by intoning, "Necessity is the mother of invention." Such "experts" are viewed as having failed to execute their legitimate statutory mandate.

Our constitutional culture teaches that keeping administrators within their delegated authority is an essential element of maintaining the rule of law, the separation of powers, and ultimately our liberal, democratic polity.[11] Fears of arbitrary and undemocratic exercises of power make delegations of administrative authority reluctant in the first instance. From this perspective, any loss of effectiveness in substantive policy caused by judicial review is but a necessary cost to pay in the crucial project of maintaining the constitutional structure. These very general institutional considerations help explain why courts have taken rulemaking review seriously and why, far from relaxing the criteria for judicial review, congressional interest in the matter focuses almost exclusively on proposals to increase the judicial role in overseeing agency rulemaking.[12]

The Instinct for Proceduralization

Yet there is still a puzzle concerning the preferred judicial technique for policing NHTSA's rulemaking efforts. That our most general constitutional arrangements promote serious review of agency rules does not tell us why we find courts reshaping the issue of regulatory reasonableness into an issue of process rationality, or why courts have jealously guarded rights of notice and participation. It is, after all, this "proceduralized" form of judicial review that is particularly debilitating from an agency's perspective. It is "proceduralism" that legitimates and empowers the full-court press. What cultural imperative has driven the courts in this direction?

The demand for a rational decision *process* is the judiciary's response to a dislocation in the legal culture. In many modern regulatory statutes Congress has required courts to decide general policy questions in a procedural context that makes it difficult for the judiciary, or anyone else for that matter, to describe judicial review as merely deciding cases according to law. The Motor Vehicle Safety Act, like most regulatory statutes adopted after 1966, permits immediate review of an agency rule, or of the withdrawal or amendment of a rule, by any party who may be adversely affected. Superficially this is only a change in the usual timing of review.[13] That a rule is invalid has always been a defense in a suit to enforce it. The consequences of the legislative shift to pre-enforcement review, nevertheless, are profound. It allows affected parties to go to court without attempting to comply with the rule and, in the absence of any attempt to enforce it against them, to obtain a declaration whether it is valid. Review in this form addresses not the particular circumstances of a rule's application but the abstract legality of its commands.

Put in this way the traditional legal view is that such abstract issues are nonjusticiable. The legal culture has historically maintained that courts declare the law only as a by-product of the adjudication of concrete controversies about the legal rights of particular parties.[14] This understanding is given constitutional status by Article III of the Constitution, which limits the federal judiciary to the adjudication of "cases or controversies." An enforcement action against Chrysler for violating the passive restraints rule, in which Chrysler argues that it cannot be required to comply because the dummy specifications are inadequate, is a conventional case or controversy. The adjudication is about individual rights and responsibilities on the basis of particular facts. The need to address the validity of the rule is a mere by-product of the need to determine individual rights. A suit by Chrysler to invalidate a rule on any of a score of grounds before the rule's effective date, and preceding any attempt at compliance or threat of enforcement, is obviously not a case cast in this same mold.

Without going further into the dense thicket of the federal jurisprudence of justiciability, we need only note here that such jurisprudence renders the type of review contemplated by the Motor Vehicle Safety Act, and pursued in the *Chrysler* case itself, problematic, if not downright suspect. In order to square the congressional command to decide cases in the abstract with the conventional and constitutionally required judicial role of deciding concrete cases, courts have been forced to identify some individual legal right that the Congress has called upon the courts to protect. What could it be?

This was in fact the question that Judge McGowan was required to answer in the *Auto Parts* case, discussed in Chapter 5. Repairing to the Administrative Procedure Act, he found that the plaintiffs' entitlement was to be free from "arbitrary" exercises of administrative power. This again is, superficially, an unremarkable legal move. Reviewing courts have traditionally employed the arbitrariness standard, and it has caused little difficulty when applied to the traditional forms of agency decision making—specific agency decisions to grant or deny a benefit or to impose a sanction. Adjudicatory decisions that are either against the preponderance of the evidence or contrary to customary policies are "arbitrary" in the straightforward sense of "not according to law." For an appellate court to say so is only to treat an agency like a lower court— which is, of course, the way in which an agency acts when adjudicating specific controversies. But the legally innovative aspect of the revolution of 1966 was to abandon traditional adjudicatory forms. How should the arbitrariness criterion be applied to general policies embodied in rules that have never been applied?

The task of translation is rhetorically simple but, given the legal culture, profoundly transformative. By analogy to adjudicatory decision making, rules are said to be arbitrary in two situations: (1) if they have no adequate factual predicate, an evidentiary interpretation of "arbitrary"; or (2) if they violate existing legal norms, in particular the statute pursuant to which they were promulgated. So far so good; but let us now examine the application of these two grounds of arbitrariness in the context of rulemaking review.

First, conformity with the statute. The Motor Vehicle Safety Act requires that rules "meet the need for motor vehicle safety," protect against "unreasonable risk," be "practicable" and "appropriate," and be stated in "objective" terms. All the quoted terms demand policy choices, not the application of legal rules. Is the court really to judge these questions? And, if so, how can it judge them without appearing to be merely substituting its policy preferences for those of the agency? For

surely neither the Motor Vehicle Safety Act, the Administrative Procedure Act, nor the Constitution gives anyone the "right" to have motor
vehicle safety policy set by federal courts.

In order to appreciate the judiciary's dilemma more fully, focus for a
moment on the statutory requirement that the agency's rules eliminate
"unreasonable risks." Remember that the passive restraints rule was
premised not on the superiority of passive restraints technology over
manual lap and shoulder belts, when used, but on the agency's despair
that any significant number of Americans could ever be convinced to
buckle up. Now suppose some litigant makes the following claim: to be
"reasonable" in most common law contexts means to behave as an
ordinarily prudent person would behave in similar circumstances. Ordinary Americans overwhelmingly decline to use restraint systems that
they already own. Put another way, we know that most Americans elect
to run the risk of being in an auto accident without the protection of a
universally available and highly effective restraint system. In short, the
risk that the passive restraints rule is designed to avoid has been demonstrated, by the very behavior upon which the rule is premised, to be a
reasonable one. It is, therefore, outside NHTSA's statutory authority to
regulate.

This straightforward claim of statutory violation presents all sorts of
questions. The fundamental issue is one of determining how the Congress intended "reasonableness" to be judged. But there are many
candidates for an appropriate methodology. Does the statute demand
that the agency analyze its rulemaking proposals on the basis of common
law standards of "reasonableness"? On the basis of the public health
consequences of maintaining the status quo? On the basis of a consideration of the ratio of costs to benefits in providing some new protection?
On the basis of current social perceptions of the acceptability of particular risks? On the basis of current social perceptions of the acceptability
of particular risks? On the basis of predictions of what those preceptions
might be after technology forcing has altered existing cultural presuppositions?

These questions and many similar ones are answered neither by the
language of the statute nor by its legislative history. Yet choosing among
them will have profound consequences for the policies actually chosen by
NHTSA. And it is this prospect that poses the judicial dilemma. If the
court chooses a particular construction of "unreasonable risk," it has in a
very substantial sense chosen the agency's regulatory program. Nothing

in our constitutional arrangements suggests that courts should play such a political role. Yet if the court permits the agency to choose any approach to unreasonableness that is reasonable, it knows that any of the candidates just mentioned, plus perhaps a host of others, will pass muster. If that is the breadth of discretion provided the agency by the statute, then the notion that NHTSA operates under law and is subject to judicial review becomes the skimpiest of fig leaves over a naked reality that is itself constitutionally unacceptable, the complete delegation of legislative policy choice to administrators.[15]

The twin shoals of judicial policymaking on the one hand and unconstrained administrative discretion on the other are hardly novel landmarks when steering for the safe harbor of judicial legitimacy. They are traversed routinely by judicial navigators. But in the context of judging the abstract legality of rules under vague statutory criteria, the task of maintaining the confidence of passengers and crew is made more difficult by the absence of some important aids to navigation. The conventional lawyerly moves for separating law and policy or for camouflaging their inseparability are largely unavailable when reviewing agency adjudications. When reviewing the abstract legality of rules it is simply preposterous to claim (1) that the court is addressing not these broad issues of policy but only the agency's application of law to fact in the adjudication of narrowly focused claims of right, or (2) that these interpretive issues are routinely decided in agency enforcement proceedings and, therefore, have long legal histories that constrain both the agency's and the judiciary's roles. To take the latter claim first, not only are the questions novel, but the norms put at issue are designed precisely to confer policy discretion on the administrator. In virtually all cases, the claim that the court is just interpreting the law, not setting (or "rubber stamping") agency policy, will convince no one.

The facts of rulemaking review proceedings similarly belie the claim that the courts are here merely engaged in reviewing run-of-the-mill administrative dispute settlements. The parties look more like legislative claimants than ordinary litigants. They often are tangentially affected business interests, such as the insurance industry, or ideological champions of the Left or Right, such as the Center for Auto Safety or the Pacific Legal Foundation. Even the directly affected manufacturers may be litigating for strategic competitive advantage (remember General Motors's absence from the *Chrysler* litigation) rather than to protect any conventional form of property interest. And no matter who is litigating, the judgment usually will bind everyone. The question is the validity of the rule, not the propriety of its application. The litigant's "rights" and the "rights" of the public are indistinguishable.

The line between law and policy can also disappear in judicial review of agency adjudication. The pre-enforcement review of rules facilitated by the Motor Vehicle Safety Act is but a recognition of the changing structure of federal administrative regulation. Yet no amount of scholarly celebration of this so-called public law litigation[16] is likely to eliminate judicial anxiety in the face of a task that calls for repeated, transparent, and general policy choices.[17] The task must be redefined to integrate it with a more conventional conception of judicial competence. For it is on that convention that the judiciary's political legitimacy depends.

From this strategic perspective the other, "evidentiary," interpretation of arbitrariness has much to recommend it. Yet here again the courts encounter an awkward gap between their traditional reviewing functions and the pre-enforcement review of rules. Judicial review of agency adjudication, like appellate court review of trial court proceedings, focuses on whether the trial record contains appropriate proofs to sustain the initial adjudicator's findings of fact. If not, the trier of fact has behaved arbitrarily. Rulemaking processes, however, are vastly different from trials. There are no obvious boundaries on the rulemaking record, no accepted standards of "proof" for policy judgments, and no procedural vehicles that sharply delineate the "issues" in a rulemaking proceeding. As Judge McGowan noted in *Auto Parts*, the agency is engaged essentially in a legislative activity. In our legal system legislatures may operate on the basis of any evidence that a majority is willing to credit—or even on no evidence at all.

Notwithstanding these difficulties, evidentiary policing of agency rulemaking threatens judicial legitimacy much less than does outright policy revision. Agencies are not legislatures. Indeed, they are substituted for legislatures precisely in order that policy may be based on a more expert understanding of the problems addressed. Agencies are supposed to get the facts right. Hence, from *Auto Parts* on, courts have experimented with a series of techniques designed to sharpen issues, reveal factual assumptions, and thereby shape a record within which judicial review of rules for factual adequacy makes sense. This story of procedural innovation has been told elsewhere[18] and need not be rehearsed in detail. The point here is only that the need to integrate a novel judicial role into the accepted legal culture helps explain the use of the particular techniques that we have witnessed in the review of NHTSA's rules.

Auto Parts creatively transformed the requirement of a "concise statement of basis and purpose" into a demand for the presentation of a rule's factual support and policy rationale. These materials constituted a "record" from which the court could judge means-ends rationality and thereby police for arbitrariness in its traditional forms: the inadequacy of the record[19] and inconsistent[20] or incoherent[21] decision making. Of course, the agency's presentation of factual material might be incomplete. The "record" therefore had to be expanded to include submissions of outsiders and the agency's responses to those submissions. As the record grew in importance, so did meaningful opportunities to participate in its formulation through adequate notice. The *Wagner*[22] decision's demand for additional rounds of notice and comment is simply the logical outgrowth of this proceduralized approach to rationality review.

So structured, judicial review necessarily transforms the image of rulemaking from a legislative-political endeavor into an analytic-policymaking enterprise[23]—Judge McGowan's language about "essentially legislative" tasks to the contrary notwithstanding. The judicial role is not to remake political choices, but instead to examine agency reasons and agency choices in the light of an appropriate factual record. This is, then, only a familiar role in a new context, or so it can be made to appear. As the conventional reviewing court remands for new trial upon discovering evidentiary gaps in the trial-court record, so the court reviewing administrative rules remands to the agency for reconsideration when the record seems inadequate to support the agency's policy choice. If this approach strongly reinforces the opposition tactic we have called the full-court press and severely burdens and delays the rulemaking process, that is perhaps unfortunate. But it is surely consistent with an adversary legal culture whose libertarian values have always given the advantage to the defendant and the status quo.[24]

The translation of legislative-political questions into analytic-policymaking issues through proceduralized judicial review, of course, never really fools the sophisticated regulatory players. Judicial review for process regularity was the opposition technique both of "conservatives" confronting the New Deal and "liberals" confronting the Reagan Administration's desire to deregulate.[25] Yet notwithstanding proceduralism's penchant for the status quo, such political shifts in some sense signal the legal culture's success in pursuing its aspiration to political neutrality. Judicial review in a proceduralist form, like lead ballast, tends to stabilize the ship of state whether the political winds blow from left or right.

All of this is to say that any chief counsel at NHTSA who believed that there was an easy way out of the legal bind revealed by *Chrysler, H & H Tire,* and similar cases would have had a poor understanding of some of the most basic features of American legal culture. Proceduralist review is a practical solution to the dilemma of judges in our modern activist state, who must maintain our great myths of the rule of law and democratic political control in an ambivalent polity. That polity demands explicitly (when providing for judicial review) that those myths be defended, but implicitly (when empowering agencies to legislate) also requires that they be abandoned. Absent a sea change in either the polity's perceptions of appropriate governmental organization or demands for governmental activism, it would be foolish to imagine that judges will abandon their project of accommodating these inconsistent demands or jettison the few legal tools with which they can do so.

The upgrading of judicial demands for agency sophistication in rulemaking has striking parallels to the development of products liability law. When new products and production technologies generated both new risks and new forms of social and economic organization, courts responded by imposing strict liability on manufacturers of defective products. This imposition was thought to be both distributively just, in a risk-spreading sense, and also just from the internal standpoint of the new forms of enterprise that had emerged. The systematic elimination of errors or defects, including errors or defects that increase injury, is after all the highest aspiration of a technical-bureaucratic mode of production. The law based liability on the manufacturer's own implicit values, notwithstanding the recognition that these aspirations to perfection could never completely be realized.

Commentators have criticized the courts for transposing this aspirational standard to judicial review[26]—for succumbing to the intellectual appeal of comprehensive or synoptic rationality as a legitimating paradigm for administrative regulation. They have urged that courts recognize the impossibility of such a decision process and the necessity of "muddling through" as a dynamic decisional technique where events unfold in real time, under uncertainty, and in face of resource constraints. But these arguments are radically incomplete.

They are incomplete first because the judiciary has not required systematically that agencies, including NHTSA, make bulletproof decisions. The bureaucratic aspiration to comprehensive rationality is tempered both in doctrinal announcement and in practice by some appreciation of reality.[27] The courts seem to be searching instead for an "agency standard" somewhat analogous to the "industry standard" in products liability cases: a product or a rule will be defective only if it fails to meet the expectations engendered by good agency practice. As Judge McGowan put the standard of review in *Auto Parts,* courts are looking for action that limits the dangers of irrationality, not for rational perfection.

The argument for judicial modesty is also incomplete because it fails to articulate a normative standard for "acceptable muddling through" that has reasonably predictable consequences. This failure is not surprising. The "muddling through" idea is a descriptive heuristic. Transformed into a normative concept it is itself a muddle. Every final decision has a history. Within that history concrete choices are always explicable. If we know enough about the concrete events, "It seemed like a good idea at the time" is almost always a plausible explanation. If that were good "muddling," judicial review would police only for bad faith or fraud.

Perhaps that is what the critics have in mind. Such a reduction in the judicial presence in regulatory affairs, however, has demonstrably not been sanctioned by the political process. Judged by the specific statutory provisions for judicial review that Congress adopts, and by the proposals it debates for general reform of judicial review of administrative action, there is no substantial constituency out there for reduction or elimination of judicial review. Eclectic, uninformed, and disabling as judicial review may be, Congress and perhaps also the electorate seem to want it to form a part of the regulatory environment.

The Heyday of Recalls

Whatever the complete explanation for judicial receptivity to NHTSA's defects determinations, congressional support and a green light from the courts produced an orgy of recall activity in the latter half of the 1970s. During some of the Carter years, 1977 through 1980, more cars were recalled for repair than were sold new in the United States. It seemed that the agency had finally discovered a regulatory activity that was both politically popular and legally legitimate. And given the ease with which NHTSA could substantiate a demand for a recall notice, the manufacturers saw little to be gained from judicial trial. Their best, perhaps only, strategy was to negotiate for moderation of the language describing the hazardousness of the defects identified in particular recall notices. Non-"alarmist" notices might not only reduce the owner response rate but also limit press coverage of recalls and the negative publicity that such coverage entailed.

The Unity of Law and Politics

The emphasis on recalls at NHTSA in the late 1970s was broadly consistent with the basic ideological premises of the Carter Administration. Jimmy Carter came to Washington promising essentially two things: first, to make the government efficient; and second, to make it responsive to the interests of the populist-consumerist constituency that Carter had identified as the "outsiders" of American politics. The central message of the Carter candidacy was that these outsiders needed representation by people who were not tarnished by long exposure to the Washington establishment.

Jimmy Carter was a politician who kept his promises. The major domestic initiatives of his administration were captured in two elaborate executive orders. The first established a major new body within the Executive Office of the President, the Council on Wage and Price Stability (COWPS), and gave it the responsibility of ensuring that all major federal regulatory actions were both cost-beneficial and cost-effective.[28] The council was to carry out this task through a technical body known as the Regulatory Analysis Review Group (RARG). Like the names of most such bodies in Washington, its acronym became a new noun. Unlike the doings of most agencies, however, RARG's activities gave rise to a new verb. Bureaucrats began to talk of the possibility that their regulatory efforts would be "rarged." To be "rarged" was to be subjected to the incessant demands for information and reanalysis by RARG's band of beady-eyed economists.

Whatever the ultimate success of the Carter regulatory analysis effort in terms of regulations reviewed and found wanting, this high-level support for a cost-conscious and economically "rationalized" regulatory posture reinforced the internal efforts that had already begun in many agencies pursuant to the much less rigorous requirements of the Ford Administration's inflation-impact program. At NHTSA, of course, the administration's concern for rationality, economically defined, also reinforced the defensive internal analysis of proposed rules for economic "practicability" that a proceduralist judicial review had spawned. The cautionary posture of lawyers still smarting from unhappy experience in judicial review proceedings was matched by the attitudes of a regulatory analysis staff that kept a sharp eye on their counterparts at RARG. Skepticism about rulemaking had been institutionalized.

Carter's second important executive order formed yet another new staff within the Executive Office of the President, the Office of Consumer Affairs.[29] It was the mission of this office to ensure that all federal agencies were responsive to the demands and complaints of consumers. Each federal agency was required to establish an office of consumer affairs of its own, structured so that it was both accessible to consumers and positioned to make the consumers' voice heard in the agency's policy councils. Disappointed consumers were, of course, the specific beneficiaries of NHTSA's recall campaigns.

If the 1974 amendments to NHTSA's recall powers and clear congressional support of an aggressive recall effort were not enough to energize NHTSA's defects efforts on behalf of disappointed vehicle purchasers, surely the Carter Administration's consumer directives, when combined with the appointment of Joan Claybrook, a well-known consumer advocate, as NHTSA's administrator, was likely to do the trick. Judicial review, the 1974 legislative experience, and the Carter Administration's program were all saying the same thing to the agency—be careful about rules, be aggressive about recalls.

The combined effect of these messages reoriented the agency profoundly. As will be discussed in the next chapter, a long-standing internal battle for the heart of the agency's program was won decisively in those years by those within the agency who believed that NHTSA's regulatory energies were better applied to recalls than to rules. The feedback from the agency's external environment demonstrated that they were correct. If in 1966 motor vehicle safety regulation could easily be equated with rulemaking, a decade later it was only mildly hyperbolic to characterize vehicle safety regulation as synonymous with NHTSA's recall program.

To be sure, NHTSA had not abandoned rulemaking. Agency resources were still being devoted to safety standards. It remained embattled over the passive restraints rule, which had been reinstated in 1977 by the new transportation secretary, Brock Adams, following the rule's suspension in the final year of the Ford Administration. The agency also devoted substantial energy to the requirement of stronger automobile bumpers, an initiative that had strong congressional, insurance industry, and consumer-advocacy support, but that had virtually nothing to do with safety. It continued to work at upgrading, modernizing, and extending its existing inventory of rules. But in 1980, when the decade and the Carter Administration ended, it was clear that NHTSA's regulatory product since 1974 would either have to be measured by its recall campaigns or run the risk of remaining invisible to whatever measuring device might be employed. A review of *New York Times* reporting on NHTSA activity for the years 1977–1980, for example, reveals only two stories concerning the agency's safety standards. By comparison there were seventy-one stories on recalls.

The Limits of the Recall Strategy

However well justified by positive and negative feedback from the relevant political and legal environment, NHTSA's shift from standard setting to recalls signaled the abandonment of its safety mission. This conclusion, however, is not necessarily a normative criticism of NHTSA's behavior. That the safety mission as conceived in 1966 may not have been doable is a subject to which we shall return in later chapters. The claim that NHTSA's emphasis on recalls abandons the motor vehicle safety mission is only an assertion about the inevitable effect of equating regulation with recalls—a claim we believe to be supported by the available evidence.

Let us begin with the concept of a "defect related to motor vehicle safety." To loosely paraphrase the judicial opinions, a defect is a failure of some part of a vehicle to perform up to the usual standards expected for that type of equipment under those circumstances. Such a failure "relates to motor vehicle safety" if it might cause (or presumably exacerbate the injuries resulting from) an accident. Motor vehicles are also defective if they fail to comply with an existing motor vehicle safety standard. In the argot of products liability law, a defect may result from either faulty manufacturing or faulty design.

What do we know about the extent to which failures in the mechnical, electrical, or hydraulic systems of motor vehicles cause or increase the severity of accidents? Not a great deal, actually. Reconstructing the causes of accidents is difficult and costly if done well, and therefore it is not done very often. Nevertheless, the highest estimate made by a reasonably well designed study is that 13 percent of accidents involve vehicle failures of some kind.[30] When combined with what we know about the rate of owner responses to recall notices—that roughly 50 percent of owners return their vehicles for repair[31]—this information leads to an obvious conclusion. If every vehicle recalled were in fact defective, every defect sure to cause an accident or injury, and every defect repair faultless, NHTSA's recall program would at most be remedying 7 percent of the vehicle safety problem.

A 7 percent reduction in injuries and deaths is hardly trivial. But 7 percent is still not a believable estimate. The same studies that allocate 13 percent of accidents to some form of vehicle failure allocate most of those failures to inadequate or faulty maintenance. In short, most accidents related to vehicle failure involve vehicles that are *not defective* within the meaning of the the Motor Vehicle Safety Act. Accidents due to "defects" in that sense are estimated in the range of 3 to 5 percent.

Again, a reduction of vehicle injury and death through recall campaigns of 1.5 to 2.5 percent (50 percent return rate × 3 to 5 percent of accidents) is not a trivial matter. But yet again, this too is not a very realistic estimate. It assumes that NHTSA's recall program will catch all the defects that would cause accidents, which surely is a heroic assumption. Finally, of course, it assumes that all repairs are faultless. Operating on that assumption is not as heroic, although it is surely false.

As least where manufacturing defects are involved, only a minuscule proportion of the cars recalled actually have a defective part. Yet all must be inspected and often partially disassembled. In many recalls the suspected unit is simply replaced in all cars because that is less expensive than determining whether a defect exists in each vehicle. And whatever the cause of the defect, manufacture or design, most defects will never cause an accident. The vehicle is "defective" because the defect *might* lead to an accident. Remember General Motors's pitman arms and Ford's windshield wipers. Taken together, these considerations yield an unhappy conclusion. A modest error rate in the repair operations of the hundreds of dealerships who must actually do the repair work for recalls could introduce more hazards than are eliminated.

It is thus not implausible to believe that the recall program is decreasing motor vehicle safety. Indeed, some agency advocates of more aggressive standard setting have earnestly contended in conversation with us that when the risks of accident added by trips to automobile dealers to obtain free repair of safety defects are factored into the safety equation, the recall program is almost certainly exposing motorists to more hazards than it is correcting.

We are not convinced by these claims. No one has the requisite data to support them. Yet the problematic effect of recalls on vehicle safety is underscored by NHTSA's steadfast failure to study the question. Since some vehicles are repaired and some are not, but all have subsequent accident histories, the agency has a perfect environment for studying the safety effects of recalls. To our knowledge, however, no portion of NHTSA's research budget has ever been allocated to discovering the safety effects of recalls. We do not argue that it should be. The effects are surely negligible, as systematic study of state vehicle inspection programs suggests.[32]

There is still one safety claim that might be made for the recall program. Perhaps the threat of recall enforcement not only induces voluntary compliance with repair obligations but also feeds back into the design and manufacturing process to reduce the overall incidence of defective vehicles. Perhaps. After all, David Halberstam reports that Lee Iacocca insisted on the first Chrysler 5/50 protection plan, not because he thought the company could produce cars that would hold up for five years or fifty thousand miles, but because he was certain that it could not. He wanted the threat of warranty liability to hold over the heads of the financial wizards who were blocking product engineers' requests for the working capital necessary to improve the product.[33]

But such anecdotes do not in any way demonstrate a systematic or substantial effect of the recall program on the incidence of vehicle defects. And though we are hardly prepared to deny that the imposition of costs on manufacturers for the production of defective products will provide an incentive to substitute engineering and quality control for repair, capital, and reputational costs, we are extremely skeptical that the incentive is of much significance. Save in one or two extreme cases, the costs—repair costs, increased capital costs, and loss of product reputation—are simply too small to be meaningful.

Consider first the out-of-pocket cost of the repair itself. Although sometimes impressive in absolute terms, these costs are trivial in relation to the overall costs of running a motor vehicle production company. To our knowledge no company has ever thought such costs sufficiently significant to report them on its required 10–K filings with the Securities and Exchange Commission as having a potentially "material" effect on the corporation's earnings.

Second, there are the increased costs of capital implied by depressed share prices. The important question is whether recalls affect share prices. One econometric study finds a significant effect on the day of (and the day preceding) a recall's announcement.[34] Another finds that there is a "rebound" effect six days later that cancels out the initial loss in value.[35] Maryanne Keller, one of the most highly regarded automobile company securities analysts, states flatly that recalls have no effect on share prices.[36]

How do recalls affect share prices? We cannot tell. We find most persuasive analyses that take a more particularistic view of the matter.[37] Some recalls may have some effect on some share prices some of the time. An expensive recall imposed on Chrysler when its quality reputation is already low and it is on the verge of bankruptcy is likely to have an effect. The run-of-the-mill recall probably has none. Moreover, whether there is an effect is not quite the right question. The real issue is whether recalls will affect safety because managers will perceive such an effect and respond to it. We are very doubtful.

It would be very hard for company managers to *see* that recalls have a negative effect on share prices. A manager looking at his own company's shares for any particular period might actually perceive that recalls are causing his share prices to go up! According to the share price data used in several studies, looked at over a fifteen-year period and considering all companies, stock prices go up 40 percent of the time on the day a recall is announced.[38] For a single company, looking at a shorter time period, it is easy to find evidence suggesting that shareholders are rewarding the production of defective cars by bidding up share prices. It is also true that nearly 60 percent of the time a recall announcement coincides with other news about the company that may affect share prices.[39] An observant manager will not know what to conclude from share price movements that coincide with recalls, and managers are certainly not studying the question econometrically.

Finally, managers may not respond even if they believe that recalls are costly both in capital markets and in product markets. And believe it they may. It is simple common sense to believe that recalls have negative reputational effects and should be avoided. But spending large amounts of money on quality assurance in an attempt to avoid recalls may also be a mistake that knowledgeable managers are unlikely to make. All manufacturers are experiencing recalls. Hence nothing short of a recall identifying a very dangerous and widespread problem in the current production line of vehicles will have much effect on a company's reputation vis-à-vis the relevant alternatives for car buyers—other car companies. Indeed, by selective, but not false, portrayal of NHTSA's recall statistics, any company can be the industry leader in quality. Ford pioneered this form of advertising, although its recall record was at that time actually the worst overall of the major producers.[40]

Moreover, recalls relating to serious and widespread defect problems in current production lines add very little to the reputational damage that has already been done by news reports that predate the recall. Audi surely was not happy to have to recall the 5000S, but the recall did not add appreciably to its problems. In any case, that recall, like many, would have occurred whether or not the 1966 and 1974 legislation had ever been passed.

Recall activity, nevertheless, may have some safety payoff. It may interact synergistically with product liability litigation to amplify the signals from both that provide incentives for greater care in engineering and production. But, given the facts as best we can know them, the effects on safety do not seem substantial. From a societal perspective, this is a shame. Recalls are a form of regulation that the American people seem to like. Recalls help give leverage to the underdog, the disappointed consumer. And in providing that leverage they reflect highly valued remedial aspects of our legal culture. It is unfortunate that we are not making ourselves a lot safer at the same time.

NINE

Inside NHTSA

In a mid-1970s portrait[1] of NHTSA Charles Pruitt pictured the agency as committed to the task of remaking the motor vehicle almost exclusively through the issuance of motor vehicle safety standards. In Pruitt's view this stance was "an inevitable . . . product of the way in which the agency has been staffed, organized and led." At the time of Pruitt's research, engineers held virtually all key posts in the agency. In his view, the agency's preference for rulemaking over alternative regulatory strategies (for example, highway redesign or the modification of driver behavior) simply reflected "the task [that engineers] do best." Pruitt portrayed NHTSA as an agency that had been "captured" by engineers.

In some sense, Pruitt's portrait was a true picture of NHTSA from the inside. He relied heavily on the perceptions of those then in the agency, and there is no reason to believe that Pruitt's informants were either systematically misled or less than candid about the "feel" of the agency's internal culture. Yet we also know that, when Pruitt wrote, the agency's rulemaking years were already behind it. How could an agency internally organized and staffed as Pruitt describes thereafter fail almost completely to promulgate any new vehicle safety rules?

The answer is that NHTSA had been and was changing rapidly, even as Pruitt wrote. An indication of how far and how fast is provided by a 1980 memorandum entitled "Why I Am Losing My Hair" from Michael Finkelstein, associate administrator for rulemaking, to his rulemaking staff.[2] The memorandum was written in a light-hearted tone, but its message was serious and unmistakable. The guard had changed. Permanently. Finkelstein got straight to the point:

To insure that intelligent regulations are issued, we must take advantage of all the talent in NHTSA and work with our colleagues, particularly those in OCC [Office of the Chief Counsel] and P & P [Office of Plans and Programs]. Moreover, neither OCC nor P & P are expected to provide automatic endorsements of our work, but must independently examine our proposals.

Many of you (and I will admit that it hits me occasionally as well) believe that P & P and OCC exist to harass us. That they are not cooperating to meet deadlines. That they continually raise issues that are without merit or fail to understand our analysis. I don't agree.

After reviewing the situation in detail (Finkelstein described the office as "festering" with an "undercurrent of discontent"), he announced new procedures to force rulemakers to respond to the objections raised by lawyers and analysts. Finkelstein then concluded his memorandum in tones that were both conciliatory and ominous:

I know that it is annoying to see documents that are acceptable to us—or are as good as we can produce under a tight deadline—seemingly being picked to death by others at their leisure.

I do not for a moment believe that we are always wrong and P & P or OCC is always right. However, there is little that we can do to correct them. I think that it will be far more productive to concentrate on eliminating some of the reasons for complaints, warranted or unwarranted.

Finkelstein's memorandum thus affirmed a defensive organizational strategy that had put the cost-benefit and legal analysts in P & P and OCC on a par with the engineers on the rulemaking staff in the final approval of motor vehicle standards. And as the frustrations of the rulemaking staff (to which Finkelstein's memo was in part addressed) attest, that new structure was an effective check on the engineers' rulemaking bias. The Finkelstein memo reflected many changes in NHTSA's internal processes and personnel over the past decade—changes that had transformed the agency's internal power structure. Within those ten years the engineering-rulemaking dominance that Pruitt described had given way to a lawyer-economist-recall dominance that was equally pronounced.

To put the story in this bold form suggests that the shift from rules to recalls at NHTSA was the outcome of professional warfare within the agency. From the inside it may well have looked that way. The professional cultures did clash, and professional orientation may often have motivated or guided the combatants. Yet this is a radically incomplete account of why the agency's regulatory technique changed. We need to know not only that lawyers and economists were in conflict with engineers—a conflict that may have been a natural outgrowth of their differing professional orientations—but also why the former seemed to have triumphed. If professional orientation provides the set of "drives" or motivations that explain the behavior of actors, that explanation has nothing to say about which professionals will or should be successful. What were the rules that governed this competition? And why did those rules—reflected in the agency's staffing and organization—tend to emerge?

Our thesis is that in this struggle for survival or preeminence, the environment, particularly the legal culture, selects the winners. Lawyers and economists as professionals are not inherently better endowed for survival or preeminence in bureaucratic settings than engineers. When the job to be done is safety engineering, one would think the opposite to be true. Nor were other possible endowments that promote organizational success—structure, decision routines, or budgetary resources—immutably fixed in 1966 in ways that systematically advantaged the engineers' antagonists in OCC and P&P. Quite the contrary; Pruitt's findings would otherwise have been inconceivable. There must have been something in the agency's regulatory environment that ultimately exalted one group over another. Recognizing, of course, that this preeminence may be reflected, strengthened, and in the short run maintained by allocations of resources and structural features within and controlled by the agency itself, we believe that "something" was the law.

Yet the output of the agency is surely something more than an interaction between the professional culture and legal constraint. Professionals have, at the very least, moral commitments, individual personalities, and organizational roles that shape their conduct. To know that a person is a lawyer or an economist is not to predict his or her behavior. And the dictates of the law or legal culture are not translated without loss into bureaucratic constraints or empowerments that determine an actor's success.

It is therefore both fundamentally correct and hopelessly incomplete to say that NHTSA's shift from rules to recalls signaled the triumph of lawyers and economists over safety engineers in a multiyear struggle mediated by the validation or invalidation of their respective efforts by the external legal culture. Professional culture, bureaucratic role, individual personality, agency structures and decision processes, judicial review, congressional amendments and appropriations, executive branch requirements, and a host of other factors, including chance, were important to that ultimate result. Yet a more detailed look inside NHTSA as events unfolded during the crucial decade of the 1970s reveals the signal importance of the law in empowering bureaucratic actors and establishing the agency's internal standards of success and failure.

The Rise of Motor Vehicle Programs

In 1971, Robert Lee Carter, aged forty-four, was named acting associate administrator for Motor Vehicle Programs. Carter's professional background perfectly suited him to the task of managing the auto safety program that Congress had envisioned in 1966. Carter had done postgraduate work in human factors engineering at Ohio State University from 1951 to 1953 and had worked on aeronautical crashworthiness programs at North American Rockwell for more than a decade. He had joined NHTSA in 1967, as director of crash survivability research, and in that capacity developed an early and passionate commitment to the airbag.

Douglas Toms, NHTSA's administrator at the time of Carter's promotion, was the new associate administrator's perfect foil. Toms knew relatively little about automotive engineering and seemed more comfortable with the Highway Safety Act side of NHTSA's operations. He was delighted to delegate responsibility to his deputies. Delegation soon became a matter of necessity, as well, as frequent visits to the regional offices, attendance at conferences on auto safety, and other out-of-town engagements earned Toms a reputation as administrator in absentia.

Carter, an ambitious, tough-minded manager with shrewd bureaucratic instincts and a low tolerance for sharing power, set about the task of filling this void. One agency colleague remembered Carter as "very dominating," a figure who "controlled information" and "couldn't tolerate disagreement." Another senior staffer stated simply that "you either got along with Bob or you were not there."[3]

The spare administrative structure at NHTSA created favorable conditions for Carter's ascendancy. The agency's few divisions, Motor Vehicle Programs (MVP), Research and Development (R & D), and Transportation Safety Programs (TSP), and congressional constraints on hiring high-level personnel meant that there were correspondingly few opportunities for rivals inside the agency to challenge Carter's control over the rulemaking and recall programs. Carter's authority was formalized in November 1972, in an internal directive—Order 800–1[4]—that vested virtually all important rulemaking activities in MVP. Under Order 800–1, MVP had initial responsibility for addressing not only engineering aspects of the rules but also analysis of lead time and economic impact, costs and benefits, expected industry and public reaction, and legal and political issues. MVP held the ultimate decisional authority as well. After MVP engineers prepared a "preliminary review paper" that summarized the proposed action, other offices were permitted to "comment" on the proposal within a strict timetable. The order gave MVP sole responsibility for adopting or rejecting the comments of other offices and for preparing a transmittal memorandum to the administrator seeking his "concurrence" to initiate rulemaking.

Once a decision was made to go forward with a rule, MVP prepared the necessary technical documents (for example, the "engineering position paper") for review by an evaluation panel. The panel was composed of representatives from all major organizational elements of the agency, including R&D, OCC, and P&P. But seven of the thirteen panel members, a working majority, were from MVP, and an MVP representative chaired the panel.

Engineers in Command

Order 800–1, drafted by MVP, was more than a statement of aspirations. It described a regulatory process that was in fact tightly controlled by the engineers within NHTSA. Carter and his colleagues in MVP determined which rulemaking initiatives would go forward and which would not. The October Plan of 1971 reflected MVP's priorities. The agency's strategy of integrating multiple safety rules into a single crashworthiness superstandard, built around Standard 208, was also a strategy conceived in MVP. Standard 208—in particular, the airbag—was Carter's top priority. Inside NHTSA, there were murmurings that MVP's commitment to the airbag was beginning to resemble a crusade. Carter was nicknamed "Associate Administrator for MVSS 208," and it was said that Carter had lured Toms into thinking that the airbag would "make him famous." Even Nader complained that NHTSA was losing its perspective on passive restraints, and that it was neglecting or compromising on recalls in order to secure manufacturer cooperation on Standard 208.[5]

This picture of engineering dominance is consistent with Pruitt's findings as of 1976. But Pruitt's conclusions failed to distinguish between professional capture and legislative intent. The preference for regulation by safety standards, after all, was implicit in provisions of the Motor Vehicle Safety Act, which required NHTSA to issue rules within a strict timetable. The prevalence of engineers followed from a clear congressional vision of NHTSA as an expert agency guided by the new science of accidents. The legislative history made clear that passive restraints were precisely the kind of engineering device that Congress had in mind when it determined to prevent the "second collision." If engineers had "captured" NHTSA for the purpose of promoting such devices, they did so with Congress's blessing.[6]

Pruitt's sketch, however, missed an even more important dimension of life inside the agency. He portrayed engineers as a "homogeneous" community whose shared norms bound members to a common cause of action, whatever their organizational affiliation within the agency. Somehow Pruitt had overlooked the abundant evidence that different groups of engineers were, in fact, at war among themselves. Indeed, conflict along internal organizational lines was making the issuance of innovative safety rules a virtually impossible task. This conflict helps to explain the gulf between Carter's state-of-the-art aspirations and the mundane reality of NHTSA's actual rules.

MVP versus R & D

Gene Manella, aged forty-one, joined NHTSA in late 1972 as associate administrator for research and development after a career that had included such positions as director of technology at NASA's Electronics Research Center and dean of the School of Architecture and Engineering at Catholic University. NHTSA was a "rudderless" agency, he found, and the R & D office in particular was in a "state of disarray." There appeared to be only one genuine leader at NHTSA: Bob Carter. MVP was a "well-knit organization" with an extensive and vigorous external constituency: private companies seeking to market the airbag, the insurance industry, Nader's public interest groups, and Hartke and his staff, among others. No other division within the agency enjoyed such support, and Carter adroitly used his contacts outside NHTSA to preserve and extend his authority within. At staff meetings, for example, Manella was impressed that only Carter seemed to know what would happen at the increasingly frequent and contentious congressional hearings, and accordingly, how to prepare for them.[7]

Despite this unsettling state of affairs, Manella found that he had arrived at an auspicious time. Belatedly fulfilling the original commitment to provide NHTSA with a research arm, the appropriations committees were now hurling bodies and dollars at the R&D office. In the context of no growth in other agency divisions, it was evident that Congress wanted the R&D office to play a more important role. At the same time, it was beginning to be clear that something had gone seriously awry in the rulemaking process. The courts—in *Wagner* (August 1972) and in *H & H Tire* and *Chrysler* (December 1972)—seemed to be sending a message that related directly to the reseach and development effort. NHTSA must do a better job researching its rules.

Inside NHTSA, tension had been building for months concerning the control of the research program. With Manella's arrival, this competition burst into open and prolonged conflict. The central issue was whether MVP had veto authority over research projects and must "sign off" on the R&D office's program. The battle lines were clearly drawn. Carter considered research to be a rulemaking support function: R&D's purpose was to act as an adjunct of MVP. Manella strongly disagreed. It was imperative that the R&D office be autonomous, he believed, in order to provide an independent appraisal of auto safety programs. The result was a stalemate.

As the months wore on, reports of trench warfare inside NHTSA filtered to the congressional committees. At Senate oversight hearings in 1972,[8] officials of the Public Interest Research Group, Clarence Ditlow and Carl Nash, reported that safety standards seemed to be "almost completely devoid of input from NHTSA's Research Institute which has spent tens of millions of dollars on motor vehicle research and the experimental safety vehicle program." To illustrate the point, Ditlow and Nash cited the infamous case of Standard 101, the standard involving "Miss Fifth Percentile." The agency had sponsored extensive research in the late 1960s and early 1970s at Man/Factors Inc. and the Guggenheim Center for Aerospace Health and Safety at the Harvard School of Public Health. Information was now available about "the size of adults, children, and pregnant women, including detailed measurements of the arm reach of adults of all sizes." Miss Fifth Percentile's measurements finally had been taken.

But no one in the rulemaking office was paying attention. Standard 101 continued to take as its point of reference "a person." Wilt Chamberlain was "a person," Nash and Ditlow complained. "One gets the distinct impression when one looks at new proposed rulemaking," Nash continued, "that nobody at NHTSA who is involved in the promulgation of standards actually reviews the research that has been done at the agency."

In January 1973, Chairman Magnuson demanded an investigation, and fifteen months later the GAO issued its report.[9] In part, the GAO said, the breakdown between the offices stemmed from the different professional orientations of the respective parties. Researchers preferred to approach projects "analytically," "whereas the MVP office believed that sufficient analytical data was available to develop structures for testing and thereby start with a more advanced phase of research." Rulemakers were driven by schedules and were impatient with vague research findings that generated further questions and delayed regulatory implementation. Rulemakers, therefore, tended to ignore R & D office reports. Researchers, by contrast, were not cast in an adversarial relationship with manufacturers, were free of deadline pressures, and spent most of their time with contractor personnel, who shared their joy of research for research's sake. Indeed, reliance on contract research greatly magnified the problem. After reviewing a sample of twelve research projects under contract, the GAO reported: "Most of the contractors' final reports included a recommendation that further work be done to confirm research conclusions."

According to the picture that the GAO painted, rulemakers were lucky to get any research at all on their priority initiatives. Missed communications and professional and personal preferences sent researchers on a frolic of their own that seemed to lead anywhere but the rulemaking docket. But no one, it seemed, was insisting on coordination. Although vehicle-handling and stability characteristics had been identified as the agency's second-highest priority in the October Plan, for example, the R & D office was collecting no data on the relationship between vehicle-handling characteristics and accidents. Nevertheless, the R & D office, GAO reported, did not seek clarification, and rulemakers did not determine why the priority was not met. Haddon and Steiglitz were gone, but their warring perspectives had now been institutionalized. The researchers were never satisfied; the rulemakers lacked sufficient data to withstand judicial review. Regulation stagnated.

Opening the Complaints Bureau

As rulemaking conflict both inside and outside the agency ground on, the Toms era at NHTSA was drawing to a close. On April 1, 1973, his last day in office, Toms granted an interview to the *New York Times* to review his accomplishments and "wax nostalgic."[10] He was proudest, he said, of the creation of NHTSA as a separate agency. This had given regulators "the independence to deal with Congress and the lobby groups" and was "his most significant achievement on behalf of traffic safety." The knowledgeable reader of the *Times* article would, of course, be puzzled by this claim. The separation from the Federal Highway Administration has been part of the March 1970 reorganization orchestrated by Ribicoff and his congressional allies; it had been planned long before Toms's arrival. The basic organization of the agency had changed very little under his supervision. There was, however, one new box in the organizational chart that represented a genuine innovation: the creation of an Office of Consumer Affairs and Public Information to handle the consumer inquiries that were flooding the agency. NHTSA, under Toms, had taken the first steps toward reconstituting itself as a complaints bureau.

As Toms had repeatedly made clear in testimony to Congress, the lines forming outside his office were growing alarmingly long. There seemed to be no respite from the swarm of angry consumers who demanded NHTSA's help in repairing their broken cars. The market in safety defect letters had turned bullish. In 1970, NHTSA received about five thousand complaints concerning defective automobiles. The following year, the number doubled. The next year, it nearly doubled again. Complaints poured in, not only from individual consumers, but from insurance companies, Congress, consumer groups, other agencies, and NHTSA's own regional offices. It soon became clear that the defects operation itself would have to be expanded if NHTSA were to have any hope of answering its mail.

The defects office had been established within MVP in late 1967 as a tiny division in the larger Office of Compliance, whose principal purpose was to enforce safety standards. Initially, the defects division was staffed by only three professionals. Toms, responding to the flood of incoming mail and complaints from Congress and Nader that recall investigations were taking too long, increased the staff to thirteen engineers and technicians by the end of 1970.

When pressures did not abate, he reassigned additional staff and gave new organizational stature to the recall effort. Effective July 1, 1971, the defects division was removed from the Office of Standards Enforcement and raised to the status of a separate office, the Office of Defects Investigation (ODI), within MVP. It now had a professional staff of twenty-four, about half the combined total of professionals working in the rulemaking offices of operating systems and crashworthiness in MVP.

If rulemaking was a source of internal stress, recalls were an administrator's delight. To a large extent, the investigation of defects simply ran itself. A study by the National Commission on Product Safety called the process "largely passive."[11] Investigations proceeded then, as now, through three basic phases, and at each step, the regulatory burdens on NHTSA were much lighter than in rulemaking. As one administrator later remarked about defects, "there was no lack finding them in my term, I mean, they just came and presented themselves to me."

There was, however, one issue that troubled NHTSA's senior managers as they transferred personnel and funds to ODI in the early 1970s. The agency could not demonstrate any safety benefits from the recall program, and repeatedly told Congress so. Administrator Toms, for example, testified in 1972 that he did not "feel the payoffs [were] high there."[12] Appearing before the House Appropriations Committee later that year, he reiterated: "We have always said that we should do what we can to be sure that the vehicles on the road were safe. We don't want to contribute to a situation where there are defective parts on cars that could injure or kill people. In the actual analysis of different programs, [however,] the whole defect situation of recalling cars does not have the kind of safety payoff that crash survivability of structures has."[13] The administrator's critique was, to say the least, understated. There were many inside NHTSA, especially in MVP, who believed that it would be no great loss to shut down ODI altogether. Robert Lee Carter was foremost among them.

OCC v. MVP

On Friday afternoon, July 12, 1974, Larry Schneider, chief counsel of NHTSA, suffered a fatal heart attack while playing tennis at East Potomac Park. His death was a shock to his colleagues at the agency. Schneider was only thirty-six. He had become an instrumental figure at the agency, especially in the aftermath of the 1974 recall amendments. Schneider had personally lobbied the bill in Congress and was eulogized by Magnuson as a "moving force in legislation to strengthen the auto safety recall provisions." Inside NHTSA, the legal staff had won significant gains in prestige and influence during the three years that Schneider presided as chief counsel. Between 1971 and 1974 OCC had nearly doubled in size, growth justified to Congress in substantial part on the basis of a "phenomenal" increase in litigation.[14] The chief counsel was now the number three administrator—right after the deputy administrator—and second in charge in the chief administrator's absence. In three years, OCC had leapfrogged ahead of every other office in the agency.[15]

Since the principal rationale for expanding OCC had been NHTSA's ever-growing caseload, it was perhaps not surprising that the agency turned to a litigator in selecting Schneider's successor. But the appointment of Frank Berndt was not by any means a foregone conclusion. Berndt had comparatively little experience in the rulemaking side of the enterprise. He had come to NHTSA in 1970, in the heyday of rulemaking, when OCC comprised only seven attorneys—six for rulemaking and one for "enforcement," that is, recalls. Berndt was NHTSA's first recall attorney. At the time of Schneider's death, the enforcement division within OCC was still comparatively small (three attorneys), and the rulemaking group (five attorneys) seemed the more likely group from which to select a replacement.

For Bob Carter, Berndt's appointment as chief counsel was hardly welcome news. There had long been tension between Carter and Berndt concerning the direction, importance, and control of the recall program. Berndt had incessantly pressed Schneider to convince the administrator to tighten OCC control over defect investigations, and it now appeared that Berndt would be in a position to lobby even more aggressively for this goal. For Carter, Berndt was a recall "zealot." Carter was baffled by the view, expressed by others in the agency, that NHTSA needed to build a constituency and that recalls were the best way to do it. In his view, agency involvement in defects was superfluous at best.[16] Berndt, in turn, regarded Carter as a devious autocrat who "wanted to control everything" and did not take the enforcement program "seriously." Berndt believed that Carter was sacrificing recalls to Standard 208, and he was furious that Carter had placed the Office of Defects Investigation under the control of a supervisor, Andrew Detrick ("No Defect Detrick," as he was known in OCC), who "didn't really believe in the program." Berndt believed the engineers and technicians in ODI "didn't know how to investigate cases" and had "pro-industry" leanings.

As the 1970s wore on, the bickering between lawyers and engineers grew steadily worse during the panel meetings that were held to determine whether an "engineering analysis" should proceed to full-fledged investigation. Lawyers felt that engineers in ODI were not sufficiently zealous or competent. Engineers in ODI felt that lawyers did not understand engineering problems. Berndt and his deputies usually wanted to go forward with the investigation. The engineers were more "conservative" and often favored closing the file. If NHTSA had no data establishing that injuries or death had occurred (as was often the case), the engineers reasoned, it made no sense to press for a recall. After all, the statute only provided for recalls if the defect presented an "unreasonable risk" of injury.

The lawyers were contemptuous of this position. The issue, as Berndt saw it, was whether NHTSA could win in court. If so, nothing in the statute required NHTSA to prove that deaths and injuries had actually occurred, and Berndt was determined that the agency should not take upon itself such an onerous burden of proof. The rulemaking cases showed where that would lead. In fact, Berndt refused even to issue a regulatory definition of the term "defect" on the ground that "the relatively broad definition of defect contained in the Safety Act is best suited to the wide variety of objective conditions that may arise."[17] But the 1966 act's definition was little more than a tautology ("defect includes any defect in performance, construction, components, or materials in motor vehicles or motor vehicle equipment"). The agency's refusal to provide a more meaningful standard, therefore, maintained maximum strategic flexibility.

Of course some operational definition was necessary for decision-making purposes. Berndt's discussions with colleagues, including an attorney who formerly had worked at the Antitrust Division of the Justice Department, led him to conclude that, under the statute, essentially any malfunction of a safety-related component (for example, wheels, brakes, lights) could be treated as a defect *per se,* just as certain practices, like price fixing, are anticompetitive under antitrust law even without a showing of actual harm to competitors. If the agency could establish that safety-related components were failing in "disproportionate" numbers, the burden of proof should shift to the manufacturer, Berndt believed, to show that accidents and injury would not result—that is, that the risk was reasonable.

Carter and Berndt were obviously speaking different languages, and neither showed any interest in gaining fluency in the idiom of the other. By late 1973, Carter had grown weary of the feud with Berndt over differences in recall policy. To break the impasse, Carter expressed a willingness to litigate test cases in order to resolve their differences through judicial clarification of the statute. On January 10, 1974, the agency notified General Motors that the steering or "pitman" arms on 1959–1960 Cadillacs constituted a defect. The courts would decide the outcome of the Berndt-Carter dispute, in part because the new administrator had been incapable of doing so.

The Perils of Neutral Leadership

James B. Gregory was administrator during the crucial years of OCC-MVP competition. Beyond driving his own car, Gregory, aged forty-eight, had no identifiable ties with auto safety. He was exceedingly uncomfortable with the feuding among the senior staff, but having little substantive background to guide him, Gregory assumed a defensive position. Rather than resolve the Carter-Manella conflict, he institutionalized it. In 1974, apparently weary of a decision-making process that produced much information but few decisions, he decided to resolve the deadlock by transferring the R&D office to MVP. Associate Administrator Manella promptly threatened to resign, and Gregory dropped the plan. Instead, minor procedural and organizational changes were adopted that required MVP and R&D to "concur" in research plans. The attempt was to force reconciliation within a set timetable and to refer irreconcilable differences to the administrator for resolution. The new procedures produced much referral and little reconciliation. Gregory was left to stew over the conflicting views presented to him on the airbag and a host of other issues.

Meanwhile, up on the tenth floor, the transportation secretary's staff was taking notice. Gregory, of course, had inherited the Carter-Manella problem from Toms, but as 1973 turned into 1974, and 1974 into 1975, the perception grew that NHTSA's internal conflict was a mess of the new administrator's own making. Strike one.

Searching for Acceptance. If indecisiveness under pressure was the problem, Gregory would have done well to refuse Secretary Brinegar's invitation to head the NHTSA. Gregory arrived at the Department of Transportation just as the first 1974 models equipped with an ignition interlock were rolling off the production line (September 1973), and his term in office, running through February 1976, was destined to embrace the Arab oil embargo (October 1973), the peaking of small car sales (1974–1976), President Nixon's resignation (August 1974), and the passage of the 1974 amendments (October 1974). To make matters worse, the new administrator had managed to arrive just as pressure was mounting on NHTSA to come to terms, finally, with its two most ambitious technology-forcing projects: the airbag (Standard 208) and the air brake (Standard 121). Caught between warring senior advisors and buffeted on all sides by conflicting demands of auto manufacturers, consumer groups, their respective allies in Congress, and others, Gregory groped for a course that would find "public acceptance." But this quest for "public acceptability" sent Gregory down a lonely, treacherous path that led, ultimately, to his resignation.

Standard 208. Many of the technical uncertainties surrounding the airbag were resolved well before or during the early part of Gregory's term in office. In the months following *Chrysler,* NHTSA and its contractors watched attentively as a series of vehicles occupied by baboons, cadavers, and instrumented manikins smashed into fixed barriers at various speeds. These tests made it reasonably clear that the technical objections most frequently voiced against the airbag—danger to out-of-position occupants, inadvertent actuation, toxicity of the propellent, and the like—did not pose a serious concern. Most observers agreed. The airbag worked.

The focus shifted to cost. The agency's own figures at the time indicated that full front protection from airbags would save $4.4 billion in annual auto accident expenditures, and that benefits could exceed costs by more than 2 to 1. But Gregory was leery. The manufacturers, of course, had produced quite different cost-benefit figures. More important, the mail from angry interlock customers had poured into NHTSA during Gregory's first days in office and convinced him, as he later said, that there was something uniquely "personal" about auto safety regulation. Would "rational" consumers be willing to pay the incremental cost of full airbag protection?

Gregory wasn't sure. Although the airbag controversy had been thoroughly aired in the press and seemed to have aroused much interest, the absence of support from individual consumers made him edgy, he reported. In testimony to Congress in 1976 Gregory remarked that he had "not yet received one letter that I can think of, from an individual citizen who thinks much of the airbag." Remembering the interlock, he was concerned. "Many good ideas, if not thoroughly looked at, and thoroughly planned, can be shot down through lack of public acceptance," he later said. "This public involvement and acceptance, is something that we must keep in mind during the preparation for new programs, or we will not succeed."[18]

To gauge public sentiment on the airbag and break the deadlock inside NHTSA, Gregory convened a public hearing on May 23, 1975. He had promised to issue a final rule that year, and the large turnout reflected the participants' concern that this might be their last opportunity to influence the outcome. Nearly three hundred people milled about the hearing room. Some fifty speakers, representing the automotive industry, insurance companies, equipment suppliers, consumer groups, and public and political sectors rose to express their views—views that staked out every conceivable position on the issue.

The contradictory testimony at the May hearing did not provide a way out of the impasse inside NHTSA, and Gregory soon despaired of finding a consensus outside. "In regulating an area such as ours," he later said, "there is no 51% majority. As a matter of fact, if I get 12½%, I consider it a landslide."[19] He would have to choose between the factions. As one agency insider later described it, an "anguished" Gregory accordingly closeted himself in his office to fashion a recommendation to the transportation secretary.[20]

There was reason to be apprehensive. Not only was the long-awaited (indeed, overdue) decision almost certain to stir controversy, but the recipient of the action memorandum would be, not Gregory's personal friend, Brinegar, but a recent arrival, William T. Coleman. Coleman, a fifty-four-year-old Philadelphia lawyer, longtime Republican party regular and civil rights activist, was a Harvard-trained lawyer with recognized expertise in transportation law. For Gregory, Coleman was another unknown factor in the Standard 208 equation.

Gregory's action memorandum reflected his uncertainty. He urged that the agency simultaneously issue two NPRMs. The first would propose a traffic safety standard requiring the states to take whatever measures were necessary—for example, mandatory seat-belt use laws (MULs)—to bring seat-belt usage to 75 percent by January 1, 1980. The second notice would propose an amendment to Standard 208 to require driver passive restraints by September 1, 1979, and full front passive protection two years later. Time was of the essence, Gregory argued. The notices should be issued no later than May 1976.

The reason for two recommendations was strategic. Either proposal might run into a political buzz saw, and both proposals would have to undergo congressional review pursuant to the 1974 amendments. In Gregory's view this was the beauty of his proposals; Congress would resolve the enigma of public acceptance.[21] In effect, he urged Secretary Coleman to force *Congress* to decide what the public really wanted.

Coleman and his senior advisors were not impressed. Some twenty state legislatures had considered but failed to pass mandatory seat-belt use legislation, and a proposal was pending in Congress to rescind NHTSA's authority to impose sanctions on states that failed to observe the agency's traffic safety standard on motorcycle helmets. Would Congress behave any differently if NHTSA tried to force reluctant states to pass MULs? Moreover, there was concern that the general public would be enraged by mandatory passive restraints. Reflecting these concerns, the assistant secretary for systems development and technology, in a memorandum to Secretary Coleman dated February 26, urged strong opposition to any passive restraint requirement "at this time."[22] Strike two.

Standard 121. Gregory found the public's attitude toward Standard 121, the large-truck braking standard, equally baffling. He reported, "despite editorials fairly late in the game, I could feel practically no interest" in the matter.[23] Yet the purposes of Standard 121 seemed to justify strong popular support. Air brakes were not designed to protect motorists from their *own* folly, after all, but from the folly of others. But lack of public support was to be the least of Standard 121's troubles.

When issued in supposedly "final" form, on February 19, 1971, the rule set forth various performance characteristics of braking systems for trucks, buses, and trailers, including stopping distances at specified speeds on wet and dry surfaces (for example, 245 feet at 60 miles per hour on a dry surface) and the requirement that vehicles stop within a lane 12 feet wide without locking any wheel except momentarily. The effective date was January 1, 1973.

Many aspects of the rule elicited the opposition of regulated industries, but the most vociferous objections were raised against the standard's controversial antilock requirement. The standard contemplated (but did not require) the use of state-of-the-art electronic computer modules that would sense impending wheel lock-up and automatically adjust air pressure in the brake chamber to maintain the wheels' rolling action. Petitions for reconsideration were received from eleven vehicle manufacturers, ten brake component suppliers, and six operator groups. The most common complaint was that the effective date could not be met, largely because more time was needed to develop and test antilock devices.

These and other complaints precipitated a seemingly endless cycle of revisions, new petitions for reconsideration, and new revisions. In 1974, for example, a year after the rule was supposed to have been in effect, the agency issued an average of one rulemaking notice on Standard 121 every two weeks. In turn, it received scores of requests for reconsideration. Between 1972 and 1975 the agency revised virtually every aspect of the standard.[24]

The flurry of notices, amendments, petitions, renotices, and further amendments created a climate of confusion that only strengthened the hand of those opposing Standard 121. The process seemed endless, and endlessly indecisive. The agency continued to revise the rule even after issuing another "final" rule, denying petitions to reopen the proceedings, and being sued by the Paccar Corporation. This pattern of activity created the impression that NHTSA was engaged in rulemaking by trial and error. On the tenth floor, it was thought that the unfolding debacle reflected poorly on the entire department.

For Gregory, Standard 121 was strike three. On February 26, 1976, President Ford publicly released his letter accepting Gregory's resignation "with sincere regret." Gregory had privately submitted his notice a few days earlier, and although some opponents of Standard 121 were said to be spreading rumors of his impending resignation, most observers inside NHTSA and elsewhere greeted the decision with surprise. Gregory categorically denied that he had been asked to resign or had been fired. "You get up one morning and you're worn out," Gregory told a *New York Times* reporter, "You think maybe it's time to lay this career to rest."[25]

Finding Acceptance. In his valedictory address to the House Subcommittee on Oversight and Investigations on March 1, Gregory indicated that he had been able to find "public acceptance" in only one of NHTSA's endeavors. Public participation in defect proceedings was "excellent." The bull market in consumer complaints had continued without interruption. In October 1975, NHTSA established a toll-free hotline on an experimental basis in ten East Coast states to disseminate information on defect investigations and to gather complaints. As one NHTSA observer later remarked, it was relatively easy to "set up a consumer hotline and have consumers do your work."[26]

Meanwhile, the agency continued to tell Congress in budget submissions that the influence of recalls on vehicle safety had "not been established."[27] A study on recall campaigns by NHTSA's own Advisory Council in 1976 concluded that: "The question naturally arises—do the safety benefits of the program justify its cost? Curiously, no one knows. Indeed, the scarcity of hard facts and the abundance of unknown factors make any definitive evaluation of the defect-recall program very difficult."[28] NHTSA nonetheless continued to press forward with the recall program. In fiscal year 1976, plans to allocate sixteen new personnel to the recall effort were announced. The staff for this purpose would be taken from the rulemaking office, specifically, the Office of Crashworthiness.[29] Carter's grip was weakening.

MVP v. P&P: or, Congress v. the President

Coleman and his staff looked upon the disarray in NHTSA with a sense of disgust. One senior Transportation Department official during this period complained contemptuously, "They [NHTSA] were formed from the dregs of the auto industry, but they still claim to be independent experts in their field and they don't have to be cost effective. The problem is that they don't have any checks and balances down there and as a result everything they do becomes a *cause célèbre*."[30] Coleman and his inner circle concluded that NHTSA would have to be placed under tighter, more direct control if any semblance of order was to be imposed on the rulemaking process. Gregory's departure presented an ideal opportunity for establishing the desired checks and balances.

In these circumstances, Coleman did not look far for a replacement. On April 21, 1976, the press reported his selection of John W. Snow, the department's deputy undersecretary, to succeed Gregory.[31] Snow, thirty-seven, held a Ph.D. in economics from the University of Virginia and a J.D. from George Washington University. An expert in economic regulation of the railroad, aviation, and motor carrier industries, he had joined the department as deputy assistant general counsel in 1972. By May 1, 1975, Snow had risen to the position of deputy undersecretary, and in that capacity he oversaw the department's "regulatory reform" program.

Snow had only modest experience in safety regulation. His substantive involvement in automobile safety regulation had been confined largely to intermittent involvement as congressional liaison in a handful of high-visibility issues, such as passive restraints and the ignition interlock. Snow's background, nevertheless, suggested a definite point of view concerning regulation. He taught cost-benefit analysis as a part-time lecturer on the economics faculty of the University of Maryland and represented the Department of Transportation on the Domestic Council's Regulatory Review Group, the interagency task force established by President Ford to coordinate regulatory reform.

Safety partisans were appalled by Snow's appointment and bore down hard on his "regulatory philosophy" at the nomination hearings held before the Senate Commerce Committee on June 26, 1976. Much of the debate focused on Snow's commitment to free-market economics and to the appropriate use of cost-benefit analysis in the formulation of auto safety rules. Congress, of course, had repeatedly refused to enact legislation requiring NHTSA to justify its auto safety rules on the basis of cost-benefit comparisons.

From 1974 forward, however, pressures, emanating largely from within the executive branch, mounted steadily on NHTSA to rationalize its standards precisely on those grounds. On November 27, 1974, President Ford signed Executive Order 11,821, which directed all executive branch departments to prepare inflationary impact statements for major rulemaking proposals.[32] The order was implemented by Office of Management and Budget Circular A–107, dated January 28, 1975, which directed each agency to develop procedures for evaluating rules in terms of quantified costs and benefits where possible.

These orders were followed in turn by three "regulatory reform" policies issued by Secretary Coleman on April 13, 1976.[33] The first required an assessment of costs, benefits, and other effects of all Transportation Department rulemaking actions prior to issuance in either proposed or final form. The second policy required agencies within the department to notify the secretary thirty days before the proposed publication of any costly or controversial regulation. The third policy described the department's recently implemented program of evaluating regulations already in effect to determine actual costs and benefits.

Without more, Carter and his staff inside NHTSA might simply have ignored this blizzard of exhortatory paperwork. That was certainly their inclination. As Carter breezily admitted, as late as February 1976, NHTSA used cost-benefit analysis in only a "limited way."[34] The tiny cost and lead time staff in MVP (six people in 1975) reflected the relatively low priority that MVP engineers attached to the effort. But in practical terms, Carter's nonchalance was becoming increasingly difficult to maintain. A new entity, statutorily created, had begun to appear on a regular basis in the agency's rulemaking proceedings—the President's Council on Wage and Price Stability. From the moment of its first appearance at the agency, COWPS had been raising hell over NHTSA's treatment of costs and benefits in rulemaking.[35]

Following the promulgation of Executive Order 11,821, the council had almost immediately identified NHTSA's standards on the airbag and the air brake as priority proceedings in which to intervene. It filed comments that were highly critical of NHTSA's proposals. Similar submissions were filed on proposed amendments to Standard 105 on hydraulic brakes (February 11, 1975), proposed cost-information reporting requirements (November 26, 1975), and the Uniform Tire Quality Grading Standard (June 9, 1975).

The Council's sudden appearance in rulemaking proceedings startled the senior staff inside NHTSA. MVP's cost and lead time branch was no match for the council at cost-benefit analysis, and as the President's personal representative, council submissions were hard even for Carter to ignore. Agency officials, in testimony before Congress in 1976, left the clear impression that they were inclined to "defer" to the council on matters of economic analysis. Indeed, under the *Auto Parts* decision NHTSA was required to make a reasoned, thorough response to the detailed cost-benefit critiques being offered by the council's staff. Through the interaction of executive branch commentary and proceduralized judicial review, NHTSA was being forced to adopt a cost-benefit methodology in setting standards, no matter what the 1966 act said.

The agency's stalwart allies in Congress, especially on the oversight committees, were outraged that the council could control NHTSA's rulemaking operations in this manner. But they were also ineffective. Senator Hartke, for example, doggedly pursued the issue at Snow's nomination hearing. Hartke's particular grievance was not so much the council's insinuation of cost-benefit considerations into rulemaking at NHTSA as the administrator-designate's own predilections in this respect. Hartke mounted a frontal attack on Snow's prehearing statement that "we should rely on marketplace incentives to the extent possible." The nominee, however, was both unapologetic and unyielding.

Snow presumably was aware of the difficulty Gregory had encountered only weeks before in hearings before Representative Moss's subcommittee. Resting the legitimacy of cost-benefit methodology at NHTSA on Executive Order 11,811, Gregory had been lectured by Moss about the precedence of congressional statutes over executive orders.[36] Adroitly skirting around those shoals, Snow made no mention of executive orders, Coleman's new regulatory policies, or the Council on Wage and Price Stability. The use of cost-benefit comparisons was a *judicially* imposed requirement, Snow explained. It derived from the courts' interpretation of the requirement of the 1966 act that standards be "reasonable" and "practicable." Snow elaborated:

> I think those words "reasonable" and "practicable" carry with them the connotation that the Administrator is to carefully analyze the alternatives available to him to advance the safety objective. In that analysis, looking at the benefits and looking at the costs, seem to me entirely appropriate.
>
> In fact, as I read, I think it is the *H & H Tire* case in DOT, and I have been reading a lot of cases—it is a brand new field for me—as I read the *H & H Tire* case, the *H & H Tire* case says that it is appropriate to use cost-benefit analysis to help inform the decision. And the failure to take into account effects of the standard on industry, the cost of the standard, can fatally—fatally affect the judicial review of the standards.[37]

Hartke's interrogation of Snow soon sputtered to an end.

Snow's appointment proved unstoppable. For safety partisans in Congress and elsewhere, however, there was nonetheless a silver lining in the cloud created by Snow's confirmation as administrator on July 2, 1976. Only three months remained before the presidential election, and it seemed clear from public opinion polls that Gerald Ford's administration was in trouble. With any luck, the safety partisans thought, Snow's tenure as administrator might be merely a momentary lapse before the arrival of reinforcements to reaffirm their conception of the original legislation.

Snow had other ideas. As he scanned the regulatory landscape, his gaze fell upon Order 800–1. The agency's proceedings on airbags and air brakes, he believed, were hardly a model of efficient administrative action. That being the case, there must be something wrong with the rulemaking process itself. By overhauling NHTSA's internal procedures for preparing rulemaking actions, Snow concluded, he could influence not only pending rulemaking actions but, perhaps, future policy as well. To help in revising Order 800–1, Snow turned to Michael Finkelstein and Frank Berndt.

Various senior staff meetings were held to consider alternative approaches. Over a winter weekend, Berndt, Finkelstein, and Snow hammered out the final revisions to Order 800–1, which were formally issued on February 2, 1977.[38] The revised order had one overriding purpose, Finkelstein later reported, and that was to free the administrator from the "captivity" of MVP.[39]

The revised order encompassed two complementary sets of reforms. The first was organizational and redefined the role of engineers in relation to the role of program analysts and attorneys. The second set of reforms was methodological and emphasized the importance of cost-benefit considerations in setting standards. Together, the reforms constituted an entirely new way of thinking about and conducting rulemaking at NHTSA.

The revised order abolished MVP's supremacy in the standard-setting process. The "evaluation panel," which MVP had dominated under the terms of the original order, was eliminated. The revised order substituted in its stead a seventeen-step "flowchart procedure" in which rulemaking responsibilities were widely dispersed among engineers in MVP, policy and cost-benefit analysis in P & P, and attorneys in OCC.

More important, under the new order, engineers could only seek, not force, consensus on a proposed rule. Whereas the original order had empowered MVP unilaterally to resolve differences with other offices, the revised order required that disputes be referred to the administrator for resolution, and explicitly stated that "unless a delegation is granted in a specific area, the Administrator is responsible for establishing, amending, or revoking vehicle safety and fuel economy standard."

In a memorandum accompanying the revised order,[40] Snow made clear that program analysts in P & P and attorneys in OCC, especially the former, were expected to exercise independent judgment and to interrogate rulemaking engineers closely concerning the rationale for their proposals. The rulemaking process was conceived as intensely reiterative. The revised order envisioned that MVP would revise rulemaking support proposals in response to comments from P & P and OCC, and that amended proposals would be subject to further review and comment. The revised order thus internalized a painstaking process of notice and comment, renotice and recomment rulemaking, simply to formulate *proposals*, whose publication in the Federal Register would commence a similar proceeding involving parties outside NHTSA.

Carter was enraged by the new procedures. He was especially incensed by the requirement for OCC concurrence on rulemaking support papers. Berndt would not sign off on rulemaking proposals until he was convinced, Carter later reported, that the supporting data were invulnerable to court challenge. Because it was impossible to eliminate the risk of losing in court, he observed, the revised order amounted to a pact not to issue rules.[41]

The Illusion of 1966

On February 13, 1977—less than two weeks after the issuance of the revised order 800–1—the new secretary of transportation, Brock Adams, announced that Joan Claybrook was President Carter's choice to head the NHTSA. The contrast between Claybrook and Snow was stark. Claybrook's credentials as a safety partisan were impressive. She was an ardent proponent of the airbag, and her experience in auto safety regulation was virtually unique. As noted earlier, Claybrook had been present at the legislation's creation, and she later served as a special assistant to Haddon. She was a close associate of Nader's, and in her subsequent position as president of Congress Watch had continued to press for auto safety programs. Few persons were more knowledgeable or experienced in auto safety regulation or apparently more committed to the revolution of 1966.

At times, Claybrook's testimony in her confirmation hearings looked like a direct refutation of Snow's fundamental commitments. She emphasized, for example, that cost-benefit analysis was a very "imperfect" rulemaking tool, in part because benefits could not be fully measured and in part because its analytic methodology did not adequately take account of distributive effects. Claybrook also claimed that cost-benefit analysis was deficient because it was "linear, not internodal," meaning that "it balances costs of a safety improvement against its benefits, not against costly, frivolous items with little or no value." Although the language was different, the sentiments were those of Abraham Ribicoff in 1966.[42]

Claybrook also challenged Snow's reading of the case law. Cost-benefit analysis was not a statutory requirement, Claybrook told Congress. A standard that cost more than the benefits it generated was lawful, she reasoned, even if issued without any analysis. In *H & H Tire*, she explained, "The court did not state that benefits of greater than unity must be shown to demonstrate 'economic practicability.'" She also pointed out that the Sixth Circuit in *Chrysler* had specifically, in a footnote, found that Congress did not require that the benefits of safety rules exceed their costs.[43] There were also passages that seemed to preview a return to the heyday of MVP. Although defect modifications and recalls were "very important," Claybrook testified, they were "not as fundamental" as the promulgation and enforcement of standards. Bob Carter, rejoice!

Now it was industry's turn to be horrified. S. L. Terry, vice president for consumer affairs at Chrysler described the prospect of Claybrook's appointment as "appalling." "She has always been against the industry," he said in comments to the press. "It certainly does not seem to be an even handed appointment. I would not expect that the Department of Transportation would appoint an industry executive, but likewise, I also wouldn't expect the appointment of an industry critic or a Nader supporter."[44]

A Power Lunch

In January of 1977 Claybrook's nomination had not yet been formally announced, but she was already making plans to take command of NHTSA. Claybrook had a number of topics on her mind when she invited Frank Berndt to lunch at a restaurant on Capitol Hill. They included, among others, the internal divisions among the agency's staff that the GAO had chronicled in 1974. Claybrook knew that the conflict persisted. As the conversation wore on, she posed a question that Berndt had been dwelling on for years. What should be done with Robert Lee Carter?

Claybrook valued Berndt's advice, as her luncheon invitation implied. Both were lawyers and, to a significant extent, both spoke the same language. They viewed regulation in win-lose terms and expected to be involved in heated contests with the industry. But there were important differences between Claybrook and Berndt, as well. He was a litigator, she was not. Claybrook's experience was almost entirely legislative, and on matters affecting litigation she showed the tendency of many "office lawyers" to defer to the litigator's judgment and instincts. Berndt's skill in court, moreover, had produced tangible results. The recall program was an unqualified legal success. NHTSA was winning every recall decision the courts were handing down, and the *per se* theory had given NHTSA, meaning Claybrook, great leverage in dealing with the manufacturers. NHTSA was now able to impose significant costs and reputational damage on recalcitrant manufacturers without a corresponding expenditure of scarce agency resources. "I have placed a powerful weapon in the Administrator's hands," Berndt later remarked, "and she's not afraid to use it."

As Claybrook knew, Berndt's success on recalls had come without much support from Bob Carter. She reportedly believed that MVP had a disastrous record running the Office of Defects Investigation. In addition, Carter had made a mess of things on the rulemaking side of the house. The principal catastrophes—the *Chrysler* decision, the Standard 121 debacle, and the interlock episode—had occurred on Carter's watch. All were strategically debilitating and politically embarrassing, as Claybrook well understood. The agency simply could not afford similar reversals in the future.

When Claybrook asked about Carter, Berndt had a ready answer. The Office of Motor Vehicle Programs had acquired too much power under Carter, Berndt replied. MVP should therefore be dismantled. Enforcement activities, in particular the recall program, should be organized as a separate unit equal in stature with the rulemaking program, but reporting to different management. Rulemaking should also be more effectively supervised and focused. A corollary principle followed, either explicitly or by implication. The checks and balances embedded in the revised Order 800–1 should be retained, whatever Claybrook's views on the propriety of cost-benefit analysis.

No immediate action was taken on Berndt's grand design, but within weeks of her arrival, Claybrook moved to adopt measures that enhanced OCC's control over the recall program. A special task force, composed wholly of lawyers, was established to clear out pending cases. Berndt was placed in charge. Results quickly followed. Over ten million vehicles were recalled in 1977, up from three million the year before. In 1978, the number climbed to over twelve million vehicles. More vehicles were being called back for repair than were coming off the production line.

Tensions between Claybrook and Carter quickly arose and mounted steadily. There was, one senior agency official later noted, "negative personal chemistry" between them. Both were strong personalities and clashes were inevitable. Carter obviously did not share Claybrook's enthusiasm for confrontation by recall. On one occasion, for example, he discreetly negotiated a settlement with a manufacturer over a suspected defect. The manufacturer agreed to fix the problem promptly, provided it was outside the glare of a high-visibility recall campaign. Claybrook was enraged over the deal that Carter had cut, and "chewed him up one side and down the other."[45] Claybrook was keeping score with the industry over recalls. Carter had forfeited agency points.

Claybrook, moreover, was her own associate administrator for rule-making. She worked long hours, enjoyed the detail of close work, and was inclined not to delegate major decisions to Carter. Besides, the decision-making forum for the agency's most important initiatives— Standards 208 and 121—had by now largely shifted to Congress and the courts. The former legislative aide and director of Nader's congressional project did not need Carter's help to find her way around on the Hill. And Carter's connections with safety constituencies outside the agency— which had so impressed Manella—were no match for Claybrook's long-standing ties. As spring turned to summer, Carter grew even more frustrated by Claybrook's domination of programs. She ran the agency more like a project officer than an administrator, he believed.

In the early winter of 1977, Claybrook decided to act on Berndt's proposal. Her reorganization of NHTSA took effect January 1, 1978, less than a year after their luncheon conversation.[46] Its purpose, Claybrook announced, was to "simplify the agency's structure and to improve the quality of its decisionmaking process." In fact, however, the new organizational chart was in some respects more complex than before. The principal feature of the reorganization, as Berndt advocated, was the separation of standard-setting authority from enforcement and investigative authority. MVP was abolished. Two new staffs were established in its place: one reporting to an associate administrator for rulemaking, the other to an associate administrator for enforcement. This set the stage for personnel shifts that told the story of revised priorities at NHTSA in unmistakable terms. In March 1978, Michael M. Finkelstein, Snow's former right-hand man and chief cost-benefit analyst, was named associate administrator for rulemaking. His deputy, Barry Felrice, an alumnus of the Federal Highway Administration, took charge of P&P. Berndt became associate administrator for enforcement. (After setting up this new unit, he returned to his post as chief counsel.) Carter was named director of the agency's test facility in East Liberty, Ohio. James Hofferberth, Carter's principal rulemaking assistant, and Andrew Detrick, head of ODI, accompanied Carter to NHTSA's version of Siberia.

The New Religion

These changes hardly stilled the discontented voices within NHTSA. It was, after all, two years after the Claybrook reorganization was implemented that Finklestein issued his "Why I Am Losing My Hair" ultimatum to the rulemaking staff. The new associate administrator hoped that his memorandum would root out two misconceptions that, he believed, were at the heart of his staff's resentment against P&P and OCC. The first concerned the long-awaited progeny of the October Plan, the Rulemaking Plan that Claybrook had issued with great fanfare in 1978 and that identified NHTSA's rulemaking priorities. The second misconception dealt with Claybrook herself.

Finkelstein called the misconceptions "the two principal myths in NHTSA" that arose every time OCC and P&P delayed a rulemaking action in order to obtain more information. Finkelstein described the myths as follows:

"Myth I"
"It is in the RULEMAKING PLAN: (capitalizing denotes an item demanding special reverence)."

"Myth II"
"JOAN wants it (see note above)."

Among the rulemaking staff, Finkelstein observed, "it is believed that the invocation of either myth should be sufficient to terminate the thought processes in P&P and OCC."

Finkelstein proceeded to dethrone these false idols. The rulemaking process, he noted, was "a rigorous search" for "the best approach to ameliorate a problem." In preparing rules, it was important to consider as many sources of information and perspectives as possible. A regulation might be warranted, but then again, it might not, depending on the results of the analysis and the reiterative effort to revalidate assumptions. "It is the RULEMAKING PROCESS that determines whether a regulation will be issued, not the fact that it is included in the rulemaking plan." Finkelstein's memorandum chided the engineers that they should be "overjoyed" if the lawyers or analysts found reasons to kill a rule, thus sparing the engineers a "never-ending" stream of petitions by regulated parties.

The second myth was even more curtly dismissed. Claybrook's exhortations should not be misinterpreted, Finkelstein cautioned. To be sure, the administrator wanted rulemaking completed "as quickly as possible," but she also wanted "the most intelligent course of action followed." Finkelstein elaborated: "I want to emphasize as strongly as I can that the rulemaking process is not a rubber stamp procedure designed to get out regulations that have been divined by Claybrook, Finkelstein, or anyone else. It is intended to produce reasonable solutions to real problems as a result of the work of a large number of professionals thinking creatively." Agency rulemaking was governed by the Order 800–1, not by the personalities of individual officials. Myths I and II accordingly were "forbidden as heresies."

By the time of the issuance of Finkelstein's memorandum, February 1980, it was clear that the new religion of auto safety was not producing a flood of important new rules. The first two years of Claybrook's administration were devoted largely to Standard 208 and to the promulgation of fuel economy rules, a task that Claybrook's deputy later characterized as "terribly diverting."[47] When Claybrook sought to press forward on other proposals in the second half of her term, she learned about the difficulties of assigning an offensive mission to a defensive team. The checks and balances of the rulemaking process, coupled with the agency's responsibility to consider the impact of its rules on the economy, the environment, small businesses, and urban communities, made it impossible to prepare and issue rules expeditiously.

It was not until the very end of her administration that Claybrook was able to issue in final form many of the proposals that had been pending since her arrival. But by then, times had changed again. The new leadership at NHTSA, appointed by the Reagan Administration, simply revoked Claybrook's eleventh-hour rules before they could take effect. Many pending proposals were similarly dropped.[48]

These difficulties had, of course, not beset the recall program. The P&P office occasionally urged that recalls be subjected to cost-benefit analysis, but that proposal made little headway during either Claybrook's administration or thereafter. Berndt brushed aside the proposal as unworthy of serious consideration. Economists simply never understood the law, he later explained.[49]

The Interaction of Legal and Bureaucratic Culture

Berndt's comment about understanding the law is a fitting, if ironic, epitaph for NHTSA's rulemaking efforts in the 1970s. Over the course of that decade the law steadily reshaped the agency's internal organization and procedures. Compliance with "proceduralized" judicial review for rationality, combined with the demands of executive orders from three presidents, pressed NHTSA relentlessly toward a defensive, checks-and-balances internal structure for proposing and acting on its rulemaking initiatives. The agency, as a matter of formal internal procedure, began to litigate with itself. Losses in court stymied, embarrassed, and ultimately delegitimated the efforts of the principal proponents of aggressive rulemaking. Meanwhile, enforcement burdens were progressively relaxed, and the external legal successes of the enforcement personnel, particularly Frank Berndt and the OCC staff, lifted them to successively higher plateaus of power within the agency.

If the redeployment of personnel from rulemaking to enforcement, the restructuring of lines of authority in favor of the recall effort, and increased procedural complexity that emphasized the cautionary propensity of lawyers and economists were the hallmarks of internal development at NHTSA in the 1970s, those developments were also undeniably shaped by other factors, in addition to the external legal culture. Public demand for recalls provided the moving force for the recall effort. Professional biases, bureaucratic ambitions, fiscal constraints, personality conflicts, and simple chance were also at work in shaping the agency's structure, processes, and behavior.

Yet we are struck by the degree to which the legitimation or delegitimation of NHTSA's efforts by the judiciary channeled the currents and cross-currents set up by other influences into a stream of ideas, arguments, and, ultimately, internal processes and personnel decisions that shifted NHTSA away from the vision of 1966. Robert Carter, after all, was nobody's patsy. By all accounts he was technically well qualified, a tough competitor in the bureaucratic trenches, and sufficiently politically astute to build a solid network of external supporters. His staff of safety engineers was committed to the rulemaking effort. Had the courts ratified Carter's efforts in *Chrysler* and in other crucial decisions of the early 1970s, while demanding that recalls be justified by demonstrable effects on safety, Joan Claybrook might well have had her January 1977 strategy lunch with Carter rather than with Berndt.

Or, to take another example, John Snow and William Coleman were committed to implementing Nixon-Ford policies concerning thorough assessment of the economic impact of regulations. But the engineering staff and the relevant congressional committees clearly were not. Moreover, in 1977 NHTSA got an administrator who had ill-disguised contempt for cost-benefit analysis. The effective establishment and retention of procedures to analyze NHTSA's rulemaking proposals ad infinitum in terms of their economic costs, benefits, and alternatives is explicable only as a defensive posture made necessary by the ultimate requirement of explaining to reviewing courts why the cost-benefit criticisms of COWPS, manufacturers, or others did not undermine the reasonableness or practicability of the motor vehicle standards adopted.

Much that was going on inside NHTSA in the 1970s was unrelated to the preoccupations of the American legal culture. The NHTSA that survived to enter the new decade, nevertheless, was powerfully shaped by the demands and the differential supports of the law.

TEN

Regulation for an Ambivalent Polity

How should motor vehicle safety regulation be explained? From the perspective of over two decades of experience under the Motor Vehicle Safety Act of 1966, both the private and the public interest explanations of regulation portrayed in Chapter 1 seem incomplete, if not naive. The private interest hypothesis encounters immediate and obvious difficulties. After all, according to interest group theory, the 1966 legislation should not have appeared on the legislative agenda, much less passed without a dissenting vote. From what has been said the public interest has hardly been served by NHTSA's switch from rules to recalls either—at least if the public interest is equated with the public safety purposes of the 1966 act. Yet further brief attention to these explanatory traditions is necessary to appreciate more precisely both where they are likely to mislead and how a focus on the constraints of the legal culture acts as a corrective.

The Private Interest Story. After 1966 the automobile manufacturers fought the agency relentlessly, but they hardly took it prisoner. The full-court press limited NHTSA's regulatory output, but the recall program flourished. Prior to the Reagan Administration, at least, there was no love lost between NHTSA and the auto industry. The Nixon Administration intervened to give the manufacturers a low-cost alternative, the interlock, in an early iteration of the passive restraints rule. But this was an example of an industry begging for relief from an agency that was anything but servile. Moreover, in this instance and elsewhere, the manufacturers' interests have not been unitary. Rules that impose costs on everyone still do not impose the same costs across the board. Those with a cost advantage tend to favor the regulation.

Nor, the Oval Office meeting aside, have we been telling a story of privileged access by a regulated group with little or no opposition from other interests. The regulatory space that auto manufacturers inhabit is also occupied by another heavyweight, the casualty insurance industry. When the Reagan Administration rescinded the passive restraints rule that had finally been adopted, the insurers went all the way to the Supreme Court to get it reinstated. When one adds to this competitive, regulatory process both the continuous presence of established safety and consumer groups and the participation of disparate, but reasonably well organized, interests like the components manufacturers, the physicians' and trial lawyers' associations and others, external capture by regulated interests could not possibly provide a cogent or complete explanation for NHTSA's quiet shift to recalls.

The friendly relations and regulatory relief provided by the Reagan Administration certainly produced effects that look something like industry capture. Remember, however, that the agency's regulatory pattern was established well before 1981. The political history of the 1980s, moreover, reveals a dynamic quite unlike the usual private interest model. The Reagan Administration's stance with respect to automobile safety regulation was not a product of low-level, interest group politics. The Reagan regulatory relief program sprang from an ideological commitment to reducing the federal government's presence. In other words, it was a commitment premised on a particular vision of the *public* interest. Far from the usual "special interest deal" scenario, the administration's position was fully disclosed, indeed marketed with patriotic zeal, in the election campaign of 1980. The promise of regulatory relief to increase the competitiveness of American industry, and of the automobile industry in particular, was fully presented to, and perhaps ratified by, the voters.

The story inside NHTSA has had a somewhat more characteristic flavor of capture. The lawyers and economists do seem to win out over the safety engineers. The problem with viewing the story as one of capture by private interests is that it is far from obvious how any professional or underlying economic interest of the participants is being served. One might hypothesize that lawyers like litigation and trial experience, but it is hard to see how the shift from rules to recalls gets them more court exposure than the reverse would provide. Nor is this an agency like the Federal Trade Commission, whose trial lawyers have a large number of alternatives in private firms and trade associations on the basis of their experience at the FTC. Motor vehicle safety regulation is a legal backwater. Virtually any government experience is marketable somewhere, but the lawyer who believed that working for NHTSA was the way to open up a broad range of employment prospects in private practice would be highly unrealistic.

The economists who do the cost-benefit analyses for the agency are surely behaving like economists. But again it is hard to see exactly how they get ahead in the profession by eliminating rules. There might be some publication opportunities for economists who came up with novel theories for measuring either costs or benefits in the context of motor vehicle safety regulation. But to the extent that the agency goes out of the rulemaking business, the opportunities for staff economists to generate new theories, or even to hone their basic skills, are reduced rather than expanded. The economists, after all, are completely closed out of the recall program.

The behavior of the lawyers and economists is much more explicable when viewed as conforming to the roles thrust upon them by the broader institutional and legal culture. Both have internal influence that is reinforced or diminished by the contribution they make to maintaining the agency's institutional position. The lawyers played out their counseling role in the usual fashion. They interpreted the external legal culture to the internal culture of the agency. Their message was straightforward: if you want to be successful legally, pursue the recall strategy.

Similarly, every president since Nixon has had something to say about the desirability of careful economic analysis of federal regulation. And the regulatory analysis that came into vogue in the Carter and Reagan administrations was the executive analogue of the rationality requirement imposed by the courts. The external legal environment thus gave the economists an important role to play. That they benefited by gaining an enhanced status within the agency hardly indicates that they had somehow "captured" the agency in pursuit of their own underlying economic interests.

Nor does the post-1966 legislative politics of auto safety regulation conform to the standard interest group paradigm. From that perspective, we should have seen over time the development of an "iron triangle" of legislative subcommittees, regulated interests, and NHTSA that controlled legislation and appropriations in the interests of particular legislators on the jurisdictionally relevant committees, the agency, and the manufacturers. This is surely not the politics of 1966 or 1974. Nor do we find the iron triangle much in evidence in periods that had no substantive legislation on the congressional agenda.

To be sure, representatives and senators who have a higher than normal commitment either to auto safety or to the protection of the automobile industry are key participants in congressional hearings. But neither group seems to be getting what it wants from the agency or, for that matter, from the rest of the Congress. Meanwhile, the other two sides of the "triangle" have regularly taken their legislative lumps. The agency has been berated continuously for regulatory laxity, but simultaneously starved for funds. And the motor vehicle manufacturers' reputation with Congress seems never to have recovered completely from the debacle of 1966. We cannot eliminate the possibility that there is a lot of "chumminess" that the public record and our interviews have not revealed. But, if so, the effects on public policy are also too subtle to discern.

Pursuing the Public Interest. The poor explanatory power of the private interest story does not, of course, establish that the public interest has been served by NHTSA's retreat from rulemaking. Indeed, there are plausible grounds for believing that the public interest has not been served, if by "public interest" we mean achieving the greatest economically beneficial reduction in motor vehicle deaths and serious injuries consistent with politically acceptable levels of regulation. The real difficulty, however, is that there is no way to give a convincing answer to the question of whether any particular regulatory initiative serves the public interest. The rhetoric of regulation focuses relentlessly on public interest issues. But if we admit (as indeed we must) that this talk could be a smoke screen, or at best a convention, then harder evidence is required. It is at just this point that the public interest explanation fails. To demonstrate that failure, the remainder of this chapter revisits and reanalyzes the tale of NHTSA's apparently most beneficial regulatory requirement, equipping automobiles with passive restraints. This story not only reveals how excruciatingly ambiguous any public interest account must be, but also sets the stage for a reevaluation of NHTSA's experience from the perspective of the demands of the legal culture.

Passive Restraints and the Public Interest

Airbags and Belts from Ford to Reagan. We last heard from Standard 208 late in the Ford Administration, as NHTSA's administrator, James

Gregory, anxiously searched for some "publicly acceptable" way to issue it.[1] After Gregory's exit from the scene, Department of Transportation Secretary William Coleman took charge of the proceeding. In fairly short order he decided not to issue any rule, even though he was convinced that air cushion restraint systems were both technically feasible and effective. Coleman's approach instead was to negotiate a deal with the auto companies. He would not issue the rule if they would build a substantial fleet of airbag-equipped cars. The point of this exercise was to permit on-the-road experience to either confirm or overcome public and congressional doubts concerning the effectiveness and costliness of the technology. Those doubts were clearly Coleman's, as well as Gregory's, preoccupation. References to the interlock episode run like a *leitmotif* through the order announcing Coleman's decision.

But Jerry Ford and Bill Coleman were not long for their respective offices. Brock Adams, the new secretary of transportation under Jimmy Carter, reopened the passive restraints rulemaking docket almost immediately upon entering the Transportation building. Adams's notice of proposed rulemaking disagreed sharply with the Coleman decision. He believed that a demonstration program was inconsistent with NHTSA's statutory responsibility to reduce highway deaths and injuries. He also disagreed with Coleman's use of public resistance as a ground for decision. In his view, the airbag and the interlock were vastly different techniques. The interlock had involved constant interference with automobile operation; airbags were not even visible to automobile passengers. Hence there was no reason to imagine that automobile owners would disable passive restraint equipment with anything approaching the frequency that they disabled the interlock device. According to Adams's notice in the Federal Register the agency had only three alternatives: continue existing manual belt requirements; move to mandatory passive protection; or attempt to generate increased belt usage through mandatory seat-belt use laws (MULs).

Secretary Adams decided quickly, on July 5, 1977, to require passive restraints in all passenger vehicles. He thus demonstrated the Carter Administration's political will in reintroducing passive restraints. But the rule's lead times left implementation to the early years of a second term that was not to be. And as it turned out, subsequent tinkering with the rule provided the rationale for abandoning passive restraints entirely.

Muddling in a Circle. NHTSA initially had required that passive belt systems be detachable by means of a push-button release mechanism.

This requirement was adopted to quell consumer fears of being trapped in burning vehicles after a crash. Indeed, the rulemaking record on emergency exit technologies is replete with speculations about consumer preferences and consumer fears. The agency debates resolved themselves into a simple trade-off between acceptability and defeatability. The push-button system was likely to be acceptable to the public because it replicated the devices currently on manual belts. But, by the same token, it could be used to make passive belts *into* manual belts, thus defeating the basic purpose of passive restraints. Technologies such as the continuous spool, however, which did not reassure consumers that they would be able to exit from their belts on demand, might produce an even greater public reaction and a greater tendency to disable the belt entirely. Unless attached to an interlock, a passive belt system could, after all, be defeated with a pair of scissors. In the end the agency yielded to the imponderables and permitted manufacturers to choose their own emergency exit technology. This seemingly innocuous decision set the stage for the Reagan Administration's rescission of the rule in 1981.

Connoisseurs of political irony might like to note that on February 2, 1981, NHTSA granted the petition of Ralph Nader for the initiation of rulemaking to raise the barrier-crash test speed in Standard 208 from 30 miles an hour to 40 miles an hour in model year 1984 and 50 miles an hour in model year 1986. Nader's petition pointed out the expected increase in fatalities accompanying the shift to smaller cars and recent technical studies indicating that airbags could be constructed that would meet the injury criteria of Standard 208 at a barrier impact speed of 50 miles per hour. In granting Nader's petition that the agency pursue the matter, NHTSA agreed with his basic position, but stated that it was in the process of analyzing accident data files to evaluate injury modes and injury distributions as a function of crash mode and crash speed. Only after it finished this analysis would the agency be in a position to reconsider the Standard 208's injury criteria in a systematic way.

While this polite exchange was going on in the Federal Register, the *Washington Post* was reporting the deregulatory proposals and initiatives of the new administration. High on Reagan's list of immediate targets were regulatory requirements affecting the automobile industry. The stagflation of the 1970s had been devastating for American automobile manufacturers and auto workers. It was actually not at all clear that regulatory relief would help reverse these trends. But candidate

Reagan had promised that if he were elected, regulatory relief would be forthcoming. The Federal Register began to reflect the new political world reported in the *Washington Post* only ten days after the grant of Nader's petition. On February 12, 1981, NHTSA proposed a one-year delay in the effective dates of its passive restraints requirements.

The stated reason for this proposal was to allow the agency to reconsider Standard 208 in the light of the major changes that had occurred since its adoption in 1977. The agency was particularly concerned that the current phase-in schedule, which began with large cars in 1981 and proceeded through mid-size to small cars in 1983, might exacerbate the economic troubles of the domestic automobile industry. In addition, the automakers' plans for compliance with Standard 208's demand for passive restraint systems had altered radically in the intervening years. Whereas airbags were the passive restraint of choice when Adams acted in 1977, it seemed clear that most manufacturers in 1981 would attempt to comply through the use of passive belts. It had made some engineering sense to introduce airbags first in large cars, where the experience was greater and the design problems were smaller, but this was not necessarily the case with passive belts. The only real experience with passive belts had been in small cars. And the need for protection became greater as cars were made smaller.

As usual, the commentary flooded in. The most comprehensive comments opposing the proposed suspension came from the insurance industry. Capitalizing on the government's increasing enthusiasm for cost-benefit analysis, State Farm Insurance Company sponsored a cost-benefit analysis by William Nordhaus of Yale University. According to the Nordhaus analysis, the economic costs of delay were five times greater than the benefits.

The automobile manufacturers' most telling argument in favor of the suspension was that the passive restraints standard might well be ineffective. The extremely high price of airbags per vehicle dictated that, under current economic conditions, the manufacturers would use passive belts. But passive belts were, in the manufacturers' view, unacceptable to the public unless they were easily detachable. If they were easily detachable, then they would probably function essentially like manual belts. And if they functioned like manual belts, the industry and consumers were being asked to spend millions of dollars for no increase in safety. NHTSA's earlier "flexibility" on the issue of detachment technology was thus turned against the passive restraints rule itself.

Predictably, the agency concluded that it should delay implementation for one year in order to reevaluate the passive restraints standard. In October 1981, having completed its reevaluation, the agency published a notice rescinding the passive restraints requirement entirely. The rescission order explained that the agency could no longer conclude that passive restraints were reasonable and practicable. Because of uncertainty about public acceptability and usage rates for detachable passive belts, the passive restraints requirement might be adding substantial costs to motor vehicles without any attendant benefits. Events since 1977 that had changed the economic and political context of rulemaking were also significantly influencing the agency's decision. There were less costly alternatives, such as public information campaigns and the Coleman demonstration project, which the agency had never seriously undertaken. NHTSA believed that these efforts, combined with the possibility of manufacturers' installation of passive belts as optional equipment, might better meet the need for automobile safety.

State Farm Insurance Company immediately sought judicial review of the rescission order in the D.C. Circuit Court of Appeals. The order was held invalid by a panel of the D.C. Circuit in a long, somewhat confusing, occasionally bizarre, opinion.[2] The government immediately appealed to the Supreme Court, which sustained the D.C. Circuit's determination, but on quite different grounds.[3]

In its decision on *State Farm,* the Supreme Court found two major faults with NHTSA's order. First, it could not understand why NHTSA believed that passive belts with an easy means for detachment would function like manual belts. After all, as long as the belts were not detached, they required no effort by motorists to provide passive protection. Hence, by contrast with manual belts, inertia favored use rather than nonuse. Given this inertial factor, how could NHTSA conclude that no increase in belt usage should be predicted? If "detachability" was a problem, why not use General Motors's preferred continuous-spool technology?

Second, the Court was baffled by NHTSA's apparent but unexplained abandonment of airbags. The agency might ultimately conclude that it could not require a passive belt technology that was both acceptable to the public and likely to increase belt usage. But that said nothing about airbags, devices that the agency had maintained for over a decade were technologically available and cost-beneficial. Why had the agency not simply eliminated passive belt systems as a means of satisfying Standard

208, leaving airbags as the only feasible means for compliance? Finding no answer to that question in the agency's rationale for its decision or in the immediate rulemaking record, the Court remanded the question to the agency for redetermination.

The Dole Finesse. Responding to the remand order, in October 1983, the agency returned to the passive restraints rule. Elizabeth Dole, the new secretary of transportation, issued an NPRM requesting comment on various alternatives for amending Standard 208. After a lengthy discussion of the regulatory history leading to the Court's decision in *State Farm,* Dole presented some of the data the department had gathered. That presentation demonstrated both how much and how little the agency had learned since 1969.

Secretary Dole's notice revealed that the agency was awash in data. Yet the critical uncertainties identified in *State Farm* remained. There was still no road experience with sufficient numbers of airbags or passive belt systems to determine their effectiveness when used and, more critically, their probable utilization rates. Nor was the agency any closer to answering the Supreme Court's, apparently sensible, questions: if detachable automatic belts might merely replicate the utilization rates of manual belts, why not make the belts nondetachable? What are the effects of inertia on the utilization rates of detachable passive belts? Why not use airbags?

There was, of course, an answer to some of these questions. Technologically there was no good reason to make belts detachable. The continuous-spool belt systems were thought to be reliable and to provide easy exit from the automobile after a crash. And airbags were considered both reliable and effective. The problem was not technology. The problem was predicting consumer behavior, or, as the issue had come to be phrased, "public acceptability." Continuous-spool belts were removable with a pair of scissors, and a significant public outcry might motivate Congress to excise the vastly more expensive airbag requirement. As the agency awaited comments on its NPRM, public acceptability loomed as the core issue in choosing among the regulatory alternatives that the agency had identified.

Comments flooded in, 7,800 of them. But, as usual, the commentators raised as many new issues as they answered. After preliminary analysis of the comments the agency felt compelled to issue a supplemental notice of proposed rulemaking requesting further information on prior issues and identifying some additional issues for comment. With all this information in hand, a special task force prepared a 700-page Final Regulatory Impact Analysis analyzing the costs and benefits, and the imponderables, of the agency's alternative proposals. On July 17, 1984, a final rule was issued. The statement of basis and purpose runs 50 pages in the Federal Register and incorporates the Final Regulatory Impact Analysis by reference. The core of the agency's decision, however, was captured in four paragraphs:

> Effectively enforced state mandatory seat belt use laws (MULs) will provide the greatest safety benefits most quickly of any of the alternatives, with almost no additional cost.
>
> Automatic occupant restraints provide demonstrable safety benefits, and, unless a sufficient number of MULs are enacted, they must be required for the most frequently used seats in passenger automobiles.
>
> Automatic occupant protection systems that do not totally rely upon belts, such as airbags or passive interiors, offer significant additional potential for preventing fatalities and injuries, at least in part because the American public is likely to find them less intrusive; their development and availability should be encouraged through appropriate incentives.
>
> As a result of these conclusions, the Department has decided to require automatic occupant protection in all passenger automobiles based on phased-in schedule beginning on September 1, 1986, with full implementation being required September 1, 1989, unless, before April 1, 1989, two-thirds of the population of the United States are covered by MULs meeting specified conditions.

How Could We Have Gotten Here from There? The July 17 decision was by any standard astonishing. Although the *State Farm* decision had seemingly narrowed the agency's range of alternatives, the July 17 rule in effect left the question of whether passive restraints would be required, and if so, what technology would be used, to the future decisions of state legislatures and automobile manufacturers. In addition, the preferred regulatory strategy now seemed to be the mandatory use law. Not only had such laws heretofore been unpopular with state legislatures and with the Congress, but they were a return to the behavior modification strategies of the pre-1966 era.

The parties who historically had pressed passive restraints technology on the agency, the insurance companies in particular, found the agency's rule not only astonishing but irrational. They were shortly back in court seeking review of the rule on numerous grounds. They were told by the D.C. Circuit Court of Appeals, however, that their suit was not ripe for review.[4] After all, their basic complaint concerned the substitution of MULs for passive restraints. That had not happened yet, and it might never happen, although a remarkable number of states had enacted MULs pursuant to the agency's invitation and a massive lobbying effort by the automobile manufacturers. But, the Court reasoned, these laws were quite diverse and the rule had given no indication of how any of them might "count" toward the required minimum level of MUL coverage.

As these words are written, it appears almost certain that the Court's sense of timing was acute. The "trapdoor" built into the July 17, 1984, version of the passive restraints rule has not sprung open and is unlikely to do so. The "Dole rule," therefore, provides an appropriate point from which to take stock of NHTSA's efforts on Standard 208. Those efforts reveal a complex interplay between two major themes of motor vehicle safety regulation—rationality and public acceptability. Has the agency once again, as the courts have found in decisions reaching from *Chrysler* to *State Farm*, failed in the straightforward, if complex, rational-analytic task allotted to it by the Motor Vehicle Safety Act? Has it failed to promote the public interest by "meeting the need" for automobile safety? Or did it instead make a Solomonic judgment in the face of irrational forces that were outside its capacity either to control or to predict, but that were, nevertheless, relevant to its regulatory task?

The Insurance Industry View. Those opposed to the Dole decision believe that the agency fundamentally misunderstood the relevance of public acceptability to its regulatory mission. In their view, public acceptability is only an issue of "practicability." The agency must consider whether motorists would so frequently defeat any technological requirement embodied in its rules that its benefits would either be lost or would be so disproportional to their costs that the rule would be unreasonable. From this perspective the agency is not meant to concern itself with whether motorists will "like" any new occupant restraint requirements.

Viewed in this way the agency's failure to eliminate the detachable belt as an option and its preference for mandatory use laws is bizarre. MULs are the most defeatable strategy available to the agency. Motorists need not cut out their belts or have their airbag sensors deactivated in order to defeat a mandatory use law. They need only not buckle up. Does the agency really believe that a population that refuses to wear its currently available belts will wear them in large numbers because failure to buckle up has become a traffic offense? This is, after all, the same population that the agency suspects may take the time and trouble to defeat passive restraint systems that provide substantial protections with no motorist effort, and the same public that makes a daily habit of violating virtually any traffic law that is temporarily inconvenient.

Stranger yet, the study of foreign mandatory use laws that was most relied upon by the department, a study by Peat, Marwick, Mitchell and Company, concluded that the most important factor affecting utilization was the level of police enforcement. One might expect therefore that an important part of NHTSA's criteria for approval of a mandatory use law would be the level of enforcement resources devoted to implementation. Yet the July 17 rule contains no such criterion. It requires merely that there be a penalty of at least $25, that the state have "a program to encourage compliance," and that there be the opportunity under state civil law to mitigate damages with respect to persons injured while violating the MUL.

The agency also had an alternative that was both unobtrusive and difficult to defeat—the airbag. Indeed, the agency's discussion of the airbag in the July 1984 Federal Register notice and in its Final Regulatory Impact Analysis does not really view motorists' defeat of the airbag as a major issue. The critical disadvantage of airbags is their cost. They have a predicted lifetime cost of $320, *net* of insurance benefits. By contrast, using mid-range predictions of utilization, the agency predicted that motorists would recapture the increased cost of passive belt systems from reduced insurance premiums alone. And of course mandatory use laws would add no incremental cost to automobiles.

Still, the agency's concise statement of basis and purpose notes that airbags may be a good buy in any event. A different approach to cost-benefit analysis, one that took into account the potential savings of lost productivity, pain and suffering, and the like, might have concluded that the airbag was a bargain at $320. Indeed, a new Nordhaus cost-benefit analysis submitted on behalf of a group of insurance companies predicted that the benefits of airbags would outweigh their cost even if they increased the percentage of motorists restrained by only 4 percent and had a unit cost of $850. If the Dole decision was based crucially on a consideration of public acceptance and on analysis of costs and benefits, why did the agency fail to adopt the most nondefeatable technology, given its apparently positive cost-benefit ratio?

The answer may reside in a single word—ideology. The administration adopting the July 17, 1984, version of Standard 208 was the same administration that had attempted to rescind it in 1981. Thwarted in that attempt by the Supreme Court, and believing itself unable factually to justify a rescission to that court's satisfaction, the agency may have chosen its next best alternative. It adopted passive restraints while putting the fewest possible restrictions on manufacturers' choice of technology and holding out the prospect that states could repeal offensive federal regulation by substituting their own legislation. The most cynical form of this explanation would also note that MULs provided the states with the opportunity to return to the discredited behavior modification techniques of the past. Such state programs, like most traffic safety regulations, can be long on exhortation and short on enforcement. If so, the MUL option is tantamount to deregulation. According to this interpretation, the public interest has been subordinated to campaign promises to a special interest group.

A (Possible) View from the Department. Although an ideological explanation cannot be dismissed, the agency's decision can also be portrayed as the shrewdest implementation of safety goals in the "public interest" that has occurred in over two decades of motor vehicle safety regulation. Consider how the world might appear to an agency that has had the experience with Standard 208 that NHTSA has had.

First, the agency is unlikely to subscribe to the insurance companies' narrow view of public acceptability. On that view the ignition interlock was a great success. At the *lowest* level of interlock utilization rates, seat-belt use was doubled. And given the low cost of the interlock technology, the net benefits were very substantial. Yet surely an agency that had its interlock rule overturned by an enraged Congress is entitled to view the entire episode as a disaster. If the 1974 amendments meant anything to NHTSA, they meant that reasonableness and practicability included consideration of possible political, not just technological, issues in its rulemaking.

Or, to take a different example, the 55-mile-an-hour speed limit may be the most effective safety regulation ever adopted. Further reductions in speed would certainly have nontrivial safety payoffs. Should NHTSA, therefore, proscribe the sale of automobiles having a top speed of over 55 miles an hour? One's intuitive and immediate response is no. And that intuition is in no small measure the product of a vision of public outrage and swift congressional reaction. Administrative rationality in implementing the 1966 act cannot consist in a fixation on safety considerations to the exclusion of attention to public acceptance. Political sensitivity to public preferences seems a necessary element of reasonableness. This agency, any agency, should always read between the lines of its statute an implicit qualification of the form: "Don't forget that this statute does not exhaust our vision of the good life or the good society. Remember that we have other goals and other purposes that will sometimes conflict with the goals and purposes of this statute. If we forgot to mention all those potential conflicting purposes in your instructions, take note of them anyway. For heaven's sake, be reasonable."

Once one begins to consider the issue of public acceptability from this broader perspective, the pursuit of the public interest becomes very complicated indeed. The liberty-security conflict engendered by automobile travel seems to produce extremely ambivalent responses on the part of the public. In pre-MUL America, a very small percentage of motorists wore their manual seat belts, but a substantially larger percentage reported that they did. Many nonusers reported that they failed to use their belts simply because they forgot. Yet a large proportion of Americans who received cars with a fail-safe reminder—the interlock—eventually disabled the system. Some public opinion polls reveal that consumers want airbags in their cars and are prepared to pay the NHTSA-estimated cost for them. The little sales experience that is available, however, has convinced the manufacturers that airbags are unmarketable except at the very high end of the price range. A substantial number of Americans, according to opinion poll data, favor mandatory use laws, unless you tell them that "mandatory" means that there is a penalty attached to nonuse. But this same populace apparently strongly favors criminal penalties for parents who fail to provide elaborate crash protection seats for their children.

Predicting how such a public will react to passive restraints is hardly a straightforward task of data analysis. From this perspective, allowing manufacturers to choose among passive restraints technologies, while encouraging a national referendum on the choice between passive restraints and mandatory use laws, begins to look more sensible. Moreover, there seems to be a political or ideological element in the public reaction that cannot be ignored. The public reaction to the interlock often emphasized reports of that device's unreliability, although by comparison with other components of the automobile the interlock system was enormously reliable. The public response thus can only be explained as including a large dollop of reaction to the mandatory and explicit limitation of driver freedom that the interlock represented. The interlock violated the first commandment of automobile law. It interfered with mobility.

Moving from required automobile technology to aspirational traffic laws, and from a federal bureaucracy to the state legislature, thus has its own complex, public interest rationale. The dynamics of state legislative enactment may prepare the populace for new public regulation in a way that is simply unavailable to a federal regulatory agency. After all, our constitutional culture teaches us to prefer self-governance in its most concrete, localized forms. State legislatures are not New England town meetings, but they are much closer to "the people" than the Department of Transportation is. Viewed in this way, predicting that seat-belt avoiders and interlock disablers will become compliant users of manual belts does not seem so improbable. Should MULs fail to alter driver behavior, they will not impose severe social costs in any event. These laws surely will be enforced very modestly. Private driving behavior thus will be allowed to contradict public safety aspirations in a way that Americans seem to find congenial.

Should MULs not reach the requisite level of adoption, the critical involvement of automobile companies in the choice of passive restraints may have similar effects on their public acceptability. Consumers may reject Ford's choice of standard equipment in favor of General Motors's. But they will not hate Ford Motor Company for its choice. They are unlikely to vandalize Ford automobiles on car dealers' lots by disabling Ford's technology. And experimentation with different devices may over time produce widespread acceptability of one or several passive restraints techniques.

There is yet a further reason for believing that the public interest concerning occupant restraint technology might be best defined through a decentralized and partially privatized process of decision making. Although most discussions view the issue as closed, it is far from clear that the analyses of costs and benefits provided by proponents of one or another passive restraints technology would stand up to searching examination. The major savings claimed for passive restraints in these analyses are the dollars assigned as the value of lives saved and injuries prevented. In insurance company estimates submitted in the course of the 1981–1984 proceedings, these values are averages of the imputed value of life taken from a series of public programs (ranging from Medicare payments for dialysis to the OSHA acrylonitrile rule). The valuation technique is computationally quite straightforward. With respect to existing health and safety programs, the estimated regulatory costs are divided by estimated fatalities prevented, to provide a per-program "imputed value" per life saved. The results from particular programs are then averaged to produce an average "social value" per life saved—in these analyses, $520,000.

This is one way to get a number. But why should it convince anyone? The imputed values in the programs surveyed range from $93,000 to $989,000,000 per life saved. This spectacular variance—by a factor of 1,000—suggests that these implicit social values are very situation-specific. Even if we imagined that per-program imputed values represented true "social perceptions" (whatever that might mean) of the value of life, why should an average, abstracted from any concrete context, be meaningful? It would seem more sensible, using this methodology, to say that the social value of the passive restraints rule must be whatever its costs of implementation are, divided by the number of premature deaths prevented. Once implemented, the rule's benefits will, by definition, precisely equal its costs. Viewed in this fashion the cost-benefit exercise cannot be an argument for or against adopting the passive restraints rule. If we have no passive restraints rule, and thus no costs, the value must be zero. If this were true, anything the agency did, including nothing, would be cost-justified (and would probably fall within the range of values established by preexisting programs).

There are, of course, other ways to approach the value-of-life question in cost-benefit analysis. The standard approach is to ask what people either pay or accept in other contexts to avoid or accept particular increases in the risk of death. If the movement from job A to job B, for example, entails an increase in risk of .001 per year, matched by an increased income of $100 per year (and the jobs are otherwise "comparable"), then the imputed value of life is $100,000. But this technique has similar defects. Risk premiums also vary widely with context. There is no reason to choose any particular context, or an average, as applicable to automobile risks.

More important, there is already a market for automobile safety equipment. Any analysis premised on "willingness to pay" (or requirements for payment) should ask what car drivers or buyers are willing to pay for increased safety equipment (or require in payment to accept increased risks). But why ask and answer these questions in terms of "shadow prices" for hypothetical risk reductions? The market is already making allocations in accordance, not with averages, but with particular marginal demands. People have preferences concerning safety equipment, and some will purchase it—including passive belt systems. Indeed, the demand seems quite pronounced among some buyers of higher-priced cars. But these purchasers represent a very small segment of the market. Most car buyers not only fail to purchase additional safety equipment but refuse to use the manual belt systems that they have been required to purchase.

None of this analysis is meant to suggest that cost-benefit analysis is a silly game or that many drivers do not in some sense "want" passive restraints and other designed-in reductions of automobile risks. The argument is merely that there is no methodology of cost-benefit analysis that will make a convincing case that they do. In a market for private goods, consumer "willingness to pay" is best measured by observing what consumers do pay, unless there is a "market failure." Are there reasonable stories of market failure to be told here? We are unconvinced by attempts to count lost additions to the gross national product or the costs of social insurance or welfare programs as "externalities" justifying regulation of individual decisions to take driving risks. If these are justifications, there literally are no limits to the social controls that might be justified.

Nevertheless, there is a market-failure problem that would be addressed by passive restraints. Under conventional automobile liability insurance, my liability costs are dependent not on how well my car protects me, but on how well your car protects you. Liability insurance savings thus provide an incentive for me to want you to purchase a crashworthy car, not for me to purchase one. But how am I to get you to buy more safety?

Consumers obviously face impossibly high transaction costs in inducing each other to purchase safety devices, even if the insurance savings are sufficient to compensate those who would have to be "bribed" to undertake the purchases. The passive restraints rule might thus be justified as a means of solving this transaction costs problem. Under the rule everyone is required to buy safety equipment that should reduce everybody's liability (and some other) insurance costs. This is in fact the approach that NHTSA's 1984 statement of basis and purpose implicitly takes when discussing the costs and benefits of passive restraints. Its analysis uses insurance cost savings as the measure of the benefits.

Notice, however, that on that analysis mandating airbags is *not* cost-justified.

But it is far from clear that this insurance externality problem really makes passive restraints the most attractive regulatory option. The transaction costs problem might be solved more cheaply by a subsidy to automakers that would cover the production costs of passive restraints. Subsidies would equal purchase price in a competitive market, but would avoid whatever additional demoralization costs attend forcing car buyers to pay for equipment they do not want. The states, too, could solve the externality problem by switching to "pure" no-fault liability systems. No-fault schemes allow all the reduced insurance costs from purchasing safer cars to be captured by car owners through reductions in their own insurance rates. That action would have the additional advantage of leaving passive restraints equipment "optional" for the purchaser. The federal government might seek either to induce the states to take this approach or might partially preempt state automobile accident law. In short, as a rational response to a perceived imperfection in insurance markets, the passive restraints rule may be inferior to other techniques of intervention.

Nor is the value-of-life issue the only difficulty besetting the passive restraints cost-benefit analyses. There is, after all, no guarantee that a single life would be saved or injury prevented by the installation of passive restraints in all new automobiles. The engineering estimates used in all the analyses fail to take account of an offsetting and predictable public reaction: as the risks and accident costs of driving are decreased, motorists both will drive more and will drive "more intensely." These increases in mobility and associated risks will increase the number of accidents and their severity. These substitution effects could reduce or even eliminate the predicted safety benefits of the passive restraints rule.

Debate about the existence and extent of risk substitution effects has been raging in the academic literature for over a decade.[5] That some substitution will occur is widely accepted, but the extent of the effect remains inconclusive. For that reason NHTSA's Final Regulatory Impact Analysis decided to ignore the "risk-substitution hypothesis" as unproved. Its terse dismissal is difficult to justify. To be sure, no particular estimate is well established. But neither are NHTSA's engineering estimates. Can an agency that views public reaction to its rules as a crucial consideration rationally ignore an aspect of driver behavior that may dramatically affect the impact of the rule?

Public Interest in Perspective. "Public interest" analysis thus leads to a rather peculiar position. Congress decided in 1966 that "we the people" wanted (or should have) safer cars. It charged NHTSA with regulating "unreasonable risks" and with "meeting the need" for automobile safety by rules that are "reasonable," "practicable," and "suitable" for the types of vehicles regulated. Presumably that statutory language refers to something—some technique of determining reasonableness or needs—but what is it? Rationalistic discourse in a cost-benefit idiom seems inadequate to resolve NHTSA's concerns. Market measures of social perception imply no regulation, which is surely not what the Congress meant.

As a matter of social interpretation it may make perfect sense to view these matters as yet another instance of psychological ambivalence or conflict—or as economists put it, of a divergence between first- and second-order preferences. We want to want safer cars. We fear, however, that when expressing our wants in the marketplace we will behave badly. We will act out our alternative preferences for style, power, convenience, or whatever, failing thereby to express our desires for safety. We therefore approve of regulation that makes it impossible for us to behave badly, to forget about safety. From this point of view, the 1971 version of the passive restraints rule might be the perfect implementation of the 1966 congressional command. We know we should wear our seat belts, but we do not, and we fear that we will not take a passive belt option, if offered; hence the government should mandate passive restraints as standard equipment.

There are, of course, standard philosophic objections to self-paternalism as a justification for social restraints. More important, for an agency like NHTSA this is a point of view that fails to discriminate between those safety initiatives that it should take and those that it should not. This is a story that can be told about any rule that reduces risk. In addition, the agency's interlock fiasco has revealed to it that not all improvements in safety are acceptable. Congress rejected an occupant restraint system that was superior in cost-benefit terms to any that the agency has since proposed. References to Ulysses tied to the mast in a statement of basis and purpose may be astute, but they probably will not sustain a rule on judicial review. It is even more problematic whether they would protect the agency from political reaction by a populace and a Congress that often seems to prefer a vision of themselves as Hercules.

MULs and Aspirational Law. These justificatory difficulties cast a somewhat different light both on the current version of Standard 208 and on the rescission decision reversed by the Supreme Court. What the Court perceived to be a failure of reason might be better understood as a failure of nerve. The agency could not justify its rescission while retaining the rationalistic, cost-benefit approach that had been its practice and that reviewing courts and OMB directives seemed to demand. It needed to take the much more radical step of insisting on the relevance, indeed the crucial importance, of political sentiment when assessing "need" and "reasonableness" under the statute. NHTSA might then have decided simply that given the 1980 election mandate, it was unwilling to conclude that the populace, already provided with seat belts that it did not use, viewed the risks of unbelted driving as "unreasonable" or "needed" further protections.

Although this would have been a high-risk strategy, we suspect that only a candid assertion of the political nature of the decision could have saved the rescission or could sustain NHTSA's further decision after the Supreme Court remand were it to be reviewed on the merits. A hard-headed "rational" appraisal of the Dole version of Standard 208 seems almost certain to find it arbitrary. The new rule simultaneously finds passive restraints to be necessary and justified and proposes to rescind the rule if states containing two-thirds of the population of the United States pass mandatory seat-belt use laws. This would be sensible from a safety standpoint only if MULs were known to be effective substitutes for passive restraints and had other characteristics that made them preferable as regulatory devices.

Neither of these positions is justified convincingly by NHTSA's statement of basis and purpose. Although initial usage rates following the passage of MULs have been impressive in many states, the effectiveness of MULs over time is far from ensured. It is well known that compliance with traffic safety rules is highly contingent on both enforcement levels and publicity.[6] The rule, however, requires neither any particular level of enforcement effort nor any achieved level of belt use. The preference for MULs articulated by the agency is based in large part on the low incremental costs of such a program. But those low costs may be the product of myopia. The agency ignores all costs of enacting and enforcing MULs.

NHTSA also ignores other grounds for skepticism about its preference for MULs. Its own accident data suggests that seat-belt usage by individuals involved in serious accidents was lower than for the population generally. Those drivers most likely to be involved in serious crashes, thus, may also be those least likely to respond to a MUL. Hence, increased belt usage may not translate directly into increased death and injury avoidance. A study of the foreign experience with MULs, upon which NHTSA relied, states: "[I]n no country in which a seat belt law has been passed have reductions in fatalities occurred which remotely approach the dramatic reductions promised . . . There have been reductions in fatalities in some countries in which seat belt laws have been passed, *but they have not been so great as the reductions that occurred in the same period in countries in which seat belt laws have not been passed*" (emphasis added).[7] Indeed, unless usage approaches 100 percent there may be little or no effect on fatalities from utilization increases induced by MULs.

There is, however, a political logic to the MUL proposal. The agency is using the only technique at its command to attempt to recast automobile safety as an issue of state law enforcement. It is only in that form that regulation of automobile safety can attend simultaneously to what we want and what we want to want. MULs insist that we behave in a safe and sane fashion while leaving compliance largely voluntary. We can thus vote for safety and live dangerously. We might even, over time, come to respect our voting sentiments. Simple "good citizenship" or "respect for law" may influence our customary behavior. Having become accustomed to "buckling up," we may continue to do so. We might also believe that each of us decided the question for ourselves. We will then have been engaged in an exercise of collective taste-shaping in which our behavior reinforces, rather than ridicules, our aspirations.

Alternatively, the state legislative process might ratify, or at least support, federal requirement of passive restraints. In some states this seems to have occurred in conjunction with the passage of MULs. Canny state legislators, for example, have drafted MULs to ensure noncompliance with Standard 208's criteria for approvable laws. They thus could not be used to spring the rule's trapdoor. Some legislators even built a reverse trapdoor into their MULs. The laws provide that if they are counted to provide sufficient national coverage to rescind the passive restraints requirement, then the MUL itself is void.

Interpreting what all this state legislative activity really means would require another book. Let us note only that it is just this kind of halting, incremental, decentralized, ambivalent, and ambiguous social process of lawgiving that was apparently rejected in 1966. We seemed to have believed then that a scientific perspective on accidents would permit a technological solution to an obvious problem involving national public health. But we forgot, when expressing our aspirations for safety, that we probably would not want to live up to them. We forgot what our legal culture told us about ourselves. We therefore gave NHTSA a task of rational implementation that it felt compelled to abandon, but no rhetorical tools with which to justify its withdrawal.

ELEVEN

Law, Politics, and Regulatory Strategy

If regulators are to be more successful, they must both understand how hostile the legal culture can be toward certain forms of regulation and develop strategies for managing that hostility. Cementing that understanding and offering strategic advice is, therefore, the task of our last chapter.

Learning from the Legal Culture

The primary demands of the legal culture of regulation—that regulatory policy be subject to the rule of law through judicial review and procedurally open to affected interests—have been much in evidence throughout the history of federal motor vehicle safety regulation. Indeed, as we have seen, these demands have been mutually reinforcing. Judicial review has been "proceduralized" in order to accord with our post–New Deal ideology of judicial policy restraint. And by focusing on "process rationality," the judiciary has leveraged both the strategic and the legal positions of regulatory participants. Not only must the agency listen with care, but participants may use their access to provide multiple grounds for later legal reversal of the agency's choices.

William Haddon's reluctance to proceed without bulletproof, scientific evidence may have been born of scientific fussiness, but it was prescient nevertheless. Frank Berndt's desire to shape policy as an adjunct to litigation strategy may have proceeded from the myopia of a traditionalist lawyer, but the legal environment ratified his instincts. Not only did his litigation successes exalt his bureaucratic position, but legal failures cast out his enemies as well. Both the agency's product—recalls in place of rules—and its internal organization came to reflect the rewards and sanctions that that legal culture, via judicial review, bestowed.

Ironically, given their explicit posture of limited intervention, the courts become crucial actors in shaping the regulatory environment. The legal culture thereby scripts the roles of the other actors in the drama of regulation. In their own decisions, moreover, the courts tend to "act out," or at least be guided by, the premises of the general legal culture rather than the more specific purposes or commitments of a particular regulatory regime. Judicial review is by "generalist" judges, not by special administrative courts. Viewing particular statutory systems through generalist legal lenses constructs the image of legitimate regulation.

"Rationality" understood from the perspective of the systems analytic premises of the 1966 Motor Vehicle Safety Act, for example, surely does not counsel the judicial acceptance of NHTSA's recall activity. Recalls make sense, if at all, only against the backdrop of the general remedial assumptions of products liability law. Nor can a technology-forcing, rulemaking enterprise possibly withstand a rationality review that evaluates technological reasonableness by reference to the legal culture's conventional standard of reasonable conduct. Where the adequacy of product design is at issue, the law generally gauges reasonableness in terms of current practice. It is just such a standard that generalist judges have imported into the review of regulatory action at NHTSA. But as we have also seen, the "state of the art" justifies the status quo, not technology forcing.

The result of judicial requirements for comprehensive rationality has been a general suppression of the use of rules. In this regard, the experience at the Consumer Product Safety Commission[1] and the Occupational Safety and Health Administration[2] is similar to NHTSA's. Even an agency like the Environmental Protection Agency, which can hardly act at all except by rule, has found its activities both halted and skewed by judicial review.[3] NHTSA's experience is not aberrational.

This is not all there is to the story. Politics, personality, external events, and many other factors also shaped regulatory output and agency structure. What may not have been so obvious, however, is the way that some of the most important of these influences also reflect basic assumptions of the legal culture and interact with judicial review to shape regulatory policymaking. The legal culture has subtle and complicated as well as direct and dramatic impact.

Notice, for example, the submerged yet powerful message in the Supreme Court's decision in *State Farm*, that the political directions of a particular administration are inadequate to justify regulatory policy. The agency must carry out the statute that Congress enacted. That, again, is one of the legal culture's firmest commitments. But looking at the act's language and legislative history, of 1974 as well as of 1966, what was Congress saying? In addition, NHTSA was an agency that witnessed many congressional actions other than the bills passed in 1966 and 1974. On Standard 208 alone congressional activity had also included appropriations' riders prohibiting the use of any budgetary resources to enforce a passive restraints rule; several failed attempts to legislate it directly; massive participation by individual representatives and senators in the rulemaking docket; and vigorous advocacy both pro and con from congressional partisans in oversight hearings. Given the legislative processes of 1966 and 1974, and the differences between the Congress as a whole and the Congress in committees, and the conflicts and ambiguities in congressional positions in all forms, whose or what will was the agency meant to follow?

As a practical legal matter, this legislative situation means that the agency is bound by the statute in judicial review proceedings, but may not be protected by it. In the absence of congressional clarity, it can rely with assurance neither on executive political direction nor on its own views. What the statute requires will ultimately be determined by the courts. As a practical political matter, this legal situation means that the agency can rely with assurance neither on congressional nor on executive support. Congress as an institution has the legal power to be determinative, but no legal duty to do so. It is generally unable or unwilling to set policy definitively. The Chief Executive, as *State Farm* makes clear, lacks constitutional authority to exercise political direction unless that direction can be articulated in terms that satisfy not just the statute but the rationalist vision of statutory implementation that the courts have adopted to guide them in judicial review.

The fundamental separation of powers that prevents the courts from insisting on congressional clarity and specificity and that keeps the President from meddling in congressional lawmaking thus leaves the regulators legally and politically exposed. They have a political job without a political mandate, and they are subject to judicial review for "legality." The basic assumptions of the rule of law and the separation of powers in our legal culture virtually make "administrative policymaking" an oxymoron. Regulation must proceed legally, therefore, under the cover of a fiction—that regulation is only the application of law to fact, the carrying out of statutory instructions. But the fictional quality of this posture becomes all too transparent in the glare of the political and legal warfare that surrounds high-stakes rulemaking. The legal culture's denial of a constitutional mandate for administrative lawmaking is awkward to say the least. Perhaps in the transportation secretary's office they thought Administrator Gregory was dithering on Standard 208. From his office the situation could easily have seemed impossible. "Public acceptability" of regulatory policy may be a necessary condition for success, but the legal culture denies administrators' appeal to such vague political supports almost by definition. They must instead insist that their policies have a political legitimacy conferred by statutory instructions, instructions that the President cannot, and the Congress often will not, provide.

It is true that although the President ordinarily may not dictate domestic law, the Chief Executive has policy influence, often verging on control, through appointments, removals, and coordination to "see that the laws are faithfully executed." Yet, sensitive to constitutional convention, this last power (or, perhaps, responsibility) tends to be exercised through structural and procedural devices designed to nudge administrators in the direction of an administration's overall views, not through attempts to mandate policy. The most conspicuous executive monitoring device in the late 1980s, for example, is OMB review of major proposed regulations through the medium of "comments" on required regulatory-impact analyses.

Peculiar notions about the separation of powers thus produce not only a proceduralized rationality review of rules in the courts, but also "proceduralized" executive oversight. The resulting multiple tiers of process can have dramatic effects on regulatory output. Put in terms of NHTSA's shift from rules to recalls, for example, even if courts gave the factual predicate for a recall the same extensive examination that they gave NHTSA's rules, the recall process would be substantially more expeditious than rulemaking. Recall activity does not have to pass through the guantlet of a regulatory flexibility analysis or OMB review. Because it does not, there is no internal staff dedicated to making the agency's rationale for its actions airtight long before they have any prospect of seeing the light of day (although the legal staff might take on this task if the courts got tougher on recalls). Nor is there an outside staff prepared to delay the process until its information demands are satisfied.

Recalls thus benefit from a major structural advantage—a smaller number of decision points within the institutional process for decision making. To see how this matters, imagine that the chances of approval for any proposed regulatory action are 50–50 at each institutional decision point. As choice points are multiplied the chances of approval rapidly approach zero. A proposal that must be approved at two bureaucratic levels has a 25 percent chance of being adopted; six levels of approvals reduce its chances to between 1 and 2 percent. Improving the chances of approval to 90–10 at each decision point helps but, even then, by the seventh decision point the chances of approval have dropped below 50 percent.[4] Additional levels of review should thus be expected to produce more than delay. And we also know that, responding in part to external legal requirements, decisions concerning recalls and regulations are structured in vastly different ways within NHTSA. Most recall proposals need only clear the chief counsel's office; regulations must jump through many more institutional hoops both within NHTSA and outside it.

The constitutional separation of powers may play a second and somewhat ironic role in regulation.[5] Competition between the executive and legislative branches (and within the two houses of the legislative branch), for example, contributed to the strengthening of the aspirations of the Motor Vehicle Safety Act of 1966. By contrast, the combination of congressional oversight and appropriations, Executive Office intervention and monitoring, and judicial review, has sharply limited the degree to which the NHTSA could translate those aspirations into concrete technological requirements. The separation of powers can thus escalate the political demands expressed in legislation, while obstructing their implementation.

Observe also how the preservation of state jurisdiction, the third major feature of the regulatory legal culture that we canvassed in Chapter 1, narrowed the regulatory choices available to the agency. Having very little enforcement machinery of its own, NHTSA catered to the demands of state enforcement personnel for equipment-specific standards long past the period in which the statute seemed to require equipment-based rulemaking. More important, when early in the life of the passive restraints rule it became clear the the simplest and cheapest way to protect occupants was effective mandatory use laws, the administrator had no usable statutory power to produce them. Driver behavior modification and other regulatory strategies such as changing accident liability rules or reforming the role of property and casualty insurance were the domain of the states.

Interestingly enough, NHTSA did have apparent power under a companion statute, the Federal Highway Safety Act of 1966, to make strong mandatory use laws a required part of state highway safety programs. But the agency's experience under the Highway Safety Act merely confirmed that the ideological commitments to federalism embodied in pre-1966 automobile law were still intact at the level of practical politics. The agency had already been down the road of attempting to force-feed state legislatures in its involvement with mandatory motorcycle helmet laws. In 1967, pursuant to the Highway Safety Act, the secretary of transportation set standards for state highway safety programs that included the requirement that each state adopt a mandatory motorcycle helmet use law. The act authorized the secretary to withhold 10 percent of federal highway construction funds and 100 percent of federal highway safety funds from noncomplying states. Prompted by the threat of losing substantial federal funding, thirty-seven states rapidly passed motorcycle helmet use laws. When added to the preexisting mandatory use laws in eleven states, these actions brought total compliance to forty-nine jurisdictions, forty-seven states plus the District of Columbia and Puerto Rico.[6]

Three states, including California, however, never complied with the federal requirements. As the Department of Transportation moved haltingly toward imposing the statutory sanctions of fund withdrawals on these states, bills began to appear in the Congress to repeal that authority. Following close on the heels of the 1974 amendments to the Motor Vehicle Safety Act, the debates on the department's requirement of motorcycle helmet use laws give an observer a strong sense of déjà vu. As in the case of the interlock, there was not much doubt that motorcycle helmets made a substantial contribution to the reduction of injuries and fatalities. There was some attempt to interpret the existing evidence as inconclusive, but virtually none of the legislative participants believed these analyses. The problem was ideological.

As Senator James Abzourek noted when introducing his bill to repeal the requirement, "people rightfully resent laws which protect them only from themselves."[7] But the objections in the Congress were to more than paternalism. Senator Alan Cranston had framed the issue when introducing his successful amendment to the Highway Safety Act: congressional action was necessary to restrain an "overbearing, overprotective bureaucracy, gratuitously trying to restrict the freedom of choice of the individual and using the clout of federal money to try to impose its views on a state government."[8]

The combination of individual and states' rights rhetoric convinced a congressional majority to act. But given the clear safety benefits of motorcycle helmets, Congress was unwilling to go on record as opposed to mandatory use laws. It compromised by merely withdrawing the Transportation Department's authority to withhold any federal funds from a state that failed to enact a qualifying statute. The department's standard remained in effect, but it was unenforceable. With astonishing swiftness, twenty-eight states repealed their motorcycle helmet use laws.[9]

NHTSA's experience with the enforcement of federal conditions on recalcitrant states is in no sense unique. Federal administrators exercise considerable influence over state policies in many schemes of "cooperative federalism." But imposition of federal sanctions for state noncompliance is very rare. State prerogative is still a powerful political symbol, and Congress will seldom support federal administrators who try to force federal policies on state political processes.

There are also important lessons to be learned from the more specific culture of automobile law. Much of NHTSA's standard setting has been virtually invisible to the affected public and, therefore, largely unobjectionable to it. Most protest has focused on visible incursions on privacy or mobility, such as the interlock. And to the extent that the agency's actions have been examples of the conventional after-the-fact, adjudicatory, and remedial approach of automobile law—that is, to the extent that regulation has meant recalls—the agency has encountered few obstacles to working its regulatory will. There is every reason to believe that NHTSA learned these lessons early. It has avoided virtually all rules that would interfere significantly with automobile styling (for example, pedestrian protection and 360-degree visibility), has abandoned its proposed technological limits on speed, and has increasingly concentrated on the regulatory technique that the public approved—recalls.

As defenders of the 1966 vision have often complained, the agency also has shifted resources and attention to older, "discredited" strategies of driver behavior modification by supporting state initiatives on drunk driving, driver education, and the like. These projects do not appear to have much effect on safety, but they fit the culturally approved paradigm of automobile law. The agency thus may not have given us what we said we wanted in 1966, or even in 1974; but it has given us what the more permanent legal environment of regulation has said is accceptable.

Yet this apologetic conclusion is not satisfactory. Perhaps NHTSA has been laboring in the face of insurmountable obstacles—the intractability of our individual and collective ambivalence about both legal regulation and the role of the "freedom machine" in our lives. Perhaps. But perhaps not. Two related questions remain. First, are there better ways to manage the inevitable conflicts inherent in safety regulation than were found by the architects of the 1966 Motor Vehicle Safety Act? If there are, we might have both more safety and more freedom. Second, if remodeling the regulatory mandate is not a promising reform strategy, what does that mean for NHTSA-style regulation? Are there shifts in regulatory technique that might prove largely acceptable and socially effective for both NHTSA and other agencies with similar public health mandates?

From Lessons to Strategies

To say that legal culture matters, that it constrains and shapes regulatory behavior, need not be a counsel of despair. The legal culture is not very malleable in the short run, but this does not imply that there are no strategies for managing the difficulties that regulation necessarily encounters. Nor need those strategies entail abandoning safety or other regulatory goals. With a slight modification in NHTSA's statute, and perhaps without it, the agency could be, and could have been, much better at negotiating the obstacles that the legal culture has deposited in its path. The examples are taken from the motor vehicle context, but the principles apply to other regulatory efforts as well.

A Message for the Congress. Since the mid-1960s NHTSA-style "command and control" regulation has developed a poor reputation. Not only have the major health and safety agencies that rely on this technique (NHTSA, EPA, OSHA, CPSC) underperformed, but critics also claim that the regulations adopted have been characterized by misdirected priorities, insensitivity to social costs, and bureaucratic rigidity. NHTSA is hardly blameless on these counts. It has promulgated a substantial number of regulations whose safety payoff is vanishingly small. Although recent studies find NHTSA standards beneficial overall, cost consciousness was hardly the agency's trademark during the heyday of its rulemaking. The courts that invalidated NHTSA's tire standards were surely correct when they found that the agency had collected no credible evidence on the economic practicability of those rules. And much of the petition and amendment overload that clogs the arteries of the standard-setting process results from the use of design-specific standards that needlessly impede automotive innovation unless given constant attention.

For some time, therefore, the search has been on to develop different regulatory techniques—techniques that would be flexible, produce safety benefits at acceptable costs, and yet also make real progress on the health and safety agenda that stretches before the nation. Suggestions for legislative improvement of the situation abound, but most fall into two radically divergent categories: to abandon "regulation" in favor of liability rules; and to force technology through congressional, rather than agency, performance requirements.

Both alternatives deserve serious consideration, both also exhibit a sort of wishful thinking not unlike that which attended the passage of the 1966 act. They concentrate to a great extent on the implementation difficulties encountered in command-and-control systems but focus very little attention on the implementation and effectiveness problems that will surely attend the proposed reforms.

Congressional Standard Setting. If more motor vehicle safety standards are desirable (and there is reason to believe that many cost-beneficial improvements are possible), then Congress has available several means for shoring up NHTSA's political and legal position. The most obvious is for Congress to adopt NHTSA's (or NHTSA-like) standards as its own, that is, to put the agency rules into legislative form. Congressional choices generally do not require rational justification before the judiciary. Thus if Congress makes the decisions itself, there is no opportunity for the industry to mount an aggressive legal defense against them; the full-court press collapses.

Congress occasionally has been willing to mandate specific safety standards. With respect to the "first generation" of safety rules and the school bus safety standards, Congress at least chose the topics that would be covered. It specifically rejected the interlock and continuous warning devices and required the adoption of certain tire labeling rules.

Responding to public outrage about the Ford Pinto's propensity to catch fire in rear-end collisions, and unhappy with NHTSA's pace on upgrading its fuel-tank integrity standard, Congress mandated that NHTSA's proposed standard take effect by a certain date.[10]

Many other attempts to legislate particular design standards have proved unsuccessful, however. Whether the particular legislative proposals have related to controversial subjects, such as airbags and passive restraints, or to more mundane initiatives, such as raised rear warning lights, increased side-impact protection, or antilacerative windshields, the results have always been the same: no final action by the Congress.

We cannot fully explain the failure of Congress to adopt most of these proposals. But congressional legislation of specific regulatory requirements is rare in any field. Neither Congress as an institution nor individual representatives within Congress seem to feel that this sort of technocratic endeavor should be pursued through legislation. It is hard to fault that judgment. The possibilities for design standards are, if not endless, certainly multiple, and standards must be kept up to date, as NHTSA has discovered to its chagrin. Although it is conceivable that Congress might effectively develop, enact, and amend specific motor vehicle safety standards, it hardly seems to hold a comparative institutional advantage to undertake such an intricate task.

There are, however, ways to achieve essentially the same result without involving Congress in the details of specific design standards. The basic idea is for Congress to adopt broad performance criteria, leaving the means for satisfying those criteria either to the automobile manufacturers or to an agency like NHTSA, working within the overall performance parameters that Congress has specified. These are the techniques used in two other areas of federal automobile regulation—the regulation of fuel economy and the regulation of automotive emissions.[11] Moreover, it it not difficult to imagine legislation that takes this approach to motor vehicle safety. By analogy to its emission control legislation, Congress might demand, for example, the survivability of the General Motors Hybrid III dummy in a barrier crash at X miles per hour. Or, borrowing a page from its fuel economy legislation, Congress might require that the vehicles produced by any manufacturer be associated with fatal accidents only at the rate of Y per 100 million miles. Or, combining both techniques, legislation could demand a reduction of X percent in fleet fatality rates over a given period, leaving the means of compliance wholly to manufacturers. Agency action would then be limited to enforcement and the provision of limited waivers or delays in compliance for "good cause."

The suggestion that Congress copy the legislative techniques it has used in other arenas of motor vehicle regulation raises an obvious question: how well have these techniques worked elsewhere? The answer, unhappily, seems to be not very well. Emission controls have, after a decade's delay, achieved the reductions that Congress initially specified by statute—at least in laboratory testing. The program's success was bought, however, at a very high price. Time constraints and the demand for substantial emissions reductions effectively locked in an expensive and rather unsatisfactory technology, the catalytic converter. This mechanism hurts fuel economy, produces additional quantities of sulphur oxides (which are themselves harmful), and loses effectiveness as a car is used. Many motorists apparently disconnect their converters in order to improve their car's performance, and the use of leaded gasoline destroys the converter's effectiveness almost immediately. As a consequence the auto emissions program, as measured by laboratory tests of the emissions of new automobiles, substantially overstates the true effectiveness of the program. The overstatement is probably in the range of 100 to 500 percent, depending on the type of pollutant sought to be controlled.[12]

The health and other benefits of emissions reductions seem extremely modest. Even if the laboratory reductions are achieved in actual use, the health benefits are close to zero. The largest benefit comes from estimated increases in property values in locations experiencing smog. Taking all benefits into account, the best estimates put the annual costs of the emissions control program at about three times its annual benefits.[13]

Public acceptance of the emissions program remains high, according to the polling data, as does public support for environmental protection generally. But at a behavioral level, the picture is not so clear. States have been very reluctant to adopt mandated emissions inspection programs that attempt to maintain the effectiveness of emissions control technology in use.[14] Most state programs would be only partially effective, given their testing and repair requirements, even if every car were submitted for testing and repaired to the extent required by law. In fact compliance ranges from only 50 to 80 percent, and the worst offending vehicles are the most likely not to comply. To put the matter in perhaps its most negative light, the emissions control requirements adopted by

Congress have required an additional and unpopular layer of state compliance-in-use regulation that, even if successful, would only enable the program to achieve benefits that are vastly outweighed by their costs.

The fuel economy experiment also seems, if not a failure, hardly a success. Much of the reduction in gasoline consumption required by the fuel economy standards was stimulated by the market, not by the regulation. Before Congress specified the first five years of mileage requirements, it was assured by the automobile industry that the industry could and would meet them. The automakers had to meet or exceed those targets if they were to maintain their market shares against foreign competitors. It is therefore not too surprising to find that careful studies of the effects of corporate average fuel economy (CAFE) standards can identify no significant influence on American manufacturers' production behavior prior to 1981.[15] The technology was already moving rapidly to adapt to a changing market—so quickly that all the manufacturers exceeded the CAFE requirements by substantial margins during the first five years of the program.

As market forces abated, however, the producers (except for Chrysler, which had substantially reduced its participation in the large car market) got into compliance trouble. From this point on, the regulatory history of the CAFE standards parallels the tale of the 55-mile-per-hour speed limit. Responding to the changed market situation, Congress first bailed out the companies by allowing "credits" earned by exceeding the CAFE requirements in prior years to be carried forward for three years.[16] When these credits became inadequate to avoid the imposition of penalties, NHTSA, again the administering agency, used its authority statute to relax the target of 27.5 miles per gallon.[17] Congress and NHTSA thus assured consumers that they would not be denied the larger automobiles that they now desired.

The CAFE standards may have influenced the speed with which some manufacturers downsized their fleets, the urgency of their redesign, and the maintenance of fuel efficient fleets beyond the point that the market justified such behavior. If so, most studies conclude that these marginal gains in fuel economy were bought at a very high cost.[18] Overall the fuel economy standards seem to have been a program that was not needed and whose "efficacy," if any, lay in imposing requirements that produced no public benefit.

What can be learned from the CAFE and emissions control experience? Were Congress to overcome its apparent reluctance to adopt a general

50-mile-per-hour crashworthiness standard, for example, we would expect the following. First, assuming that NHTSA was given very little discretion to make waiver or other decisions that might be subject to judicial review, the performance standard would be met after some delay. Second, complete success in nominal terms would produce only partial success in terms of true legislative goals. Here, as with auto emissions and auto fuel economy, the real-world effects of safety improvements depend importantly on how well testing methodologies approximate the goal of reducing deaths and injuries. No one now knows what discrepancies might turn up between laboratory tests and on-the-road experience. A recent comparison of NHTSA crash tests and insurance industry accident data suggests that the gap may be very wide indeed.[19] Third, we anticipate that whatever success was achieved would be bought at a fairly high cost, both in terms of direct outlays and in terms of side effects, such as the adoption of unsatisfactory technologies and negative effects on other goals, such as fuel economy and air quality. Draconian regulatory techniques have the vices of their virtues.

None of these problems guarantees that congressional adoption of safety performance standards would be useless or wasteful. Yet the potential disadvantages of this mode of regulation certainly argue for caution. An auto safety program modeled on either the emissions or the fuel economy statute is hardly a foolproof solution to the Motor Vehicle Safety Act's acknowledged problems.

The Products Liability System. What about liability rules? The state of the law regarding manufacturers' liability for defective automobiles in 1966 created a clear division of function between the court-administered, civil liability system and the legislative-regulatory process concerning the safe design of motor vehicles. The courts would police manufacturers' quality-control efforts and hold producers liable whenever their design or manufacture fell below industry standards. But if cars were to be made more crashworthy, if the development of safety technology was to be mandated, that effort would have to be made through legal mechanisms other than the common law.

In the space of only two years, however, the legislative revolution of 1966 was paralleled by developments in products liability law. The judicial refashioning of design-defect claims even featured the same vehicle that had figured so prominently in the legislative politics of 1966, Ralph Nader's bête noire, the Corvair. The doctrine-shattering decision was

Larsen v. General Motors Corporation,[20] handed down by the U.S. Court of Appeals for the Eighth Circuit. The plaintiff in *Larsen* had sought damages for a head injury caused when the steering column of his 1963 Corvair was thrust back into the seating compartment after a head-on collision. General Motors contended that it could not be held liable for the consequences of its design choice concerning the steering column when the car was not used as "foreseen and intended." In short, General Motors claimed that this Corvair had been used, not for driving, but for having an accident.

By 1968, however, the "second collision" idea had permeated the judicial as well as the public consciousness. The court made short work of General Motors's "intended use" argument. Noting that somewhere between one-third and three-quarters of all automobiles were involved in accidents, the court wrote: "No rational basis exists for limiting recovery to situations where the defect in design or manufacturer was the causative factor of the accident, as the accident and the resulting injury, usually caused by the so-called second collision of the passenger with the interior part of the automobile, all are foreseeable . . . The sole function of an automobile is not just to provide a means of transportation, it is to provide a means of safe transportation, or as safe as is reasonably possible under the present state of the art."[21]

Of course, that manufacturers could be held liable because of the foreseeable consequence of the second collision did not mean that they always would or should be. As with any design-defect case, the plaintiff still had to demonstrate that the manufacturer had produced an "unreasonably dangerous product" and that the defective design of the product had been the proximate cause of the plaintiff's injuries. The crucial question was what the courts would hold to be an unreasonably dangerous design.

Subsequent legal doctrine in the various states had adopted a host of criteria. It is not clear, however, that the distinctions between these different verbal formulae produce significant differences in the results of litigation. The general principles that now govern products liability law are succinctly stated in the American Law Institute's Restatement (Second) of Torts, §402A: "(1) One who sells any product in a defective condition unreasonably dangerous to the user or consumer or to his property is subject to liability for physical harm thereby caused to the ultimate user or consumer, or to his property."

In evaluating the "regulative" potential of civil liability for "defective" products, we should note four important points about the current products liability law. First, although this is nominally a "strict liability" standard, the law does not place all costs of automobile accidents on manufacturers. The crucial issue is the reasonableness of a design (whether the product is "in a defective condition unreasonably dangerous to the user"). Generally speaking this turns on two considerations: whether the product was more dangerous than the consumer might expect (the "consumer expectations test"), and whether there was an alternative design whose benefits and costs justified its use in lieu of the design that was used (the "risk-utility test"). The products liability system thus maintains the legal culture's general preference for "reasonableness" as a basis for assigning legal responsibility.

Second, even where a court would hold a manufacturer liable, the liability incentive provided by civil liability may be insufficient to generate design alterations. If, looking at the balance of costs and benefits, including the cost of paying compensation, a manufacturer is convinced that its current design is less costly than the alternatives, then it may continue that design. The inefficacy of damages to modify manufacturer behavior is not necessarily a fault, however. This aspect of liability rules illustrates one of the principal advantages claimed for regulation through the liability system. If incentives are properly focused, at least under ideal conditions, responsive behavior should be efficient.

Third, design choices are made by those presumptively best able to make them. The whole concept of design-defect litigation and product liability for defective design has been criticized as thrusting the courts inappropriately into the engineering of complex products such as the automobile. Both technically and operationally this is incorrect. The court does not issue an injunction requiring that manufacturers change their designs. The court awards damages that provides an incentive for, not a requirement that, manufacturers change the design of their products.

Finally, products liability uses the compensation claims of thousands of disparate consumers as an enforcement mechanism. The susceptibility of bureaucratic enforcement to tunnel vision, political pressures, budgetary anemia, and judicial skepticism is thus avoided.

Yet, notwithstanding these attractive features, it is doubtful that the liability system provides appropriate incentives for manufacturers' design decisions. The liability system does not operate either flawlessly or costlessly. Its incentives may be either too strong or too weak, resulting in either uneconomical "defensive design" or continued excessive injury costs.

To be sure, the institutional locus of design-defect litigation, lay juries, makes automobile manufacturers nervous that the liability system will demand too much safety. To date no manufacturer has been held liable for failure to equip its automobiles with pontoons so that they will float if driven into the water, although some strange cases have been allowed to go to the jury. For example, in *Li Puma v. County of Rockland*,[22] in 1975, the Supreme Court of New York heard a case that involved the collision of a school bus and a 40,000-ton freight train. In addition to suing the State of New York, parents of the injured and dead children sued General Motors for defectively designing the bus. General Motors moved for summary judgment on the surely plausible theory that no school bus could be designed to withstand the forces generated in such a collision. The court, however, rejected that argument. In its view the question was a question of fact: "The ultimate issue to be decided [in the action against General Motors] is whether any of the passengers sustained injuries more serious than those which would result from an impact in a reasonably designed and constructed school bus, bearing in mind . . . the physical nature of the collision . . . This critical issue . . . should properly be decided by a jury after a plenary trial."[23] The prospect of being a wealthy defendant in a jury trial brought by schoolchildren and their parents certainly makes out-of-court settlement and "defensive design" of school buses look attractive. This is true particularly if one remembers the massive punitive damages awards that were levied against Ford in the Pinto gas-tank litigation, notwithstanding Ford's careful—and by the standards of the trade, not unreasonable—analysis of the costs and benefits of redesign.

Thus it is possible that the current civil liability system is providing significant incentives for manufacturers to improve, indeed to overimprove, the safety characteristics of automobiles. It is also conceivable that these developments render the Motor Vehicle Safety Act, or indeed any specific deterrence strategy, superfluous. But we doubt it. Horror stories and fears of jury beneficence[24] do not answer the crucial question: what is the effect of design-defect litigation on the safety characteristics of American automobiles?

This question is remarkably difficult to answer. For understandable strategic reasons, the automobile industry does not disclose the precise ways in which it responds to design-defect liability. Manufacturers' representatives will provide general qualitative information, however. By their accounts, fear of design-defect liability has an occasional specific effect on design choice and a somewhat more amorphous and pervasive effect in focusing manufacturers' attention on safety concerns. All knowledgeable parties with whom we have spoken seem to agree, nevertheless, that the fear of liability provides only a modest additional incentive to those that already exist because of marketplace concerns. After all, a reputation for the production of shoddy or unsafe products is not likely to improve sales.

One would expect a major effect from defect litigation against automobile manufacturers only if litigation and litigation costs were very substantial, the information contained in litigation records were specific or revealing about design choices, and the manufacturers were organized to make use of the intelligence obtained in design-defect litigation. None of these conditions seems to hold.

Products liability litigation is increasing and design-defect litigation is increasing as a percentage of all products liability claims.[25] The financial exposure of manufacturers in design-defect claims is generally small, however, in relation to their overall economic position. The best estimates available suggest that *all* products liability exposure represents less than 0.5 percent of the revenues of the automobile manufacturers.[26] Some liability claims are sufficiently large—for example, Ford's unhappy experience both with Pinto gas tanks and with automatic transmissions—that they show up in the SEC's required 10–K filings as having a potentially material effect on the corporation's earnings. Yet virtually all defects of any substantial size are also the subject of recalls. As we saw in Chapter 8, recall campaigns have at most very modest effects on share prices, even though recalls often operate synergistically with defects litigation.

Although there are no specific studies of the effects of litigation on automotive share prices, one of the securities industry's leading automotive analysts says[27] that products liability is so well established, evenly distributed across manufacturers, and relatively predictable that it has no effect on the market for auto companies' shares. She suggests that even highly publicized and expensive litigation, like the Pinto gas-tank problems or the Ford transmission cases, do not effect the stock market. Only extraordinary products liability claims, such as those against the asbestos manufacturers and that against H. J. Robbins for the Dalkon Shield, are likely to have an appreciable effect. We remain skeptical of this no-effect thesis, but it nevertheless seems sensible to conclude that the economic incentives to redesign for safety or crashworthiness provided by design-defect liability are quite modest.

Even if automobile manufacturers paid close attention to the product liability docket, they would not get a great deal of information about how to alter the design of their automobiles. Knowledgeable observers at all the major manufacturers suggest that approximately 50 percent of their litigation involves one-of-a-kind cases. As a source of design information, therefore, half the litigation is pure noise. The other half consists of cases that have occurred at least twice. But the repetition of a particular type of case does not mean that the case contains useful information, and in fact most automotive engineers view the messages coming from the liability system as a whole as completely uninformative.[28]

It appears that Ford alone among the major manufacturers is organized to pay careful attention to the information generated by the litigation process. Litigation-savvy engineers in Ford's Automobile Safety Office carefully review all of the company's litigation and make recommendations to the product engineering staff when they believe a problem is worth consideration. However, the litigation system is only one of many sources of information reviewed by the Auto Safety Office's engineers and, according to the reports of our informants, a relatively minor one at that. One might guess that Ford's singular organizational structure is a response to its recent litigation experience, but that is incorrect; Ford's structured attention to automobile safety antedates even the *Larsen* decision.

It is difficult to imagine that the products liability system is a major influence on the safe design of automobiles. The messages from the liability system to the manufacturers are both weak and full of static. Not even a finely tuned receiver like the Ford Automobile Safety Office can make much out of the signals received.

Redesigning the Liability System. We need not, of course, rest content with the existing civil liability system. Indeed, virtually no one—save perhaps trial lawyers—is content with it. The litany of complaints ranges from erratic jury behavior to systematically exorbitant administrative costs, from excruciating delays in providing compensation to the elimination of valuable products (including products having direct and substantial health benefits, such as vaccines and pharmaceuticals) from the market. Is there a strategy that might both reform the civil liability system and address the problem of motor vehicle safety?

Oddly enough, there is. As we noted in Chapter 10, there is one real market failure with respect to automobile safety. In a third-party liability system—a system in which the party at "fault" in causing an accident pays for all damage—the purchaser of an automobile does not obtain all the rewards from buying a safer car. Some of the benefits actually go (in the form of reduced insurance premiums) to the third parties who may be legally responsible for compensating the occupants of safer vehicles involved in an accident. All of these benefits would be captured by the automobile purchaser, however, if the purchaser were the sole insurer of the safety of his or her automobile. Universal first-party insurance, or as it is commonly termed, "no-fault insurance," would produce this internalization of benefits and costs. Under such a scheme, insurers should then make premiums dependent in part upon the safety of the automobile that the insuring party purchases or drives. The potential savings in insurance costs would make it worthwhile for drivers or purchasers to demand, and auto manufacturers to market, safer vehicles.

Champions of no-fault automobile insurance have been around for years,[29] and a number of states have adopted some version of no-fault liability. The primary selling point of these schemes has been their capacity to reduce litigation costs and speed compensation for injured parties. Focusing the costs and benefits of vehicle safety in a way that feeds back into consumer demand for motor vehicle safety adds to the attractiveness of no-fault. Such a scheme combines civil liability reform with the reform of vehicle safety regulation.

Unfortunately, universal first-party insurance is probably too weak a reed upon which to rest an overall strategy of vehicle safety improvement. The "market," after all, has its own inadequacies. Chief among them is the likelihood that rating automobiles on the basis of actual road experience will be too difficult, perhaps impossible, for insurance companies to implement. The crashworthiness and crash-avoidance data for particular models necessary to make first-party insurance a market-correcting mechanism will be largely unavailable at the time of the crucial market transactions, the purchase and initial insurance on new cars. The scheme could work only if car models maintained their safety characteristics over substantial time periods. Data collected on older model years then could be used to evaluate the safety characteristics of new models.

Existing data, however, suggest that the safety characteristics of auto fleets fluctuate dramatically. *Consumer Reports,* for example, which analyzes NHTSA's crash testing each year, repeatedly warns that even minor changes in continuing models can have major effects on crashworthiness and that the data reported should be applied only to the precise body-style tested, not even to other cars carrying the same name plate. Also, whole fleets that rate well in one year's test data may perform poorly the next year. And of course as indicated earlier, data from NHTSA's crash testing do not agree with insurance company data based on actual crash reports. The chances are thus very great that insurance companies would find it impossible to differentiate reliably among vehicles for purposes of providing "safety premiums," save on the most general grounds, such as the existence or nonexistence of an air cushion or other passive restraint system. We have found no one in the insurance industry who believes otherwise.

These doubts concerning the efficacy of first-party insurance in providing market incentives for safety improvements are not necessarily determinative. There might well be a competitive advantage to a manufacturer who makes large safety improvements that are unaffected by changes in various models, body-styles, and the like. Dramatically safer technologies, the airbag being perhaps the best example, would be promoted by such a scheme. Moreover, the politics of implementation via first-party insurance certainly would have major advantages over NHTSA-style rulemaking. The latter encounters the many environmental problems that we have reviewed: a wavering political commitment in the Congress, dilatory executive monitoring, a constitutional skepticism about administrative rulemaking that it expressed through judicial review, the strategic information advantages of the regulated industry, concerns about automobile company viability and the unemployment of autoworkers, a fickle and ambivalent public, drastic variations in particular administrations' commitments to the vehicle safety crusade, and a host of other political imponderables. By contrast a no-fault regime might exert continuous, decentralized economic pressure to improve vehicle safety on parties presumptively responsive to such incentives.

Perhaps most significant, the sense that an important symbol of individual autonomy, the personal automobile, is being invaded, constrained, and perhaps made unattractive and unreliable by bumbling government bureaucrats is no part of a market strategy. The freedom machine would again seem truly free. The relentless pressure of well-designed economic incentives is, as Adam Smith so aptly put it, "invisible."

But think about getting there from here. What banners are to be carried by legislative warriors seeking to promote this general deterrence strategy? To what public values will they appeal? "Safety," "public health," and kindred slogans are available, to be sure. Claims of swifter and surer compensation can also be made. The legislative campaign might even march under the vague banner of "privatization," a rejection of centralized bureaucratic control for decentralized, claimant-activated civil justice and consumer-oriented market incentives.

Yet it is hard to imagine legions flocking to these banners. Recruiters for the opposing forces will have some attractive insignia on their flags. "Justice" is likely to lead the parade. No-fault schemes cut off existing rights to collect full compensation, including compensation for pain, suffering, and emotional distress. They also spread costs over "safe drivers." In addition, a universal no-fault program would have to be promoted state by state or would have to overcome a states' rights ideology that has always effectively defended state control of tort and compensation law and insurance regulation. Either strategy seems doomed.

Past experience with no-fault legislation in the states demonstrates that major political difficulties attend the attempt to pass relatively "pure" no-fault schemes. In fact, not one has been passed. Subsequent experience with "mixed" schemes suggests that compromise can produce the worst of both worlds—a scheme that provides inadequate compensation combined with soaring litigation and insurance costs. Nor is there any reason to believe that "safety" trumps "states' rights" in the Congress when the traditional arena of state regulation is at issue; witness the evisceration of the Highway Safety Act's enforcement provisions.

Although universal first-party insurance may have significant social advantages, the history of no-fault in this country suggests that the defenders of the status quo have a decided political advantage. So far as we can determine, no major organized economic interest can anticipate clear gains from the shift to no-fault insurance. If the scheme successfully reduces accident costs, the insurance industry loses. Indeed, overall levels of compensable loss shrink by the elimination of noneconomic losses. Even if accident experience is unaffected, casualty insurance premiums and associated investment income thus decline. The insurance industry will see this as the first step toward one of its most persistent nightmares—federal regulation of the industry. Other powerful groups are likely to join the opposition. The American Trial Lawyers

Association's views on no-fault insurance are well known, and it has been highly successful in blocking "pure" first-party insurance schemes in state legislatures.

This is not to say that well-devised first-party insurance proposals have no prospect for legislative adoption. A similar appraisal in 1966 would not have given the Nader-Ribicoff team much chance of putting through the Motor Vehicle Safety Act. But there is some very rough political sledding here. When combined with doubts about efficacy in action, the political economy of the enactment of universal first-party insurance makes reliance on that strategy deeply problematic.

A More Modest Reform Agenda. What then should be done? Is there a radically new solution to the vehicle safety dilemma? Alas, we are doubtful. We urge Congress to have the courage instead to think small, to use a scalpel instead of a cleaver. Indeed, for Congress we have but one modest proposal: Congress should amend the Motor Vehicle Safety Act to provide for judicial review of NHTSA's rules only in the context of a proceeding to enforce a regulatory standard. Some may think this proposal little more than minor, technical tinkering. But we believe such a change would have substantial beneficial effects.

Consider the dynamics of delaying review until the time of enforcement. First, a manufacturer faced with such a legal regime will be required to consider whether it wants to risk both possible sanctions and bad publicity by noncompliance. This is not trivial, because a manufacturer also knows that its challenge might well be decided at a time when other manufacturers have complied. Altering the timing of review shifts the incentives of manufacturers strongly in the direction of serious attempts at compliance.

Second, because delaying review shifts incentives, it promotes the development of more credible information on both compliance costs and engineering feasibility. Judicial review will be better informed on the critical issues that are now routinely presented but seldom substantiated by more than industry and agency conjecture. Third, in such a regime, if real problems of implementation develop, NHTSA will have every reason to delay enforcement and modify the rule. If problems are relatively tractable, manufacturers will have incentives to comply. Negotiation between the two parties who are best informed should thus resolve most conflicts, and the need to present them to a decidedly second-best form of institutional decision making—litigation—should occur much less frequently.

Fourth, in those cases that are presented to the judiciary, the questions would tend to be focused, limited, and practical rather than diffuse, multiple, and abstract. This not only limits the prospects for agency exhaustion and judicial error but transforms the remedial situation as well. Under this scheme, for example, the *Chrysler* case would almost certainly never have appeared before the courts. If it had, and if the dummy were the real issue, that issue would have been the focus of attention, not an apparent irrelevancy that bemused the agency and befuddled the court. And in the context of an enforcement proceeding, there would have been good evidence of whether the agency was behaving reasonably given existing technological understanding and industry efforts at compliance. "Objectivity" would have taken on concrete meaning. If there were any unfair surprises for the manufacturers in the agency's enforcement approach, they would have been dealt with specifically. There would almost certainly have been no need to take the draconian step of suspending the rule.

In short, delaying judicial review of NHTSA's vehicle safety standards until the enforcement stage limits dysfunctional incentives to procrastinate and to litigate, places decision making in the hands of the best-informed parties, better informs the processes of both negotiation and judicial review, and limits the disruptive effects of judicial remedies. There is then only one remaining issue. If enforcement review is such a good idea, why did Congress fail to provide it in 1966, and why does Congress persist in not providing it?

In our view, Congress made the error because it lacked critical information. In 1966 Congress was giving NHTSA apparently massive powers over the auto industry, with only modest guidance about how to use them. Systematic executive oversight of important rules had not yet been put in place. A sober second look via immediate judicial review seemed a sensible way to restrain the exercise of administrative power. At that time Congress also had very little information about the dynamics or content of pre-enforcement judicial review of rulemaking. That judicial review would so dramatically leverage the full-court press was hardly predictable in 1966. Provision of immediate judicial review looked more like the creation of what banking regulators now call a "level playing field."

There are, in general, some good arguments for immediate judicial review of administrative rulemaking. Costs of compliance with invalid rules are saved, uncertainty about the legality of regulation is more quickly removed, all affected parties receive similar treatment (no one need comply while a challenge is pending, and weak or disfavored organizations cannot be singled out by the agency for enforcement action), and regulators are held strictly accountable because they cannot suppress legal contests through enforcement compromises. From the perspective of 1966 these general considerations seemed entirely persuasive.

We now have more information and experience. The particulars of NHTSA's regulatory history, as well as the histories we have cited relating to other agencies, convince us that the reality of judicial review is much different from that embedded in the general vision of regulatory reform circa 1966. Why has Congress not responded? Part of the answer may be that the evidence, until now, has not been persuasive. One purpose of this inquiry has been to provide such evidence.

A Message for Would-Be Regulators

But that has not been our only purpose. We have also sought to understand the dynamics of regulatory implementation, and having understood them, to say something about how regulators themselves might perform better. Given that there are no legislative "silver bullets" that will make auto safety regulation simultaneously more effective, beneficial, and acceptable, reform must rely to an important degree on better administrative performance. For such reforms to be "true" reforms, they must be premised on an understanding of administrators' "true" position in regulatory politics. Administrative managers must learn from both the successes and the failures of the past. They ultimately also must translate a better theoretical understanding of the structural and inertial forces of the legal culture into concrete political-administrative action.

Lesson One. The image of top-down, rational-technocratic regulation that danced before the eyes of reformers in 1966 was an illusion. Congress stated a goal—"promote vehicle safety"—and it established a regulatory mechanism for accomplishing that goal—standard setting—that was meant to rely on scientific evidence. But twenty-plus years' experience reveal that understanding the regulation game by attending to its technical underpinnings is about as effective as trying to give foreign visitors a feel for American football by introducing them to the NCAA rulebook. Regulatory agencies are in politics. They must pursue their objectives by political means, that is, by developing and employing political resources. Statutory policies and powers are political resources, but what the statute tells an agency to do is at most the beginning of a sound regulatory strategy.

Lesson Two. Legislative history is not history. The politics of 1966 suggested a sharp, indeed a dramatic, break with the past. The legislative history of most statutes is similar. Congress rarely acts unless a crisis (economic, moral, or whatever) can be described, and it inevitably claims that it is taking a radically new direction. This sort of rhetoric now seems to be the essential predicate for virtually all national lawmaking.

American statutory history, however, is not characterized by frequent revolutions. It is instead a history of incremental change. The past is seldom decisively rejected. Old values, old institutions, and persistent interests will continue to influence brave new worlds of legislative policymaking, even as they are ignored, or rhetorically rejected, on the way to legislative action. The political resources contained in any piece of legislation must be understood and evaluated against the broader and more permanent political-institutional environment.

To be sure, the Motor Vehicle Safety Act of 1966 was a more ambitious redirection of regulatory policy than most statutes. It contained substantive and institutional visions that were radically discontinuous with most prior automobile law. But such discontinuities should themselves serve to caution an agency given the task of implementation. The prior shape of the law was not accidental. It mediated safety-mobility conflicts and embodied political-institutional commitments that could not be "repealed" simply by the passage of a new statute.

Lesson Three. Regulatory administrators have few reliable political allies. "Public interest," as well as supportive "private interest," groups have limited resources and their own institutional agendas. They will seldom supply needed technical information and they will often need to bolster their own institutional position by scolding the agency, preferably in terms that will gain them press coverage. Congress is spectacularly fickle. Its members generally are much more interested in pursuing new issues than in nurturing old institutions. Even those who maintain a concern with particular issues over time may not deliver much support when political winds are rising. Some will join the agency's critics out of frustration with the pace of regulatory progress. Even the staunchest supporters may lack the legislative-institutional resources to provide effective political protection. The presidency combines great political influence with serious constitutional disabilities—disabilities that may force executive monitoring into obstructionist procedural forms.

Lesson Four. The courts are the legal embodiment of political inertia. Their foremost institutional commitment is to the protection of individual rights against unjustified governmental intrusion. When governmental action is socially repressive, impinging, for example, on the liberty of minorities and dissenters, judicial vindication of constitutional or statutory rights suggests an "activist" or "liberal" political agenda. This is an illusion. Even when "rights" are given new meanings to accommodate changed social, economic, and political circumstances, the protection of rights is the protection of the status quo. When the rights affected are those altered by "progressive" social legislation, judicial review will operate in a similar fashion. It will demand that the alteration of these preexisting rights be justified in terms that can be harmonized with the maintenance of the rule of law.

In the context of agency rulemaking the courts have been even more obstructionist than one might have expected. But this was a function of stress on their own institutional legitimacy. Determining the abstract legality of regulatory policy, rather than the fairness or reasonableness of specific enforcement or licensing judgments, after all, is not conventional judicial activity. To weave the new jurisdiction that Congress thrust upon them into the fabric of customary legal expectations about the judicial role, the courts were forced to "proceduralize" their review—to search for procedural unfairness or gaps in the evidentiary record. Thus was rulemaking review assimilated to tasks that are conventional and widely accepted when reviewing the judgments of either lower courts or agency adjudications. Yet however necessary it was to the maintenance of an appropriate judicial role, proceduralization imposed a debilitating, defensive posture on agency standard setting. The judiciary's scrupulous search in the rulemaking record for fair treatment of all "adversaries," including reasoned responses to all participants' claims, provided colossal advantages to those opposing standard setting. Changing the status quo by rule came to entail much the same legal trench warfare as did the inefficient adjudicatory policymaking that rulemaking was supposed to supplant.

Lesson Five. Public support for regulation on issues of health and safety is widespread, but very thin. The public favors safer cars (as well as safer products, safer workplaces, and a cleaner environment), but it does not favor restrictions on its freedom or comfort. Although it relishes the morality play of trying to tame dangerous drivers, it probably does not want to think very much about how well vehicles protect their occupants in case of a crash. The press will provide the public with only episodic reporting on regulatory action, and it prefers stories with simple plot lines. Bureaucratic bungling, villainous private behavior, and dangerous defects are the stuff of good copy. Systems-oriented regulatory agendas produce little of interest even for print journalists, much less their broadcast colleagues.

Lesson Six. Lessons one through five add up to a single conclusion: if a regulatory agency like NHTSA wants to be more successful in promoting safety design, it must attempt to accommodate, if not co-opt, its adversaries. This is not to say that NHTSA should fail to cultivate political support in the public, the press, Congress, and public interest and private interest groups. Such support is crucial if "accommodation" is to be more than surrender. Nor do we mean to suggest that the agency should refrain from using the legal resources at its disposal. Structuring an accommodation with regulated parties requires sticks as well as carrots.

What we do mean is that NHTSA and automobile manufacturers (including equipment manufacturers) are of necessity in an uneasy partnership. They occupy the same policy space. They also have some common interests: both want safer cars. Neither wants to make technological errors, to enrage consumers, or to appear to be a patsy. And of course both are in a position to cause each other a lot of trouble. We believe that this "partnership" can be exploited to serve the public interest in beneficial safety improvements.

But we can find very little in the public record of NHTSA's regulatory history suggesting a serious understanding of these facts of regulatory life. Initial political resources in the form of strong legislative backing were squandered in the name of scientific method. Instead of trading long lead times for stronger substantive standards, the agency recognized the industry's production difficulties by trivializing its regulatory requirements. A crucial opportunity for further cooperative action was missed.

Then, as the agency's political resources dwindled and its technical resources failed to grow at expected rates, it began to alienate its friends without cultivating its enemies. The development and acceptance of air cushion technology is, yet again, emblematic of strategic failure. In 1972, when the *Chrysler* decision suspended Standard 208,

General Motors strongly supported the air cushion technology. It was still the leading industry proponent in 1975, when William Coleman sought a cooperative demonstration project with the manufacturers. By 1980, however, General Motors had become the industry's leading opponent of passive restraints. In 1990, when all of Chrysler's and half of Ford's production runs will contain driver-side airbags, only one-seventh of General Motors's cars will be similarly equipped.

The reasons for General Motors's defection (and subsequent disaffection) are many, but one stands out: NHTSA failed to reward it for either innovation or cooperation. Worse, the agency dithered, amended, and backtracked in a fashion that made compliance risky. Not only was the air cushion, even as a demonstration, abandoned for a set of alternative compliance technologies, the menu was changed to put another General Motors creation, continuous-spool belts, at a disadvantage. If this was a partnership, one of the partners was revealing itself to be quite unreliable. Cooperation seemed to be punished rather than rewarded.

Only Secretaries Coleman and Dole seem to have understood that NHTSA was in the business of promoting social learning and that cooperation, at least acquiescence, from all segments of the public was a necessary political condition for success. Coleman's demonstration project looked like a "weak" regulatory posture. But in fact it had a crucial element of strength: cooperativeness, the willingness to withhold formal legal power to accommodate public fears and industry tradition. The public's fears were probably groundless, and the industry tradition of first producing and marketing *any* innovation in small production runs was not sacrosanct. But humoring and enlisting these interests probably would have achieved the agency's safety goals much more expeditiously than did Secretary Adams's reversion to the "strategy" of coercion. A similar demonstration approach might well have saved Standard 121, the truck antilock braking standard, and yet another might have enlisted the support of the tire industry for tire performance standards.

If Coleman's demonstration looked weak, Secretary Dole's "trapdoor" rule looked bizarre. Its technical justification for the efficacy of mandatory seat-belt use laws had the solidity of pudding. From a safety perspective it seemed to trade the destruction of twenty years' work on a proven lifesaving technology for a behavior modification substitute of uncertain, indeed highly dubious, efficacy. Yet it is Dole's rule that is now pushing passive restraints into new cars and that has inspired a nationwide MUL revolution. Moreover, these changes have been accomplished through a process of widespread political debate that gave them the political and legal legitimacy to induce compliance. The inherent weakness of national regulation in a federalist system was converted into a strength.

Without belaboring these or other examples we think NHTSA has often failed in the essential task of developing a strategy that economizes on its limited political and legal resources. More specifically, the agency failed to take seriously the industry's need for a clear sense of the agency's regulatory direction and a reduction of production and marketing uncertainties with respect to the introduction of new technologies. NHTSA thus failed to enlist the cooperation of those elements of the industry that might stand to gain from safety innovation and thereby failed also to use the power of those potential "allies" against additional elements that might otherwise be uncooperative.

Industry accommodation need not be inconsistent with agency accomplishment. The regulated sector's desire for clearer direction can be accommodated in part by making the agency's objectives understandable. But NHTSA has seldom announced determinate safety goals, much less any indication of how much it thought achieving them was worth or how it intended to reach them. The systems-based approach of the October Plan, the RSV, and the switch to performance-based rulemaking have all apparently faded into the regulatory mists. With them seem to have gone possibilities for public and congressional as well as industry understanding of how and toward what the agency intends to proceed.

Given the imponderables of determining the safety effects of standards, the failure to state numerical goals may be as sensible for NHTSA as it is for Congress. But the agency can indicate the types of performance characteristics that it wants to see in automobiles in controlled tests. It can use only performance-based standards, in order to promote innovation and reduce its own inventory maintenance tasks. It can indicate when it believes those general requirements should be met. It can make clear that it will routinely proceed by demonstration projects before mandating across-the-board changes as long as manufacturers are forthcoming participants in those projects. (And, of course, the agency might garner a great deal more cooperation if Congress would delay judicial review of regulations until the enforcement stage.)

Beyond enhancing its credibility with the industry through clearer statement of its goals and the adoption of cooperative techniques of regulatory action, NHTSA must also attend to its other constituencies.

The agency should present its overall regulatory strategy to Congress, to OMB's executive watchdogs, and to reviewing courts at every appropriate occasion. Individual actions cannot be understood and, therefore, may not be supported unless they are placed in context. The institutional actors who make up NHTSA's regulatory environment and shape its fiscal, policy, and legal constraints must understand how particular proposals, limits, ratifications, or remands affect the agency's capacity to implement its overall program. If these actors then decide to "stop the agency in its tracks," so be it. That is often their legal prerogative. But they should not do so inadvertently because they did not understand the general stakes embedded in a particular issue.

Finally, NHTSA should devote more agency resources to serious comparative study of what works on the road—vehicle standards, behavior modification programs, and road improvements. The current state of knowledge is lamentable,[30] and none of the other major actors on the auto safety scene has a jurisdiction that stretches across all of the available strategies. If the agency is to regulate responsibly over the long term, it must also strengthen its capacity to evaluate the efficacy of performance-based standards in operation. This also entails serious study of the efficacy of recalls in relation to their costs. The results will be predictable and politically disappointing, but this is a necessary first step toward rationalizing the recall program.

In addition, NHTSA should make sustained and serious inquiry into the feasibility of replacing all vehicle standards by a first-party insurance scheme, combined with appropriate behavior modification strategies. This might be implemented without congressional action by generalizing the trapdoor provision of Standard 208. If all or most states adopted qualifying legal regimes, NHTSA would rescind all its standards and devote its energies to keeping car buyers and insurance markets well informed about the safety performance of vehicles. The first-party insurance approach may be an unworkable strategy. But if it is feasible and effective, NHTSA should announce that it is prepared formally to go out of the vehicle standard-setting business.

These proposals contain some tall orders for an agency as beset and beleaguered as the NHTSA. They seem to imagine that an agency can maintain and implement a long-term strategy in a political and legal environment that is not only hostile but also often narrowly focused on shifting, short-term, even irrelevant political or legal issues. Worse, our proposals may seem to suggest that many of these approaches have never been tried or even considered by the agency. This sort of Monday-morning quarterbacking is possible for outside kibitzers precisely because so much information is lost to us—and because we stand outside the heat of the political battles and the time constraints of regulatory decisionmaking.

Fair enough. In the end, the job may not be doable. Safety may be too uncertain a value in a culture that also prizes risk taking. Bureaucratic regulation may be too suspect in a polity that prizes freedom. Cooperative approaches and long-term strategies may be inadequate armaments in legal and political wars where power and short-term advantage count.

But if that is true, then the game is up. If progress cannot be made by combining clear, steady goals with strategically deployed incentives for cooperative action, then NHTSA should throw in the towel. Repeal of the Motor Vehicle Safety Act of 1966 would at least represent a candid admission that "technology forcing" is not really an available regulatory strategy; and it might, therefore, promote a heightened search for alternative forms of collective action in pursuit of the act's other public health goals. A proposal to put NHTSA formally out of the vehicle safety business also has the advantages of candor and incrementalism. It would not be a major alteration of the agency's current posture.

Notes · Index

Notes

1. Regulation and Legal Culture

1. *National Traffic and Motor Vehicle Safety Act: Hearings on H.R. 13228 before the House Comm. on Interstate and Foreign Commerce,* 89th Cong., 2d Sess. 1319 (1966).
2. See description in J. Eastman, *Styling vs. Safety: The American Automobile Industry and the Development of Automobile Safety, 1900–1966* 177–208 (1984).
3. For early pronouncements of the new perspective, see W. Haddon, E. Suchman, and D. Klein eds., *Accident Research: Methods and Approaches* (1964); Gordon, "The Epidemiology of Accidents," 39 *Am. J. Pub. Health* 504 (1949) (accidents conform to same biological laws as disease).
4. W. Haddon, *Selected Works of William Haddon, Jr.,* Vols. 1–2 (Insurance Institute for Highway Safety comp. 1987).
5. Goddard and Haddon, "An Introduction to the Discussion of the Vehicle in Relation to Highway Safety," in *Passenger Car Design and Highway Safety: Proceedings of a Conference on Research* 1, 5 (1962).
6. See, for example, De Haven, "Mechanical Analysis of Survival in Falls from Fifty to One Hundred Fifty Feet," 2 *War Medicine* 586 (1942). See also Hasbrook, "The Historical Development of the Crash-Impact Engineering Point of View," 8 *Clinical Orthopaedics* 268 (1956).
7. For a contemporary argument in favor of broader administrative rulemaking authority, see Shapiro, "The Choice of Rulemaking or Adjudication in the Development of Administrative Policy," 78 *Harv. L. Rev.* 921 (1965) (suggesting that greater rulemaking authority would allow agencies to develop policy in a more coherent and forthright fashion). See also R. Melnick, *Regulation and the Courts: The Case of the Clean Air Act* 5–9 (1983) (describing "new regulation" in general terms); Stewart, "Vermont Yankee and the Evolution of Administrative Procedure," 91 *Harv. L. Rev.* 1804, 1811 (1978) (noting that "burdens of trial-type hearings . . . led . . . federal agencies to turn from case-by-case

adjudication to general rulemaking proceedings in order to develop administrative policy").

8. Two early and influential works were M. Bernstein, *Regulation by Independent Commission* (1955) and G. Kolko, *The Triumph of Conservatism* (1963).

9. See, for example, *Senate Comm. on the Judiciary, 86th Cong., 2d Sess., Report on the Regulatory Agencies to the President-Elect* (James M. Landis) (1960).

10. Brown v. Board of Educ., 347 U.S. 483 (1954); Brown v. Board of Educ., 349 U.S. 294 (1955).

11. Pub. L. No. 88–352, 78 Stat. 241 (1964) (codified as amended at 42 U.S.C. §§2000a–2000d–6 (1982)).

A strong egalitarian impulse conceived of automobile safety as an "entitlement" whose content was defined by "the average person's" limited capacities. See, for example, *Traffic Safety: Hearings on S. 3005 before the Senate Comm. on Commerce,* 89th Cong., 2d Sess. 50 (1966) (remarks of Sen. Ribicoff) (person driving Plymouth, Ford, or Chevrolet is "entitled" to "certain basic things" "just as much as a person driving a Cadillac," including collapsible steering wheels and dual brakes); id. at 181–182 (remarks of William Steiglitz) (automobiles driven not only by "professional test drivers," but by "average person" and car is causally related to accident when it conflicts with "basic human characteristics" and "places demands on the driver that are beyond his capability").

The asserted need for equal protection and the promise of governmental efficacy submerged concerns that legislation would infringe upon "states' rights." Id. at 41–42 (remarks of Sen. Ribicoff) ("we have been sucked in with the propaganda that the Federal Government has no place in traffic safety; that we should leave this up to the states. There isn't a state in the country that has the facilities or the qualifications to go into the complexities of the automobile"); *National Traffic and Motor Vehicle Safety Act: Hearings on H.R. 13228 before the House Comm. on Interstate and Foreign Commerce,* 89th Cong., 2d Sess. 785 (1966) (remarks of Rep. MacKay) ("chaos will result if 50 different states set 50 different sets of standards").

12. See, for example, *Traffic Safety: Hearings on S. 3005 before the Senate Comm. on Commerce,* 89th Cong., 2d Sess. 208 (1966) (remarks of Robert F. Kennedy) (urging application of "same imaginative techniques that we are using to win the race to the moon to eliminate the most deadly features of today's cars"); *National Traffic and Motor Vehicle Safety Act: Hearings on H.R. 13228 before the House Comm. on Interstate and Foreign Commerce,* 89th Cong., 2d Sess. 450 (1966) (remarks of N.Y. State Rep. Edward Speno) ("[I]f we can send a man to the moon and back, why can't we design a safe automobile here on earth?"); id. at 781 (remarks of Col. John P. Stapp) (urging that "most completely regulated form of transportation by the federal government is space flight" and that "the international record in space flight today" is "17 flights, 733 orbits, 1,163 hours, 31 minutes, 28 seconds" and "19,033,250 miles covered without a single injury or fatality"). Amazement over the nation's progress toward reaching the moon subdued concern over the costs of auto safety regulation. See *Traffic Safety:*

Hearings on S. 3005 before the Senate Comm. on Commerce, 89th Cong., 2d Sess. 211 (1966) (remarks of Robert F. Kennedy) (country can afford to spend $150 million on auto safety, if NASA is spending several billion dollars to ensure astronauts' safety).

13. See, for example, *National Traffic and Motor Vehicle Safety Act: Hearings on H.R. 13228 before the House Comm. on Interstate and Foreign Commerce*, 89th Cong., 2d Sess. 321 (1966) (remarks of Rep. Macdonald) (auto industry has responsibility to give people not only what they want but what they can handle); Traffic Safety Act of 1966, S. Rep. on Pub. L. No. 89–1301, 1966 *U.S. Code Cong. & Admin. News* 2709 (reporting "disturbing evidence of the automobile industry's chronic subordination of safe design to promotional styling and of overriding stress on power, acceleration, speed and 'ride' to the relative neglect of safe performance or collision protection"); C. McCarry, *Citizen Nader* 13–96 (1972).

14. Indeed, it has been argued that the manufacturers for years had supported both politically and financially a governmental response to auto safety that focused ineffectually on driver behavior, while making only limited use of the results of research into safer vehicle designs that they also had partially funded. See Eastman, *Styling vs. Safety* 209–233 (1984).

15. 112 *Cong. Rec.* S. 14256 (1966) (Senate vote); 112 *Cong. Rec.* H. 19669 (1966) (House of Representatives vote).

16. University of California Regents vs. Bakke, 438 U.S. 265 (1978) (holding that reservation of specific number of medical school positions for minority candidates invalid absent finding of past discrimination).

17. *Staff of the National Commission on Product Safety, Federal Consumer Safety Legislation* 21 (1970) (safety standards require features that originated in industry and were already incorporated in many vehicles); P. Lorang and L. Linden, *Automobile Safety Regulation: Technological Change and the Regulatory Process*, 64–65 (safety technology "remarkably similar to what it was in 1968, the first year federal rules took effect"); Office of Technology Assessment, Technological Innovation and Health, Safety, and Environmental Regulation, IX–43 (1981) (compliance with federal safety standards described as having "slight influence" on overall pattern of innovation in auto industry).

18. Institute for Research in Public Safety, *Tri-Level Study of the Causes of Accidents* 7–9, 18–23 (1979) (study prepared by private consulting group for NHTSA).

19. Data on the recall completion rate for the period 1966 to 1981 were provided by NHTSA officials. See also Tobin, note 21 below, at 293–294 (suggesting that approximately 40 percent of recalled vehicles were never repaired); General Accounting Office, *The Auto Safety Problem: Identifying Defects and Recalling Defective Vehicles* 5–6 (1975) (reporting recall response rates from 34 to 60 percent).

20. See, for example, R. Crandall, H. Greenspecht, T. Keeler, and L. Lowe, *Regulating the Automobile* 55, 69 (1986).

21. The NHTSA's safety standards are set out at 49 C.F.R. §§571.1–571.302 (1986)

(codifying twenty-six crash-avoidance standards, twenty-one crashworthiness standards, and two postcrash standards). The statistics on agency regulations were compiled by examining Federal Register notices issued by the agency from its inception until July 1, 1985. Recall data were derived from the agency's annual reports. Additional recall information was examined from a data base compiled by Richard Tobin at the State University of New York at Buffalo; his assistance is gratefully acknowledged. See also Tobin, "Recalls and the Remediation of Hazardous or Defective Consumer Products: The Experiences of the Consumer Product Safety Commission and the National Highway Traffic Safety Administration," 16 *J. Cons. Aff.* 278, 288–289 (1982) (reporting number of vehicles recalled and number of recall campaigns initiated by NHTSA between 1966 and 1982).

22. *NHTSA Oversight: Hearings before the Subcomm. on Surface Transportation of the Senate Comm. on Commerce,* 97th Cong., 2d Sess. 50–53 (1982) (statement of Clarence Ditlow, director, Center for Auto Safety) (during the first sixteen months of Reagan Administration, NHTSA rescinded or relaxed existing rules or terminated pending rulemaking in nineteen instances, and proposed similar actions in an additional twenty-one instances).

23. 49 C.F.R. §571.201 (1986).

24. There are engineering estimates as well as regression analyses of the impact of NHTSA's safety standards on injuries and deaths. See, for example, Crandall et al., supra note 20, at 45–84 (1986).

25. The Bureau of Labor Statistics issues annual reports on the value of "quality changes" in automobiles, in order to exclude such values from its calculations of price increases attributable solely to inflation. In making these calculations, BLS separately identifies increases and decreases in auto prices attributable to new safety requirements (or revocations of requirements), whether in the form of new rules or amendments to old rules. The BLS data include NHTSA's bumper standard, which is both a safety measure and a property protection measure. Bureau of Labor Statistics, *Report on Quality Changes for 1986 Model Passenger Year* (1985). See also National Highway Traffic Safety Administration, *Preliminary Report: The Cost of Automobile Safety Standards* 17 (1982) (tabulating BLS data for model years 1968–1982).

26. For critical reviews of the "public interest" theory of government regulation, see R. Noll, *Reforming Regulation* 33–46 (1971); Posner, "Theories of Economic Regulation," 5 *Bell J. Econ. & Mgmt. Sci.* 335 (1974).

27. R. Katzman, *Regulatory Bureaucracy* (1985).

28. This approach is not entirely novel. It has strong echoes of Allison's Model III, G. Allison, *Essence of Decision* 144–184 (1971), and Steinbruner's cybernetic decisionmaking models, J. Steinbruner, *The Cybernetic Theory of Decisionmaking* (1974). Nor is it parsimonious. Because the analysis in this book focuses only on one portion of the agency's environment, the usefulness or comparative advantage of this approach cannot be demonstrated. The "environmental hypothesis" therefore serves merely as a label to identify our general perspective on the way that one should seek to understand regulatory behavior.

29. E. Schein, *Organizational Culture and Leadership* 9 (1985).

2. The Law of a Mobile Society

1. Morris, "On Going from Here to There," *Collier's* 511 (Jan. 6, 1912), quoted in J. Eastman, *Styling vs. Safety* 9 (1984).
2. Ibid.
3. *The Nomination of Charles E. Wilson: Hearing before the Senate Comm. on Armed Services,* 83d Cong., 2d Sess. 26 (1953).
4. J. F. Duryea, *Horseless Age* 2 (July 1897) (quoted in Eastman, supra note 1, at 115).
5. J. R. Doolittle, *The Romance of the Automobile Industry* 440 (1916) (quoted in Eastman, supra note 1, at 118).
6. J. F. Duryea, *Horseless Age* 492 (November 5, 1902) (quoted in Eastman, supra note 1, at x).
7. T. C. Willet, *Criminal on the Road* 65–66 (1964).
8. Netherton, "Intergovernmental Relations under the Federal Highway Program," 1 *Urban L. Annual* 15–32 (1968).
9. *Hearings before the Subcomm. on D.O.T. and Related Agencies of the House Comm. on Appropriations,* 93d Cong., 1st Sess. 89 (1973).
10. 402 U.S. 535 (1971).
11. *Cong. Globe,* 25th Cong., 2d Sess. 455 (1837).
12. 10 Stat. 61–75 (1852).
13. Burke, "Bursting Boilers and the Federal Power," 7 *Technology & Culture* 1 (1966).
14. O. W. Holmes, Jr., *The Common Law* 75–129 (1881).
15. Rabin, "The Historical Interpretation of the Fault Principle: A Reinterpretation," 15 *Ga. L. Rev.* 925, 927–961 (1981).
16. Eastman, *Styling vs. Safety;* S. Merrill, "Professionals and Automobile Accident Losses: A Study of Issue Conceptualization" (1986) (Ph.D. dissertation, Dept. of Political Science, Yale University).
17. Merrill, supra note 16, at 105.
18. Moynihan, in *Passenger Car Design and Highway Safety: Proceedings of a Conference on Research* at 273–275 (1962).
19. Id. at 273.
20. See generally A. D. Little, Inc., *The State of the Art of Traffic Safety* 286–288 (1970).
21. Winterbottom v. Wright 10 M. & W. 109, 152 E.R. 402 (Ex. 1842).
22. Id. at 404–405.
23. Note: "Products Liability and the Problem of Proof," 21 *Stanford L. Rev.* 1777 (1969); Green, "The Thrust of Tort Law: Part II," 64 *W. Va. L. Rev.* 115, 118–119 (1962); W. Prosser, *Handbook of the Law of Torts* (4th ed.) at 96 (1971).
24. The account here draws heavily on Heaton, "Industrial Revolution," in 8 *Encyclopedia of Social Science* 3 (1932); Fleck, "Technology and Its Social Consequences," in 5 *A History of Technology* 818 (C. Singer ed. 1958); Walker, "The Social Effects of Mass Production," in 2 *Technology in Western Civilization* (M. Krantzberg and C. Purcell eds. 1967).
25. R. Epstein, *The Automobile Industry* 39–40 (1928); J. Flink, *The Car Culture* 43 (1975); J. Rae, *The American Automobile: A Brief History* (1965).

26. Kirby, "Motor Vehicle Accidents," in 11 *Encyclopedia of Social Science* 71 (1933).
27. 111 N.E. 1050 (Ct. App. N.Y. 1916).
28. 359 F.2d 822 (7th Cir. 1966).
29. Id. at 825.

3. Science, Safety, and the Politics of Righteousness

1. "Motor vehicle safety" is a defined term in §102 (1) of the act. It means "the performance of motor vehicles or motor vehicle equipment in such a manner that the public is protected against unreasonable risk of accidents occurring as a result of the design, construction or performance of motor vehicles and is also protected against unreasonable risk of death or injury to persons in the event accidents do occur and includes nonoperational safety of such vehicles."
2. "The President's Message to Congress March 2, 1966," Weekly Compilation of Presidential Documents, Monday, March 7, 1966. Johnson's rhetoric was a call to arms:

   > Last year the highway death toll set a new record. The prediction for this year is that more than 50,000 persons will die on our streets and highways—more than 50,000 useful and promising lives will be lost, and as many families stung by grief.
   >   The toll of Americans killed in this way since the introduction of the automobile is truly unbelievable. It is 1.5 million—more than all the combat deaths suffered in all wars . . .
   >   The carnage on the highways must be arrested . . . we must replace suicide with sanity and anarchy with safety.

3. National Safety Council, *Accident Facts* 59 (1980).
4. Ibid.
5. G. Bloomquist, *Traffic Safety Regulation by NHTSA* IV–14 (A.E.I. Working Paper 1981) (citing Gallup data).
6. Automobile Manufacturers Association, *Automobile Facts and Figures* (1968).
7. *Traffic Safety: Hearings on S. 3005 before the Senate Comm. on Commerce*, 89th Cong., 2d Sess. 30 (1966).
8. *Examination of Public and Private Agencies' Activities and Role of the Federal Government: Hearings before the Subcomm. on Traffic Safety of the Senate Comm. on Government Operations*, 89th Cong., 1st Sess. (1965). Quotations in this chapter not otherwise identified are taken from testimony in the House and Senate hearings preceding the passage of the Motor Vehicle Safety Act of 1966 and from the Senate and House debates on the bill.
9. *Examination of Public and Private Agencies' Activities and Role of the Federal Government: Hearings before the Subcomm. on Traffic Safety of the Senate Comm. on Government Operations*, 89th Cong., 2d Sess. 96 (1966).
10. *Bills to Establish a Department of Transportation: Hearings on S. 3010, S. 1122, and H.R. 13228 before the Subcomm. on Traffic Safety of the Senate Comm. on Commerce*, 89th Cong., 2d Sess. (1966).
11. *Federal Role in Traffic Safety: Hearings before the Subcomm. on Executive Reor-*

ganization of the Senate Comm. on Government Operations, 89th Cong., 2d Sess. (1966).

12. Drew, "The Politics of Auto Safety," 218 *Atlantic Monthly* 96 (1966).

13. Cordtz, "The Face in the Mirror at General Motors," 74 *Fortune* 117 (1966).

14. *National Traffic and Motor Vehicle Safety Act: Hearings on H.R. 13228 before the House Comm. on Interstate and Foreign Commerce,* 89th Cong., 2d Sess. (1966).

15. 112 *Cong. Rec.,* S. 14219 (daily ed. June 24, 1966).

16. 112 *Cong. Rec.,* H. 19668–19669 (daily ed. Aug. 17, 1966).

17. Remarks of the President at signing of the Highway Safety Act and the Traffic Safety Act in 1 *NHTSA Legislative History* (1985) at 32–33.

18. This account of the legislative milieu is drawn largely from the weekly reports of the *Congressional Quarterly Almanac* for the years 1964–1966.

19. "Congress 1964: The Year in Review," 1964 *Cong. Q. Almanac* 66.

20. "Congress 1965: The Year in Review," 1965 *Cong. Q. Almanac* 65.

21. Civil Rights Act of 1964, Pub. L. No. 88–352, 78 Stat. 241 (1966).

22. Heart of Atlanta Motel, Inc. v. U.S., 379 U.S., 241 (1964).

23. "Congress 1964: The Year in Review," 1964 *Cong. Q. Almanac* 66.

24. Pub. L. 89–234, 79 Stat. 903 (1965).

25. Government Motor Vehicles: Safety Standards, Pub. L. No. 88–515, 78 Stat. 696, 791 (1964).

26. J. Eastman, *Styling vs. Safety* 38 (1984).

27. Rapaport, "Some Comments on Accident Research," in *Accident Research* 261 (W. Haddon, E. Suchman, and D. Klein eds. 1964).

28. Preface to Haddon, Suchman, and Klein eds., *Accident Research* 7.

29. W. Haddon, 1 *Selected Works* 451, 456 (Insurance Institute for Highway Safety comp. 1987); Haddon, "The Changing Approach to the Epidemiology, Prevention, and Amelioration of Trauma: The Transition to Approaches Etiologically Rather Than Descriptively Based," 58 *Am. J. Pub. Health* 1431, 1433, 1438 (1968).

4. Promise and Performance

1. *Federal Regulation and Regulatory Reform: Report by the House Subcomm. on Oversight and Investigations of the Comm. on Interstate and Foreign Commerce,* 94th Cong., 2d Sess. 168 (1976).

2. Congress amended the statute in 1968 to permit relaxation of general rules on a case-by-case basis. Pub. L. No. 90–283, 82 Stat. 72 (1968).

3. National Commission on Product Safety, *Federal Consumer Safety Legislation: A Study of the Scope and Adequacy of the Automobile Safety, Flammable Fabrics, and Hazardous Substance Programs* 60 (June 1970).

4. *U.S. Department of Commerce: National Technical Information Service, Regulating the Automobile* (L. Lawrence, D. Iverach 1977).

5. Office of Technology Assessment, *U.S. Industrial Competitiveness: A Comparison of Steel, Electronics, and Automobiles* 121 (1981).

6. *Oversight Hearings on the Highway Safety Program: The Report of the President's Task Force on Highway Safety,* 92d Cong., 1st Sess. 337–522 (1971).

7. *Motor Vehicle Safety Standards: Hearings before the Senate Comm. on Commerce*, 90th Cong., 1st Sess. 141 (1967).
8. Ralph Nader, *Unsafe at Any Speed II* xviii (2d ed. 1972).
9. *Motor Vehicle Safety Standards: Hearings before the Senate Comm. on Commerce*, 90th Cong., 1st Sess. 146 (1967).
10. Id. at 246.
11. Id. at 235.
12. W. Haddon, E. Suchman, and D. Klein eds., *Accident Research* 4–5 (1964).
13. *Motor Vehicle Safety Standards: Hearings before the Senate Comm. on Commerce*, 90th Cong., 1st Sess. 160 (1967).
14. Id. at 175.
15. Id. at 86.
16. Id. at 210.
17. National Commission on Product Safety, *Federal Consumer Safety Legislation* (January 1970).
18. Id. at 30–31.
19. Id. at 50.
20. *S. Rep. No. 1301*, 89th Cong., 2d Sess. 6 (1966).
21. National Transportation Safety Board, *Safety Effectiveness Evaluation of the National Highway Traffic Safety Administration Rulemaking Process*, Vol. 3: *Current Rulemaking* 25–26 (1980).
22. C. McCarry, *Citizen Nader* 95 (1972).
23. Expenditure Control Act, Pub. L. No. 90–364, §201, 82 Stat. 270–271 (1966).
24. McCarry, supra note 22.

5. The Great Leap Forward

1. The Highway Safety Act of 1970 codified this arrangement. Highway Safety Act, Pub. L. No. 91–605, §2, 80 Stat. 460, 1739–1743 (1970).
2. National Highway Traffic Safety Administration, *Program Plan for Motor Vehicle Safety Standards* (1971).
3. 472 F.2d 659 (6th Cir. 1972).
4. 472 F.2d at 671–673.
5. 472 F.2d at 676.
6. *H.R. Rep. No. 1776*, 89th Cong., 2d Sess. 16 (1966).
7. Brief for Respondent at 105–106, Chrysler Corp. v. DOT, 472 F.2d 659 (6th Cir. 1972).
8. 472 F.2d at 692.
9. *Motor Vehicle Safety Oversight: Hearings before the Senate Comm. on Commerce*, 93d Cong., 2d Sess. 162 (1974).
10. Id. at 235–236.
11. Id. at 180.
12. 471 F.2d 350 (7th Cir. 1972).
13. 471 F.2d at 354.
14. Ibid.
15. 471 F.2d at 355.

16. Pub. L. No. 93–492, §105, 88 Stat. 1470, 1481 (codified as amended at 15 U.S.C. §1402(a) (1982)).
17. *Amendments to the National Traffic and Motor Vehicle Safety Act of 1966: Hearings on H.R. 7505, H.R. 5529, and S. 355 before the House Subcomm. on Commerce and Finance of the Comm. on Interstate and Foreign Commerce*, 93d Cong., 1st Sess. 196 (1973).
18. 407 F.2d 330 (D.C. Cir. 1968).
19. 407 F.2d at 338.
20. Ibid.
21. 466 F.2d 1013 (3d Cir. 1972).
22. 36 Fed. Reg. 1913 (1971).
23. 466 F.2d at 1013.
24. 573 F.2d 632 (9th Cir. 1978), *cert. denied*, 439 U.S. 862 (1979).
25. 573 F.2d at 643.
26. *Federal Regulation and Regulatory Reform: Report by the House Subcomm. on Oversight and Investigations of the Comm. on Interstate and Foreign Commerce*, 94th Cong., 2d Sess. 172–173 (Subcomm. Print 1976).
27. *National Traffic and Motor Vehicle Safety Authorization Act of 1972: Hearings before the Senate Comm. on Commerce*, 92d Cong., 2d Sess. 40 (1972).
28. General Accounting Office, *Improvements Needed in Planning and Using Motor Vehicle Safety Research* 36 (1974).
29. Id. at 40.

6. The Crumbling Consensus

1. General Accounting Office, *Effectiveness, Benefits, and Costs of Federal Safety Standards for Protection of Passenger Car Occupants* 34 (1974).
2. See discussion in chapters 10 and 11.
3. *Motor Vehicle Safety Oversight: Hearings before the Senate Comm. on Commerce*, 93d Cong., 2d Sess. 86 (1974).
4. Id. at 40.
5. Id. at 41.
6. Id. at 80.
7. Id. at 95.
8. National Traffic and Motor Vehicle Safety Act, 15 U.S.C. §1381 *et seq.* (1966) *as amended by* Act of Oct. 27, 1974, Pub. L. No. 93–492 (1974).
9. *Traffic Safety, Part 2: Hearings on H.R. 13228 before the House Comm. on Interstate and Foreign Commerce*, 89th Cong., 2d Sess. 858 (1966).
10. *S. Rep. No. 150*, 93d Cong., 1st Sess. 7 (1973).
11. *Traffic Safety: Hearings on S. 3005 before the Senate Comm. on Commerce*, 89th Cong., 2d Sess. 36 (1966).
12. Id. at 45.
13. *Ad Hoc Committee on the Cumulative Regulatory Effects on the Cost of Automotive Transportation: Final Report Prepared for the Office of Science and Technology* 74 (1972).
14. Id. at 41.

15. *Auto Safety Repairs at No Cost: Hearings before the Senate Comm. on Commerce*, 93d Cong., 2d Sess. (1974).

16. Even the manufacturers did not complain loudly about the financial ramifications of making repairs "at no charge," in part because they did not wish to be drawn into public discussion of the issue. The companies did not disclose cost data or other facets of recall campaigns, as a matter of corporate policy. The details were sensitive, both from a consumer goodwill and product liability standpoint.

17. *Auto Safety Repairs at No Cost: Hearings on S. 355 before the Senate Comm. on Commerce*, 93d Cong., 1st Sess. 10–11 (1973).

18. *Motor Vehicle Safety Oversight: Hearings before the Senate Comm. on Commerce*, 93d Cong., 2d Sess. 158 (1974).

19. 42 U.S.C. §7403, *as amended by* Act of Dec. 31, 1970, Pub. L. No. 91–604 (1970), 84 Stat. 1676; Occupational Safety and Health Act, Pub. L. No. 91–596, 84 Stat. 1590 (1970); Noise Control Act, Pub. L. No. 92–574, 86 Stat. 1234 (1972); Motor Vehicle Information and Cost Savings Act, Pub. L. No. 92–513, 86 Stat. 947 (1972).

20. *Motor Vehicle Safety Oversight: Hearings before the Senate Comm. on Commerce*, 93d Cong., 2d Sess. 142 (1974).

21. Id. at 153.

22. Id. at 59.

23. Id. at 18.

24. Id. at 32.

25. Id. at 280.

26. Id. at 131.

27. Id. at 137.

28. Id. at 76.

29. Id. at 109–110.

30. Id. at 84.

31. Id. at 28.

32. Id. at 82–83.

33. Id. at 316.

7. Legislating Liberty

1. *S. Rep. No. 150*, 93d Cong., 1st Sess. (1973).

2. *H.R. Rep. No. 1191*, 93d Cong., 2d Sess. (1974).

3. *Auto Safety Repairs at No Cost: Hearings before the Senate Comm. on Commerce*, 93d Cong., 1st Sess. 2 (1973).

4. Transcript of a conversation among President Nixon, Lide Anthony Iacocca, Henry Ford II, and John D. Ehrlichman in the Oval Office on April 27, 1971, between 11:08 and 11:43 A.M., Nixon Presidential Papers, National Archives, Washington, D.C.

5. Transcript of interview by Byron Bloch, KABC-TV, Los Angeles, with John Ehrlichman, President Nixon's Domestic Affairs Advisor, November 9, 1982.

6. *Regulatory Reform*, Vol. 4: *Hearings before the Subcomm. on Oversight and Investigations of the House Comm. on Interstate and Foreign Commerce*, 94th Cong., 2d Sess. 438 (1976).

7. *H.R. Rep. No. 781*, 94th Cong., 2d Sess. 188 (1976).
8. Occupant Crash Protection, 39 Fed. Reg. 10272 (1974) (codified at 49 C.F.R. §571.208).
9. 120 *Cong. Rec.* H. 27815 (daily ed. Aug. 12, 1974) (statement of Rep. Wyman).
10. Id. at H. 27817.
11. 120 *Cong. Rec.* H. 30838 (daily ed. Sept. 9, 1974).
12. Id. at H. 30839.
13. 120 *Cong. Rec.* S. 30848 (daily ed. Sept. 11, 1974).
14. 120 *Cong. Rec.* H. 27819 (daily ed. Aug. 12, 1974).
15. 120 *Cong. Rec.* S. 30848 (daily ed. Sept. 11, 1974).
16. "Auto Safety: Buckley Introduces Bill to Make Seat Belt Interlocks Optional," *Product Safety & Liability Reporter* 66 (1974).
17. 120 *Cong. Rec.* H. 30429 (daily ed. Sept. 9, 1974).
18. 120 *Cong. Rec.* S. 30557 (daily ed. Sept. 10, 1974).
19. 120 *Cong. Rec.* S. 30837 (daily ed. Sept. 11, 1974).
20. 120 *Cong. Rec.* H. 27817 (daily ed. Aug. 12, 1974).
21. Id. at H. 27806.
22. Id. at H. 27820.
23. Ibid.
24. 120 *Cong. Rec.* S. 30587 (daily ed. Sept. 10, 1974).
25. 120 *Cong. Rec.* H. 27818 (daily ed. Aug. 12, 1974).
26. Id. at H. 27816, and 120 *Cong. Rec.* S. 30842 (daily ed. Sept. 11, 1974).
27. 120 *Cong. Rec.* S. 30841 (daily ed. Sept. 11, 1974).
28. Id. at S. 30840.
29. Id. at S. 30846–47.
30. *Amendments to the National Traffic and Motor Vehicle Safety Act of 1966: Hearings on H.R. 7505, H.R. 5529, and S. 355 before the Subcomm. on Commerce and Finance of the House Comm. on Interstate and Foreign Relations*, 93d Cong., 1st Sess. 84–85 (1973).
31. *Motor Vehicle Safety Oversight: Hearings before the Senate Comm. on Commerce*, 93d Cong., 2d Sess. 84–85 (1974).
32. *Amendments to the National Traffic and Motor Vehicle Safety Act of 1966: Hearings on H.R. 7505, H.R. 5529, and S. 355 before the Subcomm. on Commerce and Finance of the House Comm. on Interstate and Foreign Relations*, 93d Cong., 1st Sess. 547 (1973).
33. 119 *Cong. Rec.* S. 4019 (daily ed. Feb. 8, 1973).
34. 119 *Cong. Rec.* S. 9705 (daily ed. Mar. 27, 1973).
35. *Amendments to the National Traffic and Motor Vehicle Safety Act of 1966: Hearings on H.R. 7505, H.R. 5529, and S. 355 before the Subcomm. on Commerce and Finance of the House Comm. on Interstate and Foreign Relations*, 93d Cong., 1st Sess. 814 (1973).
36. Id. at 864.
37. Ibid.
38. Swann v. Charlotte-Mecklenburg Board of Education, 402 U.S. 1 (1971).
39. "Congressional Anti-Busing Sentiment Mounts in 1972," 28 *Cong. Q.* 119 (1972).

40. "Opponents to Major Legislation Score Success," 28 *Cong. Q.* 119 (1972).
41. Id. at 1075.

8. Regulation as Recalls

1. *Department of Transportation and Related Agencies Appropriations for 1980: Hearings before the Subcomm. on Transportation Appropriations of the House Appropriations Comm.*, 96th Cong., 1st Sess. 561–562 (1979).
2. 518 F.2d 420 (D.C. Cir. 1975).
3. 561 F.2d 923 (D.C. Cir. 1977).
4. "Summary judgment" is available to a litigant prior to trial when the factual submissions agreed to by both parties leave open no "material" issues of fact. At that point there remain only issues of law, and a trial to establish the facts would be an expensive irrelevancy.
5. 453 F. Supp. 1240 (D.D.C. 1978).
6. NHTSA's one recall "loss," United States v. General Motors Corp. (two cases), 841 F.2d 400 (D.C. Cir. 1988), made no new defects law. The court of appeals merely affirmed the district court's "highly fact-specific" conclusion that NHTSA's evidence, consisting entirely of consumer complaints that their brakes had locked "prematurely," could not establish a defect for which extensive, controlled tests by both NHTSA and General Motors consistently found the suspect vehicles superior in braking balance to all "peer-group vehicles" produced by competitors.
7. M. Shapiro, *The Supreme Court and Administrative Agencies* 270–271 (1968).
8. Gardner, "Federal Courts and Agencies: An Audit of the Partnership Books," 75 *Colum. L. Rev.* 800 (1975).
9. See generally Priest, "The Invention of Enterprise Liability," 14 *J. Leg. Stud.* 461 (1985) (arguing that development of strict liability tort standard is product of an intellectual movement in legal scholarship).
10. Center for Auto Safety v. Lewis, 685 F.2d 656 (D.C. Cir. 1982).
11. For two of many developments of this theme, see J. Freedman, *Crisis and Legitimacy in the Administrative State* (1978) (arguing that fair administrative procedure will supply legitimacy that agencies need to function efficiently); Stewart, "The Reformation of American Administrative Law," 88 *Harv. L. Rev.* 1667 (1975) (suggesting that current administrative process inadequately represents various interests).
12. See, for example, O'Reilly, "Deference Makes a Difference: A Study of Impacts of the Bumpers Judicial Review Amendments," 49 *U. Cinn. L. Rev.* 739 (1980); Woodward and Levin, "In Defense of Deference: Judicial Review of Agency Action," 31 *Admin. L. Rev.* 329 (1979).
13. One year after the enactment of the Motor Vehicle Safety Act, the Supreme Court gave hesitant approval to the pre-enforcement review of agency regulations under the Administrative Procedure Act. But it is far from obvious that many of the lawsuits contesting NHTSA's rules would have been ripe for review without the specific statutory authorization provided by the National Traffic and Motor Vehicle Safety Act. Compare Abbott Laboratories v. Gardner, 387 U.S.

136 (1967) (holding pre-enforcement review of FDA drug-labeling requirements justified given substantial impact of regulations on petitioners) with Toilet Goods Assoc. v. Gardner, 387 U.S. 158 (1967) (holding pre-enforcement review of FDA inspection procedures unnecessary, since injury to petitioners speculative). As a reading of *Automotive Parts and Accessories Association v. Boyd* reveals, the parties to the case recognized the novelty of the issues and put a wide variety of claims before the court. Judge McGowan was particularly troubled by the fact that the plaintiffs were attempting to have the rule overturned on the basis of arguments that directly contradicted the positions that they had taken in the rulemaking proceeding itself. Characterizing the plaintiff's position as "a soaringly expansive concept of the scope to be afforded on judicial review to a participant in a rulemaking proceeding," and noting that the court found it "hard to take the petitioners seriously on this score," the court nevertheless addressed the issues. 407 F.2d at 342. Although unhappy with the plaintiff's "effort to analogize themselves to private attorneys general with unlimited right to expose all danger to the public interest," the court seemed to believe that the judicial review provisions of the Motor Vehicle Safety Act demanded a judicial answer on the merits. Id.

14. See Marbury v. Madison, 5 U.S. 137, 177 (1803) ("It is emphatically the province and duty of the judicial department to say what the law is. Those who apply the rule to particular cases, must of necessity expound and interpret the rule").

15. For an appreciation of the Supreme Court's difficulties in mediating these contradictory impulses compare Chevron U.S.A. v. National Resources Defense Council, 467 U.S. 837 (1984), with NLRB v. United Food and Commercial Workers' Union, Local 23, AFL-CIO, 108 S. Ct. 413 (1987).

16. See, for example, Fiss, "Forward: The Forms of Justice," 93 *Harv. L. Rev.* 1 (1979); Chayes, "The Role of the Judge in Public Law Litigation," 89 *Harv. L. Rev.* 1281 (1976).

17. Critics of such efforts are quick to point out the errors of the courts' ways. See, for example, D. Horowitz, *The Courts and Social Policy* (1977); Glazer, "Should Judges Administer Social Services?" 50 *Pub. Interest* 64 (1978).

18. See, for example, DeLong, "Informal Rulemaking and the Integration of Law and Policy," 65 *Va. L. Rev.* 257 (1979) (examining criticisms of informal and "hybrid" rulemaking and suggesting alternative approaches for judicial review).

19. National Tire Dealers & Retreaders Association v. Brinegar, 491 F.2d 31 (D.C. Cir. 1974).

20. Public Citizen v. Steed, 733 F.2d 93 (D.C. Cir. 1984).

21. Motor Vehicle Mfrs. Ass'n v. State Farm Mutual Ins. Co., 463 U.S. 29 (1983).

22. Wagner Elec. Corp. v. Volpe, 466 F.2d 1013 (3d Cir. 1972).

23. See generally Diver, "Policymaking Paradigms in Administrative Law," 95 *Harv. L. Rev.* 393 (1981) (arguing that incremental decision making should be the norm except where irreparable harm will ensue).

24. See generally Galanter, "Why the 'Haves' Come Out Ahead: Speculations on the Limits of Legal Change," 9 *L. & Soc'y Rev.* 95 (1974) (arguing that nature of legal system limits possibility of redistribution).

25. See, for example, Shapiro, "APA: Past, Present and Future," 72 *Va. L. Rev.* 447 (1986) (arguing that courts' demand of synoptic rationality in administrative decision making reflects judicial preference for status quo).

26. See, for example, Diver, supra note 23, at 434; see also Rodgers, "Judicial Review of Risk Assessments: The Role of Decision Theory in Unscrambling the Benzene Decision," 11 *Envtl. L.* 301 (1981).

27. See the discussion in Gifford, "Rulemaking and Rulemaking Review: Struggling Toward a New Paradigm," 32 *Admin. L. Rev.* 577, 598–603 (1980).

28. Executive Order No. 12044: Improving Government Relations, 3 C.F.R. §152 (1978).

29. Executive Order No. 12160: Providing for Enhancement and Coordination of Federal Consumer Programs, 3 C.F.R. §430 (1979).

30. Institute for Research in Public Safety, *Tri-Level Study of the Causes of Accidents* 7–9, 18–23, (1979) (study prepared by private consulting group for NHTSA). NHTSA itself has generally put the figure at about half that—in a range of 5–7 percent. See *Department of Transportation and Related Agencies Appropriations for FY '75: Hearings before the Subcomm. on DOT and Related Agencies Appropriations of the House Comm. on Appropriations,* 93d Cong., 2d Sess. 120 (1974).

31. Data on the recall completion rate for the period of 1966 to 1981 were provided by NHTSA officials. See also Tobin, "Recalls and the Remediation of Hazardous or Defective Consumer Products: The Experiences of the Consumer Product Safety Commission and the National Highway Traffic Safety Administration," 16 *J. Cons. Aff.* 278, 293–294 (1982) (suggesting that approximately 40 percent of recalled vehicles are never repaired); General Accounting Office, *The Auto Safety Problem: Identifying Defects and Recalling Defective Vehicles* 5–6 (1975) (reporting recall response rates from 34 to 60 percent).

32. W. Crain, *Vehicle Safety Inspection Systems: How Effective?* (1980).

33. D. Halberstam, *The Reckoning* 558–559 (1986).

34. Jarrell and Peltzman, "The Impact of Product Recalls on the Wealth of Sellers," 93 *J. Pol. Econ.* 512 (1985).

35. Marcus and Bromiley, "The Rationale for Regulation: Shareholder Losses under Various Assumptions about Managerial Cognition," 4 *J. L. Econ. & Org.* 357, 367 (1988).

36. Telephone interview with Vilas Fischer Associates (April 30, 1986).

37. See Marcus and Bromiley supra note 35.

38. Id. at 369.

39. Id. at 369.

40. Id. at 368.

9. *Inside NHTSA*

1. Pruitt, "People Doing What They Do Best: The Professional Engineers and NHTSA," 39 *Pub. Admin. Rev.* 363 (1979).

2. Memorandum from Associate Administrator for Rulemaking to All Rulemaking Staff (February 1, 1980) (on file with authors).

3. The authors conducted interviews with approximately forty current or former agency officials over the period December 1980 to June 1987. Notes and other interview materials are on file with the authors.
4. NHTSA, Order 800–1 (November 7, 1972).
5. *Nominations—June, Hearings before the Senate Comm. on Commerce,* 94th Cong., 2d Sess. 85 (1976) (Nader criticizing Administrator Toms for having "put all his eggs in one basket here, the airbag, and avoided paying much attention to other safety standards") [hereinafter *Snow Nomination Hearings*].
6. For a critique of Pruitt's analysis, see Robertson, "The National Highway Traffic Safety Administration: Evidence Contrary to Pruitt's Characterizations," 40 *Pub. Admin. Rev.* 294 (June 1980).
7. Personal interview with Gene G. Mannella (June 19, 1987).
8. *National Traffic and Motor Vehicle Safety Authorization Act of 1972: Hearings before the Senate Comm. on Commerce,* 92d Cong., 2d Sess. 69–72 (1972).
9. General Accounting Office, *Improvements Needed in Planning and Using Motor Vehicle Safety Research* (September 16, 1974).
10. *New York Times,* April 2, 1973 at 29.
11. National Commission on Product Safety, *Federal Consumer Safety Legislation: A Study of the Scope and Adequacy of the Automobile Safety, Flammable Fabrics, and Hazardous Substances Program* (June 1970).
12. *Hearings on S. 3474 before the Senate Commerce Comm.,* 92d Cong., 2d Sess. 47 (1972).
13. *Department of Transportation and Related Agencies Appropriations for 1973: Hearings before a Subcomm. of the House Appropriations Comm.,* 92d Cong., 2d Sess., Part 1, 943 (1972).
14. *Department of Transportation and Related Agencies Appropriations for 1974: Hearings before a Subcomm. of the House Appropriations Comm.,* 93d Cong., 1st Sess., Part 3, 174 (1973).
15. Compare 49 C.F.R. §501.4 (1972) (naming chief counsel as seventh official in line of succession) with 49 C.F.R. §501.4 (1974).
16. Personal interview with Robert L. Carter (June 9, 1987).
17. 38 Fed. Reg. 9510 (April 17, 1973).
18. *Regulatory Reform,* Vol. 4: *Hearings before the Subcomm. on Oversight and Investigations of the House Comm. on Interstate and Foreign Commerce,* 94th Cong., 2d Sess. 446 (1976).
19. Id. at 465.
20. Personal interview with Howard Dugoff (June 12, 1987).
21. Untitled and undated memorandum prepared by Administrator James Gregory (on file with authors).
22. For an account of NHTSA's handling of Standard 208 from 1969 to 1979, see National Transportation Safety Board, *Safety Effectiveness Evaluation of the National Highway Traffic Safety Administration Rulemaking Process,* Vol. 2: *Case History of Federal Motor Vehicle Safety Standard 208 Protection* (September 1979).
23. *Regulatory Reform Hearings,* supra note 18, at 466.

24. For a general account of the agency's handling of Standard 121, see National Transportation Safety Board, *Safety Effectiveness Evaluation of the National Highway Traffic Safety Administration's Rulemaking Process*, Vol. 1: *Case History of Federal Motor Vehicle Safety Standard 121—Air Brake Systems* (August 1979).

25. *New York Times*, February 28, 1976, at 30.

26. Personal interview with Brian O'Neill (June 11, 1987).

27. *Department of Transportation and Related Agencies Appropriations for 1976: Hearings before a Subcomm. of the House Appropriations Comm.*, 94th Cong., 1st Sess., Part 2, 200, 208 (1975).

28. Department of Transportation National Motor Vehicle Safety Advisory Council, *Safety Defect Recall Report* i (November 1976).

29. *Department of Transportation and Related Agencies Appropriations for 1977: Hearings before a Subcomm. of the House Appropriations Comm.*, 94th Cong., 2d Sess., Part 2, 452 (1976).

30. Pruitt, supra note 1, at 367.

31. *New York Times*, April 22, 1978, at 53.

32. 39 Fed. Reg. 41501 (November 29, 1974).

33. 41 Fed. Reg. 16200 (April 16, 1976).

34. *Federal Regulation and Regulatory Reform: Report by the House Subcomm. on Oversight and Investigations of the Committee on Interstate and Foreign Commerce*, 94th Cong., 2d Sess. 176 n. 72 (1976).

35. Id. at 176–177.

36. *Regulatory Reform Hearings*, supra note 18, at 448–449.

37. *Snow Nomination Hearings*, supra note 5, at 72.

38. NHTSA, Rev. Order 800–1 (February 2, 1977).

39. Personal interview with Michael M. Finkelstein (February 25, 1981).

40. Memorandum from Administrator to Distribution (February 2, 1977) (on file with authors).

41. Personal interview with Robert L. Carter (June 9, 1987).

42. *Nominations—March, Hearings before the Senate Comm. on Commerce*, 95th Cong., 1st Sess. 10 (1977).

43. Id. at 9.

44. *New York Times*, March 19, 1977, at 12.

45. Personal interview with Robert L. Carter (June 9, 1987).

46. 43 Fed. Reg. 8525 (March 2, 1978); NHTSA Reorganization Information (undated mimeo) (on file with authors).

47. Personal interview with Howard Dugoff (June 12, 1987).

48. *NHTSA Oversight: Hearings before the Subcomm. on Surface Transportation of the Senate Comm. on Commerce*, 97th Cong., 2d Sess. 50–53 (1982) (statement of Clarence Ditlow, director, Center for Auto Safety) (during the first sixteen months of Reagan Administration, NHTSA rescinded or relaxed existing rules or terminated pending rulemaking in nineteen instances, and proposed similar actions in an additional twenty-one instances).

49. Personal interview with Frank Berndt (June 4, 1987).

10. Regulation for an Ambivalent Polity

1. We will not cite individually the more than seventy Federal Register issuances related to Standard 208 on which we draw in describing its regulatory history. The dates of most major issuances are included in the text and may be found in the Federal Register for that date.
2. State Farm Mutual Automobile Ins. Co. v. DOT, 680 F.2d 206 (D.C. Cir. 1982).
3. Motor Vehicle Mfrs. Ass'n v. State Farm Mutual Automobile Ins. Co., 463 U.S. 29 (1983).
4. State Farm Mutual Auto. Ins. Co. v. Dole, 802 F.2d 474 (D.C. Cir. 1986).
5. For a flavor of this sometimes rancorous debate, compare O'Neill, Lund, Zador, and Ashton, "Mandatory Belt Use and Driver Risk Taking: An Empirical Evaluation of the Risk-Compensation Hypothesis," in *Human Behavior and Traffic Safety* 93 (L. Evans and R. Schwing eds. 1985) with Wilde, Klaxton-Oldfield, and Platenius, "Risk Homeostasis in an Experimental Context," id. at 119. On the more specific relationship between risk compensation and NHTSA's rules, compare Peltzman, "The Effects of Automobile Safety Regulation," 83 *J. of Pol. Econ.* 677 (1975) with Graham and Garber, "Evaluating the Effects of Automobile Safety Regulation," 3 *J. of Pol'y Analysis & Mgmt.* 206 (1984), and Robertson, "A Critical Analysis of Peltzman's 'The Effects of Automobile Safety Regulation,'" 11 *J. of Econ. Issues* 587 (1977).
6. For some of the recent literature, see Campbell and Campbell, "Injury Reduction and Belt Use Associated with Compulsory Belt Use Legislation," in *Preventing Automobile Injury* (J. D. Graham ed. 1988); Partyka, "Mandatory Belt Use in 1985," 9 *J. of Am. Assoc. for Automotive Med.* 10 (1987); Wagenaar, Maybee, and Sullivan, "Effects of Mandatory Seat Belt Laws on Traffic Fatalities in the First Eight States Enacting Seat Belt Laws," Working Paper, University of Michigan Transportation Research Institute (1987).
7. J. Adams, *Risk and Freedom* 51 (1985).

11. Law, Politics, and Regulatory Strategy

1. See *Federal Regulation and Regulatory Reform: Report by the House Subcomm. on Oversight and Investigations of the Comm. on Interstate and Foreign Commerce,* 94th Cong., 2d Sess. 195 (1976); Merrill, "CPSC Regulation of Cancer Risks and Consumer Products: 1970–1981," 67 *Va. L. Rev.* 1261 (1981).
2. J. Mendeloff, *The Dilemma of Toxic Substance Regulation* (1988).
3. S. Melnick, *Regulation and the Courts* (1983).
4. For a more extended discussion of this point, see J. Pressman and A. Wildavsky, *Implementation,* 87–124 (2d ed. 1979).
5. For a similar point in another context, see Elliott, Ackerman, and Millian, "Toward a Theory of Statutory Evolution: The Federalization of Environmental Law," 1 *J. of Law, Econ. & Org.* 313 (1985).
6. See generally Robertson, "An Instance of Effective Legal Regulation: Motorcyclist Helmet and Daytime Head Lamp Laws," 10 *L. & Soc'y Rev.* 467 (1976);

Russo, "Easy Rider—Hard Facts Motorcycle Helmet Laws," 299 *New England J. of Med.* 1074 (1978).

7. 121 *Cong. Rec. S.* 26552 (1975).
8. 121 *Cong. Rec. S.* 40262 (1975).
9. Hortunian et al., "The Economics of Safety Deregulation: Lives and Dollars Lost Due to Repeal of Motorcycle Helmet Laws," 8 *J. of Health, Politics, Pol'y & Law* 76 (1983).
10. National Traffic and Motor Vehicle Safety Act §108, 15 U.S.C. §1389 (1966).
11. See generally Office of Technology Assessment, *Technological Innovation and Health, Safety, and Environmental Regulation* (1981).
12. R. Crandall, H. Greenspecht, T. Keeler, and L. Lowe, *Regulating the Automobile* 92 (1986).
13. Id. at 109–115.
14. L. White, *The Regulation of Air Pollutant Emissions from Motor Vehicles* 70 (1982).
15. See, for example, Crandall, "Why Should We Regulate Fuel Economy at All?" 3 *Brookings Rev.* 3 (1985).
16. The Automobile Fuel Efficiency Act, Pub. L. No. 96–425, 94 Stat. 1821 (1980).
17. 50 Fed. Reg. 22912 (1985). The fuel economy standard for the 1986 model year was relaxed to 26 miles per gallon in October 1985. 50 Fed. Reg. 40528.
18. See generally Crandall et al., supra note 12, at 117–140; A. Kleit, "The Economics of Automobile Fuel Economy Standards" (mimeo, 1987) (Ph.D. dissertation, Yale University Economics Department).
19. Indeed, NHTSA's worst vehicle was the Highway Loss Institute's best. See Schlesinger, "Automobiles," *Wall St. J.*, Aug. 29, 1988, at 14, col. 1. See also Hinds, "Value of Car Crash Tests Is Contested," *New York Times*, April 15, 1989, at 52, col. 3.
20. 391 F.2d 495 (8th Cir. 1968).
21. 391 F.2d at 502.
22. 367 N.Y.S. 2d 149 (Sup. Ct. 1975).
23. 367 N.Y.S. 2d at 153 (quoting in part Bolm v. Triumph Corp., 33 N.Y.S. 2d 151, 157 (1973)).
24. See, for example, Grimshaw v. Ford Motor Co., 119 Cal. App. 3d 757, 174 Cal. Rep. 348 (4th Dist. 1981) (jury award of $125 million in punitive damages subsequently remitted to $3.5 million).
25. This statement is based on a LEXIS search of reported products liability cases over the period 1965–1985. All cases against automobile manufacturers were identified, and a sample was drawn and reviewed to determine the precise form of the claims involved. For the period 1975 to 1985, for example, claims that automobiles were defective because they had a design defect that impaired their crashworthiness represented 44 percent of the products liability cases reported in the United States in which an automobile manufacturer was a defendant. Moreover, this type of litigation is clearly on the increase. Design-defect litigation represented only about 40 percent of the defect claims in the period 1965 to 1975, but by 1984, design-defect claims had become nearly 60 percent of the defect-claim population.

26. A Risk and Insurance Management Society survey, *1983 Cost of Risk Survey* 39, Table 36, Group 16 (1984), puts the average figure for all transportation companies at 0.44 percent for 1983, and the percentage declines with firm size.
27. Telephone interview with Maryanne Keller, Vilas Fischer Associates (April 30, 1986).
28. Telephone interview with John Eppel, assistant general counsel, Ford Motor Co. (May 6, 1986).
29. The now classic work is R. Kecton and J. O'Connell, *Basic Protection for the Traffic Victim* (1965).
30. M. Freidland, M. Trebilcock, and K. Roach, *Regulating Traffic Safety* (1989). See also *Human Behavior and Traffic Safety* (L. Evans and R. Schwing eds. 1985).

Index